SVEN CARLS

AND JONAS LEIJO

THE
SPOTIFY
PLAY

HOW CEO AND FOUNDER DANIEL EK
BEAT APPLE, GOOGLE, AND AMAZON
IN THE RACE FOR AUDIO DOMINANCE

DIVERSION
BOOKS

For more information, email info@diversionbooks.com

Diversion Books
A division of Diversion Publishing Corp.
www.diversionbooks.com

First Diversion Books edition, January 2021
Paperback ISBN: 978-1-63576-744-5
eBook ISBN: 978-1-63576-745-2

Printed in The United States of America

1   3   5   7   9   10   8   6   4   2

Library of Congress cataloging-in-publication data is available on file

CONTENTS

PROLOGUE

Toward the end of 2010, Spotify had spent two years amassing seven million users in Europe. But the company's crucial US launch faced massive delays. Founder and CEO Daniel Ek was struggling to understand why.

"He called and breathed down the line," he told one of his staff members, who would later recount the conversation.

"Who?" the colleague said.

"Steve Jobs," Daniel replied.

Daniel's colleague wondered if his boss was serious. "What do you mean? He didn't say anything? How do you know it's him?"

"I know that it was him," Daniel said.

After years of frustrating negotiations with the major record labels, Spotify's founder was beginning to understand who truly called the shots in the music industry. Apple's resistance to Daniel's free music streaming was becoming clear, and it was starting to burden him. The industry power dynamics at play weighed heavily on his mind as he walked to Spotify's headquarters in Stockholm, and on his many flights to New York, London, and Los Angeles.

The long shadow of Steve Jobs had towered over Spotify since the startup was founded in 2006. At that point, Apple was already the world's largest platform for digital music distribution, with iTunes and the iPod music player working hand in glove. Now, seven years after the launch of the iTunes store, Apple's grip was even firmer.

While Daniel Ek was fretting over iTunes in Stockholm, Steve Jobs was in Cupertino, California, obsessing over his own arch rival. The iPhone had become a huge success after launching in 2007. But three years later, his iconic product was under siege from a growing fleet of Android smartphones powered by Google. To Steve Jobs, music was a crucial weapon in a "holy war" against the search giant and its operating system.

The iTunes model, based on downloads for 99 cents per song, worked on any Apple device, and on PCs. But Android phones were not part of the iTunes ecosystem, and Steve Jobs liked it that way. He had spent years building Apple's lucrative walled garden.

And he would be damned if one of his key competitive advantages—easily accessible music—was compromised by some upstart from Europe streaming music for pennies on the dollar.

In this context, Spotify was a threat. The Swedish service was catching on in several European countries, and had created a lot of buzz in the US. Spotify had the potential to become a major challenger on Apple's home turf. What if the startup was acquired by Microsoft or, even worse, Google?

For Daniel, access to the US was a matter of survival. After more than four years of growth and constant label negotiations, he was so close to being the world's largest music market that he could almost taste it. By now, the 27-year-old Swede had powerful allies in the music industry. He had earned the support of Sean Parker, Napster's outspoken co-founder, and he was on a first-name basis with Facebook's Mark Zuckerberg, who had promised to help Spotify with their launch. Daniel had even lined up a deal with Universal Music, the label with the closest personal ties to Steve Jobs. But suddenly, Universal's executives refused to sign. The machine ground to a halt, and Spotify's investors were becoming nervous. In fact, Spotify would soon start to see negative user growth for the first time. It could all come crashing down.

Perhaps Daniel's only option was to talk directly with Steve Jobs. According to several sources, however, the Spotify CEO never got to meet his counterpart in Cupertino.

Despite his failing health, Steve Jobs continued to fight for his vision. He aimed to shift iTunes over to the cloud, and he wasn't afraid to badmouth Spotify and ad-funded music streaming to any label executive who would listen. As this book will show, many of them did.

At Spotify's headquarters, the air was thick with tension in late 2010. Their launch in the US kept meeting delays that nobody could explain. The company's top brass whispered about the bosses at Apple, Universal, Warner, and Sony. But only a few select people had any firm details.

Daniel's colleague would never find out if it really was Steve Jobs who made that fateful phone call. The Spotify CEO was, after all, known to sometimes tell stories that were hard to verify.

WHAT HAPPENED IN the following years now belongs to history. Since launching in Sweden in 2008, Spotify can rightfully claim to have saved the record labels from piracy, returned the music industry to growth, and forced Apple—a tech industry behemoth—to change its business model.

While Steve Jobs broke the album down into tracks and playlists, Daniel Ek popularized the freemium subscription model, and laid the groundwork for a new era of playlist by algorithm.

With a market cap in the tens of billions on Wall Street, Spotify is the largest music streaming company in the world, with more than fifty million songs, over a million podcasts, business in more than ninety countries, and a user base expected to surpass 350 million in 2021. Nearly half of its users now pay for the ad-free version, making the platform the industry's most important source of revenue, with billions of dollars delivered every year. But what really happened during the company's spectacular journey to the top?

The Spotify Play is an unofficial corporate biography detailing how a secretive startup from the Stockholm suburb of Rågsved revolutionized music distribution.

As Swedish business journalists, the two of us have met and interviewed Daniel Ek and his co-founder, Martin Lorentzon, several times over the years. They have, however, declined to partake in any exclusive interviews for this book.

But in August 2018, as we were writing the Swedish edition of *The Spotify Play*, we were among the journalists invited to Spotify's new, state-of-the-art headquarters in Stockholm. During a brief question-and-answer session, we asked Daniel Ek to name the single most important reason for his company's success.

"I'll give you two reasons," he replied. "First of all, we were committed to the freemium business model when no one else was. This was very controversial.

"Second, we started in Sweden, proved our model, opened up in more European countries, and grew organically one country at a time. That's what finally made the music industry realize that our model was the future."

Daniel Ek has been reluctant to tell the full Spotify story. He has talked about certain aspects in the press, while carefully guarding the rest. So, to put this book together, we interviewed more than eighty sources—some on the record, some on background—who have been along for the journey. Many of those we asked declined out of a sense of allegiance. Others felt compelled to contribute, despite their loyalties. Some of our interviewees have served as executives at Spotify. Others have been board members, investors, or music industry decision makers. A few are direct competitors.

We have also relied on mountains of documents—some public, such as annual reports, and some confidential. We have pored over the interviews and public appearances that many other Spotify employees have made over the years.

The Spotify Play is a story of how strong convictions, unrelenting will, and big dreams can help small players take on tech titans and change an industry forever.

Sven Carlsson and Jonas Leijonhufvud
Fåglarö, Stockholm
August 2020

1

A SECRET IDEA

N THE FALL OF 2005, Daniel Ek passed through Vasastan in central Stockholm. His thoughts were brimming with an idea for a new company. He had a plan and a potential partner, but the timing still wasn't right. What he needed right now was a job and an income.

The past few years had taken their toll on him. He had been working full-time since he graduated from high school. His was a world where new ideas sprung up all the time, and the work never really stopped. Daniel's hustle included formal roles at tech companies, where he would get paid to apply his skills in online advertising and search-engine optimization, but he was also constantly developing other ideas, putting small teams to work on projects that he would often fund himself.

It was a taxing lifestyle. His hair was thinning, his clothes were unkempt, and he looked older than his twenty-two years. But none of that mattered much to him. He was a man with big ideas, and a mind fixated firmly on the future.

Daniel walked down Tegnérgatan until he arrived at the site of his job interview, a pub called Man in the Moon. It was furnished in a British style, with dark wood paneling lining the walls and sofas covered in green leather upholstery. After a moment, he fixed his gaze on a bespectacled man in his late thirties who waved him forward.

Mattias Miksche was dressed like your average tech entrepreneur—t-shirt and suit jacket. He had just become CEO of Stardoll, a website full of virtual paper dolls that catered to young girls. Stardoll had new investors, and the site's user growth was impressive. Now, Miksche needed to recruit staff, rebuild the back end, and scale up the company for the international market.

The two shook hands and sat down. At first, the low-key Daniel Ek didn't make much of an impression. But as the conversation unfolded, Mattias Miksche felt the young man growing in confidence. The disheveled twenty-two-year-old offered a variety of interesting thoughts on where the industry was heading.

"I'd like you to be our new CTO," Mattias Miksche said, at last.

Daniel was ready and willing, but he wanted to join only as a consultant, not as a full-time employee.

"I have another thing that I'll need to take care of," he explained.

Mattias Miksche accepted, and the meeting ended with a handshake.

LIGHT MY FIRE

To manifest his secret idea, Daniel Ek knew he needed a partner. He had recently met Martin Lorentzon, a thirty-six-year-old entrepreneur with a crooked grin and slicked-back hair. Lorentzon had moved to Stockholm from the textile city of Borås near Sweden's west coast in the late nineties, and elbowed his way through the capital's resurging tech scene. And if everything went as planned, he would soon be a very wealthy man.

When the tech bubble burst in March 2000, things had turned sour for nearly the entire industry. Martin, however, had been lucky enough to build a company in one of the few corners of the sector that survived the crash and thrived in the years that followed. With his partner Felix Hagnö, he had founded an affiliate marketing company called Tradedoubler, which offered a partially automated system for banner placement, in which advertisers paid for results rather than exposure. The company had taken off since its inception in 1999 and was now—near the end of 2005—poised for an initial public offering on the Stockholm Stock Exchange.

When the two first met, Daniel was only three years out of high school, but he already had a good deal of experience in Sweden's fledgling online advertising business. In a recent side project, he had gathered a few programmers to create a new service he called Advertigo. The system was said to know what advertisement best fit a given space online. Advertisers could opt to pay only when the ad generated the phone number of a potential customer.

With the economy rebounding, Daniel was seeking new opportunities, which led him to Tradedoubler's head office on Norra Bantorget in Stockholm, and into Martin's orbit.

The pair first met in summer 2005, when Daniel tried to pitch Tradedoubler on a product search engine akin to Google's "Froogle" (later redubbed Google Product Search). According to his own retelling, Martin wasn't very impressed, but the two of them stayed in touch. Not long after, Daniel organized a game of *Counter-Strike* between his employer, the search-engine optimization firm Jajja, and Tradedoubler. Daniel's team won the challenge handily, making a strong impression on Martin. Years later, he found out that Daniel had secretly enlisted the help of several professional gamers from the renowned Swedish *Counter-Strike* team Ninjas in Pyjamas in order to win.

Martin had no formal title at Tradedoubler. Instead, he took the role of an omnipresent founder, boosting the morale of his employees and troubleshooting various challenges. One former colleague would later describe him as the company's "flying goalkeeper," using a metaphor from two of Sweden's favorite pastime sports: soccer and ice hockey. Martin had a brash, competitive spirit about him. Unwilling to be pinned down by specific responsibilities, he was ready to assist as negotiator, salesperson, problem solver, and cheerleader. Now, in the fall of 2005, his main goal was to take Tradedoubler public. After nearly seven years with the company, he was ready to sell off his shares and move on to something new.

Despite an age difference of almost fourteen years, Daniel and Martin hit it off. They found common ground discussing search engines, metadata, and how to generate large amounts of online traffic to sell advertising. More importantly, they bonded over the potential of peer-to-peer technology, in which files are distributed directly between users' own hard drives without needing to transfer through a central server.

The soon-to-be partners also had several friends in common. One was Jacob de Geer, a social acquaintance of Daniel and one of Tradedoubler's first employees. Much later, Jacob de Geer would make hundreds of millions of dollars by selling his payments company, iZettle, to PayPal.

In the fall, Daniel Ek and Martin Lorentzon began meeting regularly to discuss business ideas. Slowly, Daniel opened up about how he wanted to merge peer-to-peer technology with commercial content. Martin liked what he heard and seemed eager to give it a shot. But first, he had to list his company and sell off a large portion of his shares.

TRUE COLORS

A month or so after his job interview in Vasastan, Daniel Ek started to work as chief technology officer (CTO) at Stardoll. He quickly recruited several programmers out of his own network, and the team started to rebuild the website from scratch.

Colleagues found Daniel to be an introvert who avoided conflicts. He never wore a button-down shirt, preferring instead jeans and yesterday's t-shirt. He'd often forget to clean up after himself. Once, allegedly, a sign proclaiming that "Daniel Ek's mom doesn't work here" appeared in the office kitchen. Soon, it disappeared, without any mention from Daniel.

After a few weeks, however, the twenty-two-year-old's coworkers began to see how gifted he was. Mattias Miksche delighted at Daniel's progression and at his own recruitment of the new CTO. As the weeks wore on, Daniel ensured that traffic to the website was through the roof. And when his shyness gave way, he could be both funny and fascinating.

Stardoll.com became one of the internet's biggest playgrounds for girls between the ages of ten and seventeen. The website suddenly had millions of weekly users and was raking in cash by selling virtual clothing and accessories. Mattias Miksche now ran one of the hottest startups in Stockholm. He started recruiting the best engineering students in town, fresh out of the KTH Royal Institute of Technology, widely recognized as the MIT of Sweden. He also secured $10 million in financing from two of the world's leading venture capital firms: Index Ventures in London and Sequoia Capital in Silicon Valley.

Despite this success, Daniel was committed to leaving Stardoll as soon as he could. His head and heart were in getting his own company on its feet. He also considered taking some of his colleagues with him on his new adventure. One candidate was a twenty-seven-year-old development director named Henrik Torstensson. Another was the company's artistic director, Christian Wilsson, a tall and lanky guy with a dry sense of humor. But above all, Daniel wanted to recruit Andreas Ehn, a phenomenal programmer with side-swept bangs who dressed in carefully ironed shirts. Andreas had attended the private prep school Tyska Skolan in Stockholm, spoke with a posh accent, and had a worldly air about him. He'd recently interned at the software company BEA Systems in Silicon Valley as a part of his final year at the KTH Royal Institute of Technology. He never completed his degree, opting instead to work at Stardoll. When Daniel opened up about his side project, the ambitious Andreas Ehn was more than a little curious.

PARADISE CITY

On November 8, 2005, Tradedoubler was listed on the Stockholm Stock Exchange. Martin Lorentzon was now able to sell a large portion of his shares for nearly $12 million. Felix Hagnö, who owned approximately twice as much of the company, raked in even more.

The two founders were now in the public eye. They gave an interview with the Swedish business paper *Dagens industri* and posed for photographs in Tradedoubler's office and in the Norra Bantorget square. In the photos, Martin is dressed in a pinstripe suit and a striped shirt. He holds a Sony Ericsson P910i cell phone in one hand, and the stylus used to navigate the screen in the other.

Tradedoubler's founders were quick to transfer their newfound wealth to Cyprus, where they had registered holding companies two months earlier. A few weeks after Tradedoubler went public, Daniel Ek established a holding company in the tax haven as well, likely with Martin's help. Martin dubbed his company Rosello Company Limited. Daniel's company was named Instructus Limited. By 2005, Martin and Daniel were ready to invest in a new project together.

There was just one snag: per the usual initial public offering (IPO) restrictions, the Tradedoubler founders' shares were locked up, meaning they couldn't sell all of their holdings immediately. Both Martin and Felix had to wait at least six more months. After that, the plan was to sell and reinvest in Martin and Daniel's new venture.

FEELING HOT HOT HOT

In early 2006, Martin Lorentzon and Daniel Ek met frequently outside of work. Martin, now a multimillionaire, would take the green subway line to the grey suburb of Rågsved to visit his protégé. Daniel still lived in the apartment he grew up in, part of a three-story building atop a hill on Stövargatan, a few blocks from Rågsved's subway station. His mother, Elisabet, and stepfather, Hasse, had moved out, but were still registered at the address. A hundred yards away, a few concrete high-rise apartment buildings shot up toward the sky. In Martin's eyes, the rundown suburb would have contrasted sharply with the lush suburban area of Borås where he'd grown up in the 1970s.

The duo bonded by watching movies. At one point, ahead of Martin traveling out to Rågsved, Daniel jokingly gave him the same advice that Michael Corleone gives Enzo the Baker in the first film of the *Godfather* trilogy: "Put your hand in your pocket like you have a gun."

Daniel's apartment in Rågsved quickly became an impromptu workshop. Servers hummed in the closet, downloading countless pirated files at all hours of the day, warming the apartment to tropical levels. As they spitballed business ideas, Daniel and Martin would sometimes sit in front of their computers wearing nothing but underwear. They had now agreed to start a company, but Daniel still wasn't sure he could count on Martin's financial investment. He wondered what the next step was.

"I'll put in ten million crowns," Martin said at one point.

Daniel would later describe how he checked his bank account the next day and found the money, a sum worth more than a million dollars, sitting there. Martin's decisiveness and dedication must have excited the twenty-three-year-old computer wiz.

They would later tell the story of them sitting in Daniel's apartment, calling out words in the hope of naming their company something great that wasn't already taken. Martin thought he heard Daniel call out, "Spotify" from another room. He typed "spotify.com" into his browser and nothing came up. He proceeded to purchase the domain name all over the world. Daniel, however, would maintain that Martin must have misheard him. He doesn't remember saying "Spotify."

POKER FACE

As winter gave way to spring, Daniel Ek frequently had lunch with his Stardoll colleague Andreas Ehn. The young programmer had quickly taken on an informal leadership role at the company and looked like Daniel's natural successor as CTO. During these informal chats, the pair talked about new business opportunities and the future of technology.

Gradually, Daniel opened up about his other projects. He wouldn't say exactly what he was up to, but Andreas would recall how Daniel enjoyed discussing the possibilities of BitTorrent, a type of peer-to-peer technology which broke files down into smaller pieces, sent them between computers in a network, and then reassembled them on arrival. The technology allowed fast transfers, even over networks with lower bandwidth, and had been made popular by The Pirate Bay, the infamous Swedish file-sharing website. In essence, Daniel wanted to do something similar to The Pirate Bay, but legally. During that spring of '06, Daniel revealed more details to Andreas, at one point proclaiming that it should be possible to build an ad-funded streaming service for video, music, and other media.

Around the same time, Daniel gave his colleague Christian Wilsson two small freelance assignments. One was to construct a graphic profile for his side project, Advertigo. Daniel mentioned that he was going to show the product to a representative from Google, with whom he had scheduled a meeting at Arlanda Airport north of Stockholm, as one source would recall. The second assignment was to create a logo for a new company that had "something to do with streaming." Daniel told Wilsson that he was tossing the idea around with someone else, but he didn't say whom.

"It's important that the logo is 'web 2.0,'" Daniel explained.

When Christian Wilsson created Spotify's first logo, he was inspired by the graphic profile of Skype, the voice-over internet company founded by the Swede Niklas Zennström and the Dane Janus Friis in 2003. He used the same type of bubbly, playful font, and added three wavy lines above the "o" in Spotify to illustrate streaming. In a couple of days, he'd created Spotify's first, light-green logo, with the wavy lines that would later become its app icon. He invoiced Daniel $770 for his work.

In late March 2006, Daniel Ek sold Advertigo to Tradedoubler for $1.3 million. The company had no income and basically consisted of some advertising technology and a few tech consultants. Advertigo's services would have little impact on Tradedoubler's operations, according to several executives serving at the time. Then again, the purchase price was small compared to Tradedoubler's market cap of around $360 million. The deal hardly made a blip on anyone's radar.

For Daniel, however, the windfall was more than welcome. Within a matter of weeks he and Martin Lorentzon would sign the paperwork and start their new company together.

Spotify was still in its conceptual stage, but Daniel now had his own funds to kickstart the project. In the coming months, he moved from his rundown apartment in Rågsved to a condo on Hagagatan in Vasastan, not far from Martin's place in central Stockholm. There, he furnished a home office, installed a massive TV in the living room, and equipped his new digs with the latest home technology. He also left Stardoll to dedicate all his time to his new company.

In later interviews, Daniel would describe a period of partying in which he, newly rich, bought a Ferrari sports car and hung out at the nightclubs around Stockholm's central business district of Stureplan. But the girls he wanted to impress turned out to be fake and shallow. The adventure ended with Daniel isolating himself in a house in the countryside, close to his mom, strumming his guitar. As he came out of his depression, he decided to dedicate his life to Spotify, a company that married his love for technology with his love for music.

The timing of this is unclear. More than a decade later, Swedish motor vehicle records contained no trace of a Ferrari, though an agency representative admitted that their historical data was sometimes spotty.

Perhaps Daniel's origin story should not be interpreted literally. Many people who know him attest to his tendency, particularly in his early years, to embellish and add spice to his stories. As a young man, two people would recall, he earned the nickname "Spicer"—or "Kryddan" in Swedish—among some of his close friends.

GOOD VIBRATIONS

According to Martin Lorentzon's official story, Spotify was founded on his 37th birthday, on April 1, 2006. The paperwork was filed a couple of weeks later. For a brief period, the Swedish company, Spotify AB, acted as Spotify's parent company. It was, in turn, owned by Martin and Daniel's holding companies on Cyprus.

With the Advertigo deal behind them, and the paperwork complete, the pieces quickly fell into place. On May 3, Tradedoubler announced that Martin had sold half of his remaining shares in the company for almost $11 million. Felix Hagnö had sold shares worth twice that. To calm the market, the founders promised not to sell any more shares for the next six months. The stock price took a hit, but would soon bounce back and climb to new heights. Between them, Tradedoubler's founders had now amassed around $70 million.

At about the same time, Daniel Ek went to see his successor at Stardoll, Andreas Ehn, to make him an offer.

"We're starting a company. You want in?" he said.

Andreas didn't need much time to decide. Pioneering the international market for virtual paper dolls was not a bad gig for an engineer in his early twenties, but here was an irresistible opportunity. He soon became Spotify's first CTO, with enough stock options to eventually make him independently wealthy.

Andreas Ehn's departure from Stardoll was a blow to its CEO, Mattias Miksche. In the years to come, he would find himself in an uphill battle with Daniel and Andreas for Stockholm's top programming talent. Stardoll was no longer the hottest startup in town.

THE ENGINEERS

DANIEL EK AND ANDREAS EHN spent much of the summer of 2006 recruiting the best engineers around. Daniel attracted some of the consultants who had helped him at Stardoll. Andreas proved invaluable in drawing engineers from KTH, where he'd earned a reputation as one of the brightest students in his graduating class.

In August, a small group of engineers flew to Barcelona for Spotify's kick-off. Over tapas and red wine, Daniel and Martin Lorentzon explained that they wanted to create a legal, torrent-based platform for the distribution of music, and possibly video. The service would be ad-funded but free to use, they explained, because that was the only way to fight piracy.

They also made it clear that developing the product would be their top priority. Commercial licenses and agreements could wait. Fortunately, the gang in Barcelona didn't grasp how difficult those final challenges would prove to be. If they had, they may never have attempted to build the platform. In the era of Kazaa and The Pirate Bay, the word "free" caused record label executives' eyes to roll, their heads to shake, and their doors to close. Spotify's founders had never negotiated licenses before. They had no idea how strongly the industry would resist their attempt to build an ad-based streaming service by employing the same technology that was being used for illegal file sharing.

Yet the gang munching tapas on the coast of Catalonia had at least three things going for it: Martin's experience and considerable wealth; Daniel's clear and unwavering vision of a product; and Andreas's ability to attract and inspire Sweden's best programmers.

In the fall of 2006, the Spotify engineers moved into the company's first office. It was located on the second floor of an apartment building on Riddargatan, where Stockholm's central business district meets the posh residential area of Östermalm. Here, the Spotify crew spent their first week lugging IKEA flat packs up the stairs and assembling office furniture. They unpacked whiteboards and installed computers and servers. It was a humbling task, literally building a company from scratch. No one could know that the work they'd started would, over time, turn hundreds of Spotify employees into millionaires.

YOU'RE THE ONE THAT I WANT

The king of torrent technology at this time was a Swede named Ludvig Strigeus. He was a self-taught, twenty-five-year-old hacker who had single-handedly built μTorrent (pronounced "microtorrent"), one of the world's most popular file-sharing clients. The ultralight program was used to download files rapidly from file websites such as The Pirate Bay. Early on, Daniel Ek and Martin Lorentzon realized that "Ludde," as he was called, could be key to Spotify's success.

Martin had set up a meeting through an acquaintance named Niklas Ivarsson, a charismatic engineer from Borås and head of the European division of ATI, a company that sold software to the automotive industry. He had worked with Ludde and was blown away by the young programmer's talent for analyzing code and quickly building his own programs.

Ludvig Strigeus was the kind of genius who, as a child, would spend time disassembling household appliances to see how they worked. His mother told a story of how, in kindergarten, he was able to fix a broken dishwasher before the repairman showed up. But the young Ludde also suffered from a tragic medical condition. As a toddler, his parents had noticed that something wasn't right with his hips. The doctors determined that he had spinal muscular atrophy, an incurable disease that breaks down the body over time. By the time Ludde was eight years old, he was confined to a wheelchair.

Ludde's first computer was a Commodore VIC-20. He later inherited a PC, learned to code in Basic, and began creating simple programs and games. In his teens, he became a hacker and, quite famously, cloned Scumm, a popular gaming engine used to build computer games in the late 1980s. Scumm ran on protected source code, which stopped most young coders from looking under the hood. But Ludde was able to analyze the underlying assembler code, which had passed through a compiler and been translated to a language that only computer processors could understand. Line by line, he deciphered the code and translated the information back into a human programming language. It took him several years, but in the end Ludde had built something he called "ScummVM." Its users could now convert Scumm games into any desired operating system. Ludde then released his clone as open source code so that anyone could contribute. It was a remarkable feat of programming, especially for a teenager.

Ludde's youthful antics made him a phenomenal and unconventional programmer. He preferred to code in C++, an older language that was considerably more difficult than popular alternatives like Java and C-sharp. But when used properly, C++ resulted in fast and lightweight programs. In 2005, when Ludde released μTorrent, the entire file weighed only fifty kilobytes, approximately half as much as a low-resolution photograph. It was the kind of stuff that turns hackers into legends.

Daniel Ek and Martin Lorentzon began to woo Ludvig Strigeus in the summer of 2006. They traveled to ATI's offices in the Gårda business district of Gothenburg, where Niklas Ivarsson made the introduction. The two founders explained that Spotify's system would be based on bittorrent technology. They needed his help to build it, and they were willing to buy μTorrent in order to recruit him. They were proposing an "acquihire" long before the term became widely used in the tech world.

Ludde thought the idea sounded cool enough, but he was hesitant. Spotify's offer was low on cash, and he already had two American suitors. One was BitTorrent Inc, founded by the programming legend Bram Cohen, who had authored the original protocol. The other was Azureus, who had a competing bittorrent client that was popular, but not as fast as the one Ludde had built.

CAN'T BUY ME LOVE

By the early fall of 2006, Ludvig Strigeus felt overwhelmed by his options. Should he sell μTorrent to Spotify and start working there, or accept one of his American offers? The people from Azureus had already flown into Gothenburg to wine and dine him at the Elite Hotel. Representatives from BitTorrent Inc had gifted him a trip to the film festival in Cannes, all expenses paid. All three of his bidders seemed impatient. The problem was too much for Ludde's analytical mind. There were too many unknown variables.

Azureus sent a contract full of American legalese that Ludde struggled to comprehend. The ramifications of selling his company to a US operation were making him nervous. After all, his program was being used for illegal downloading. Just a few months earlier, The Pirate Bay had been the target of a police raid in Sweden. What if he, too, was sued? All things considered, Ludde decided to accept the offer from Spotify. It felt reassuring to work for a Swedish company, close to his colleagues.

In mid-October 2006, Spotify finalized the deal with μTorrent. At the same time, Niklas Ivarsson left ATI to join Spotify. He would soon prove an asset in the difficult negotiations with the record labels.

Spotify paid Ludvig Strigeus a small amount of cash, and enough shares to make him Spotify's fourth-largest shareholder.

Martin Lorentzon–42.8%
Daniel Ek–42.8%
Felix Hagnö–9.5%
Ludvig Strigeus–4.9%*

A few weeks after the deal, Spotify sold μTorrent to BitTorrent Inc. Over the years, Ludde's shares would be diluted as new investors came on board,

---

* Spotify's cap table in April 2007.

but his stake was large enough to be valued in the hundreds of millions of dollars by the time Spotify went public.

INDESTRUCTIBLE

From the start, Daniel Ek knew what he expected of his CTO, Andreas Ehn. Spotify's client needed to be quick and nimble. There was no room for the types of glitches often found in other media players on the market. The music needed to flow like water from a faucet. Delays due to buffering would not be tolerated at Spotify. It's "not cool to have to wait," as an early version of the Spotify.com website put it.

The plan was to base the system on bittorrent technology. The users would download the Spotify client and offload its own servers by storing parts of the songs on their own hard drives, sharing them with other users in the network. The arrangement would speed up the system and outsource some of Spotify's broadband expenses. Unlike The Pirate Bay, Spotify intended to share a part of its advertising revenue with artists and record companies. But the founders clearly felt their users shouldn't have to pay for music.

"Our service is ad-funded, so it costs you nothing to use," the website stated, long before the service had been launched.

Programming chops were paramount to Andreas as he expanded his team. He made one key recruitment in October 2006, when he called Fredrik Niemelä, a 27-year-old doctoral student at KTH, and offered him a job. Fredrik was a soft-spoken computer scientist from Norrland, in the north of Sweden. He sported a ponytail and goatee, and had been captain of a coding team at KTH that would soon win a world championship in programming.

Fredrik Niemelä would recall how Andreas, over dinner in Stockholm's bourgeois district of Vasastan, painted a grand vision of Spotify's future. The goal was to build an "agnostic" streaming platform, Andreas explained. Music was just the first step. After that, Spotify would expand into streaming television, film, and more. They were building a company, sure, but the product would be technically sophisticated, and ideologically akin to the file-sharing movement.

The Spotify CTO made a profound first impression on Fredrik, who was immediately drawn in by the prospect of applying his knowledge to solve a contemporary problem. After all, the battle between young file-sharers and record companies was on everyone's lips. Fredrik also had a great deal of respect for many of the other engineers who had left KTH to join Spotify.

To start, Fredrik agreed to take on a part-time role as "technical advisor." A few months later, he started working full-time. Soon, he was staying at work late into the night. Eventually, he would stay behind until the early morning, taking cabs back to his apartment in the suburb of Rinkeby. A few hours later he would wake up, take the subway back into the city, and start over. Daniel Ek tracked his progress, and figured Fredrik Niemelä would soon be due for a promotion.

WE ARE FAMILY

The office on Riddargatan quickly became a second home for the young engineers building Spotify's desktop client. Many of them were in their mid-twenties working their first real job. They would show up late in the morning but work long hours. The staffers had squeezed a foosball table into the office, and some would stay behind for some late-night poker, too.

The guys working on the "back end" technology had camped out in the apartment's largest room, past the closet with the humming servers. Floral-patterned curtains hung over the windows, right next to a whiteboard that Andreas Ehn presided over. Fredrik Niemelä had quickly become his right-hand man, primarily dedicated to building the streaming technology. Others were occupied with the database or the advertising platform. A programmer named Magnus Hult was in charge of all the metadata that threaded together songs, artists, and album art. The team would organize Spotify's music database like books in a library. Users would be able to search by artist or song, and discover other music by the same artist. They could also find cover songs, guest appearances, and songs by the same producer. Later, Spotify would pay for short biographical texts and become a sort of encyclopedia for music. Eventually, the company would develop algorithms that made recommendations, pushing music by Rihanna on Beyoncé fans.

There was a smaller room for those working on the "front end" of the client. This was the domain of Ludvig Strigeus, who built the user interface for Windows, and then for Mac, all by himself. Ludde worked out of Gothenburg but made regular visits to the team in Stockholm. He worked closely with Rasmus Andersson, a designer who would touch up his work and create Spotify's graphic design.

At Spotify's first offices on Riddargatan 20.
Daniel Ek and Rasmus Andersson (seated). *(Rasmus Andersson)*

A third room housed the rest of the Spotify team. That included Petra Hansson, Spotify's general counsel, and Daniel Ek, when he wasn't out negotiating licenses with the record labels. In February 2007, they were joined by Jonathan Forster, Spotify's first director of sales. He soon realized that his job wouldn't be easy, complaining that clients didn't see the value of targeted ads.

"You can't sell steak to people who want ground beef," the Brit would tell his colleagues.

It fell on Martin Lorentzon to deal with investors and venture capital firms. On a regular day, he would hit the gym and go out for lunch with a business acquaintance. Now and then, he would drop by the office and crack jokes with the engineers.

"What's up, slackers?" he'd say, teasingly.

Co-founder Martin Lorentzon interrupting a meeting in
Spotify's second offices with a little dance. *(Rasmus Andersson)*

The programmers chuckled. They knew he was up to something important, but not exactly what. Then again, he didn't really have a clear grasp of
what they were up to, either.

Martin would set the tone for a culture of pranks and practical jokes
around the office. He would later describe how employees slipped inappropriate magazines into one another's bags, or entered fake status updates on
one another's Facebook pages.

At one point during an early pitch at a venture capital firm in the US,
Lorentzon recalled opening his laptop and unleashing a pre-installed program that performed a Google search for the term "How to enlarge a
small penis."

The prank, initiated by an employee, caught Daniel off guard and the
pitch ended up failing.

SLICE ME NICE

Spotify's engineers were now forging ahead to build a first-class product.
Daniel Ek had insisted that users should be able to find a song instantly and
play it without delay. Soon, all the technical discussions revolved around
latency, which had a number: 200 milliseconds. Fredrik Niemelä had read
that if a song started playing within 0.2 seconds of a button being pushed,
people would experience it as immediate. The bandwidth in Sweden's
broadband networks was already good enough for songs to load faster than
they were being played. So, in theory, it should be possible to start playing
a song while it was still loading.

The challenge with bittorrent was that the files were broken down into
pieces that arrived in a "torrent," so in no particular order. Forcing the protocol to change this would slow the process down. As Andreas Ehn's team
worked on solving this challenge, his "back end" team turned their office
into a war room. For weeks, the engineers scribbled on the white board,
vigorously debating how the bittorrent technology could be repurposed to
suit their needs. Finally, one of the sketches seemed to make sense. The
solution even looked elegant.

One illustration showed how the existing torrent system cut the music
files vertically, like a loaf of bread. These pieces were downloaded, assembled,

and then played from left to right, or beginning to end. Since the pieces arrived in random order, they all needed to be in place for the song to begin to play without interruption. Another illustration showed the same music file cut lengthwise, like the layers of a submarine sandwich. It was sliced vertically, too, but only four times. That meant that whatever piece of the song arrived first, it was far more likely to contain a part of the first few seconds—hence the song could start streaming more quickly. The team tested the theory, which worked in practice. The files were streamed from the servers in the nearby closet, and the music played instantly.

With this major challenge solved, the engineers started developing a patchwork of solutions that would ensure that the music kept playing, even when the connection was shaky. The main trick was to load, or buffer, the songs that the user was likely to want to hear next. The very first selection would always be hard to anticipate. But if the user was listening to a playlist, the next song on the list would likely follow. The system, the engineers reasoned, could thus start loading the next few anticipated songs into the computer's cache memory, and simply clear it if the user made another selection.

After a bit of trial and error, the coders figured that any unexpected selection would have to stream from Spotify's own, high-end servers. The peer-to-peer technology was used only for song choices that were easy to predict, such as the next few songs on an album or a playlist. This division of labor also cut costs, as the other users' computers helped store and transfer slices of songs. Another trick was to download a user's favorite songs and store them in their own computer's memory. These hacks would ensure a smooth user experience and guard against glitches and delays. Spotify's first protocol became a sort of hybrid. It was a torrent network supported by a central server, bolstered by a bunch of homespun features. It wasn't flawless, but it was close enough.

In January 2007, the first demo of Spotify's music player was ready. Everyone who tried it found the experience magical. The engineers could hardly believe what they had accomplished in just a few months. Spotify's client was better than anything else on the current market.

"It was rocket science, for real," an early admirer would express. Daniel was delighted with his engineering team and quickly promoted Fredrik Niemelä to the role of Chief Product Officer, CPO.

At this point, practically all the songs in Spotify's database were pirated music files from The Pirate Bay and similar websites. The irony escaped no one at the company. Spotify, after all, aimed to be a legal alternative to piracy. But what were they supposed to do—buy millions of songs on iTunes to fill up the database? Even if they did, the service still wouldn't be legal when the beta version came out.

Spotify needed to finish building the product, patent its newly developed technology, and seal licensing deals with the record companies. Then, everything would probably work out. With a little luck, Daniel Ek hoped to launch the service in the fall of 2007.

POLICE & THIEVES

As Spotify was building its music player, music industry executives were growing increasingly frustrated with all the file-sharing in Sweden. Per Sundin, the Nordic head of Sony BMG, would recall how he lost it at a dinner in Stockholm with some newfound acquaintances.

"So what you're saying is that you're a family of thieves?" the 43-year-old blurted out over the table.

He and his wife Jenny were guests at the home of a couple they'd recently gotten to know, and the subject of piracy was about to ruin yet another pleasant evening. Jenny rolled her eyes. She often found herself wishing her husband would shut up about what he did for a living.

"Yes, but everyone downloads stuff. We download. We've stopped buying CDs altogether," the husband on the other side of the table said.

Moments like these made Per Sundin's blood boil. He knew that his wife would chastise him when they got home, but he couldn't contain himself. A new flood of accusations came pouring out.

"How would you feel if your kids shoplifted at the local convenience store? Would that be okay, just because it's easy? What do you think artists are supposed to live on?"

By early 2007, piracy had caused the record industry's revenue to decline for six years straight. Nowhere in Europe was the problem worse than in Sweden, where 1.2 of the nation's 9 million people were said to share pirated music files. Per Sundin had already been forced to lay off staff a number of times during the past few years.

When his international colleagues within Sony BMG asked him why file-sharing was so common in his country, he'd point to several factors. One was the late arrival of iTunes. Apple's music store didn't launch in Sweden until 2005, and by then, the nation had already given the world Kazaa, The Pirate Bay, and µTorrent. Another reason was Sweden's "home PC reform" from 1998, a government program that subsidized home computers and spawned all kinds of computer literacy, including hacking and file-sharing. Then there were all the incentives that Swedish politicians had provided for the expansion of broadband networks. Most American households could only dream of the high speeds and low prices readily available in Sweden.

But it wasn't just the prevalence of piracy that bothered Per Sundin. It was the lax attitude toward the problem, shown by lawmakers and the public alike. For him, the low-water mark arrived with the national elections of 2006. A newly formed political party called The Pirate Party was gaining support among young voters. As a result, neither leader of the country's two major political parties was willing to slam file-sharing.

"We need to make sure that young people who do this downloading don't see themselves as criminals," Prime Minister Göran Persson said in a live television debate a few weeks ahead of the election.

Instead of criticizing his opponent, Fredrik Reinfeldt, the leader of the conservative opposition party, wavered on the issue.

"Are you watching the debate?" Per Sundin's mother said when she called him on the phone. "You need to quit the record industry!"

Per Sundin would soon leave Sony BMG, but he would remain in the industry. He was about to become the head of Universal Music in Sweden. Soon, a new streaming service called Spotify would pop up on his radar.

SAVE TONIGHT

In March 2007, a few members of Spotify's engineering team had just pulled another all-nighter at the office. By the early morning, Andreas Ehn, Fredrik Niemelä, and a developer named Mattias de Zalenski had put together the music player's back and front ends, thus giving birth to the service. When it was time to register the first account, Andreas and Fredrik exchanged glances. After a tense moment, Fredrik conceded to the man who had recruited him.

"CTO goes before product," the CPO said.

Andreas would recall that, indeed, he registered Spotify's very first account. Soon, the team would create more, selectively distributing beta invites among their friends. These soon sought-after invites were even said to be sold for money on the KTH campus. Sophia Bendz, the now-head of information and marketing at Spotify who had been recruited from the PR firm Prime, was in charge of generating hype in the right circles.

Late night at Spotify's Stockholm headquarters in 2007.
Seated: Sophia Bendz. To her right: Martin Lorentzon. *(Rasmus Andersson)*

Ludvig Strigeus and Rasmus Andersson had built a sleek client. Spotify's beta users could search for music and create playlists. There were separate pages for artists and albums, and links between the two. And, most importantly, the music began streaming immediately. It felt like pressing play on a locally stored file in iTunes. In the Spotify client, encrypted files were temporarily saved in the cache memory on the user's computer. The decryption key wasn't saved on the hard disk, but in the cloud. Users gained access to the music, but they didn't own it. The age of music streaming was born.

Daniel Ek was amazed by the progress, but he was also plagued by a guilty conscience. He was one of few people at Spotify who knew how poorly the negotiations with the record labels and music publishers were going. Still, after paying a lump sum to Sweden's performance-rights organization, STIM, he was able to secure test licenses for a limited beta-release.

Spotify's beta version hit the market in April 2007. To mark the occasion, the team gathered for a group photo. In it, fourteen nerdy-looking young men are seen smiling into the camera. Developer Gunnar Kreitz is wearing a black t-shirt with KTH's logo on the chest. Next to him stands Andreas Ehn, in one of his neatly pressed shirts. Further back stands Jonathan Forster, the only one to wear a suit jacket. Daniel Ek's friend from high school, Martin Birkeldh, tasked with administrative duties around the office, looks over the shoulder of the lanky Fredrik Niemelä, who is sporting his goatee and wearing his long hair pulled back. Crouching in the front row is the designer Rasmus Andersson, dressed in a blue and white striped shirt.

The Spotify team in April 2007. Standing from left: Mattias Arrelid, Gunnar Kreitz, Andreas Ehn, Per Malm, Jonathan Forster, Magnus Hult, Daniel Ekberger, Tommie Gannert, Martin Birkeldh, Fredrik Niemelä. Crouching from left: Rasmus Andersson, Jon Åslund, Andreas Mattsson. Front row: Daniel Ek. *(Rasmus Andersson)*

Spotify's twenty-four-year-old co-founder, Daniel Ek, is crouched in the very front, dressed in a blue polo shirt, with tousled hair and a bald spot. The young chief executive is grinning. His co-founder Martin Lorentzon is not in the picture.

INVISIBLE TOUCH

Pär-Jörgen Pärson stared into the glow of the laptop computer. To him, the music player looked like a dark gray version of iTunes. But when he typed in his favorite band, Killswitch Engage, and pressed play, the song started immediately, without the slightest delay. It didn't seem to download or buffer. It was just there.

On the other side of the table sat Martin Lorentzon, smiling wryly. Pär-Jörgen Pärson had once been his boss at the venture capital firm Cell Ventures. That firm no longer existed, but Pär-Jörgen was now a partner at the venture capital firm Northzone, with offices in one of the five high rises near the Hötorget square in central Stockholm. Martin had come there to dazzle him, and had clearly succeeded.

"Where do the songs come from?" Pär-Jörgen asked.

Martin showed him that the computer was connected to the internet through his cell phone. Pär-Jörgen was taken aback. Over the years, he'd seen hundreds of investors burn their fingers on tech companies promising to reshape the music industry, but what he had in front of him could turn into something truly great, he thought. Eight years ago, Pär-Jörgen had missed his chance to invest in Martin's ad-tech company Tradedoubler. He didn't want to make the same mistake again. Spotify, he thought, could be the biggest thing to come out of Sweden since Skype.

The seasoned investor did his best to maintain his poker face. He didn't want to seem too interested. He knew that negotiating with Martin wasn't going to be easy, since he was already so goddamn rich.

Finally, the Northzone partner hinted that he would consider investing in Spotify. But Martin didn't want to state the terms quite yet. He just smiled and said he'd get back in touch.

RÅGSVED

ANIEL EK GREW UP IN Rågsved, one of Stockholm's first concrete suburbs situated along the subway's green line going south. His father was out of the picture early on. Before Daniel was born, the elder Ek had chosen to live with another woman he was seeing. Daniel had a half-sister who was only three months younger than him, and another two half-siblings on his father's side. There seems to have been very little, if any, interaction between the two families. Later in life, Daniel would describe how he and his father were barely in touch.

Daniel was raised by his mother, Elisabet. Early on, he learned how to keep himself occupied. Eventually, Elisabet met her new husband, Hasse, who became Daniel's stepdad. When Daniel was ten years old, Hasse and Elisabet had a child together, Daniel's half-brother Felix.

Elisabet worked at an after-school center just across the park from their three-story apartment building. Next door was Daniel's grade school, Snösätraskolan. The family didn't have much money, but Daniel would describe his childhood as happy and full of music. Elisabet listened to The Bee Gees, Diana Ross, and the Swedish singer-songwriter Ted Gärdestad. At an early age, Daniel learned how to play the family's Spanish guitar with nylon strings. He played children's songs to start, but gradually advanced to music by The Beatles and Nirvana. In school, he took music lessons and learned how to play drums, bass, piano, and the accordion. As a teenager, he played in a couple of local bands and took lead roles in school musicals.

While an avid musician, Daniel was a computer virtuoso. He received his first computer, an old Commodore VIC-20 which hooked up to the television, as a five-year-old. It would soon be replaced by a Commodore 64, complete with games that kept him occupied for hours every day. Early on, when he had trouble loading one of the games from the external tape deck, he asked his mother for help.

"You'll have to solve that yourself," she said, as Daniel would recall.

Eventually, Daniel's stepdad gave him a PC. He started coding at the age of nine. By the age of eleven, he was imagining a career in technology and telling people that he was going to be "bigger than Bill Gates."

Below the hill, a short walk from the family's apartment, lay Rågsved's city center. Next to it was the local youth center, with a facade covered in a renowned 1989 graffiti mural. It had a gym and rehearsal space, and local kids would play table tennis and floorball there. Daniel Ek was often seen there in his early teens. Micke Johansson, a staff member, would remember Daniel as a kind and well-behaved kid. He recalled how Daniel would often arrive on his own, and sometimes practice bass guitar.

Daniel was reserved, at least compared to his mother. Elisabet was more of a straight talker, one of few parents that really got involved in the youth club's activities. Center manager Rickard "Ricky" Klemming, a man in his 60s, ran a tight ship and was fond of involving the local talent. When he needed to install computers with fast internet connections, he turned to Daniel, who had earned a reputation as a computer wiz. In a show of initiative and salesmanship, Daniel rose to the occasion and secured what he would describe as his first professional gig. He had overpromised, and needed the support of his stepdad to get the job done, but they managed to do it. It felt good. Daniel Ek was on his way to becoming Rågsved's youngest IT consultant.

STATEN OCH KAPITALET

When Rågsved was built at the end of the 1950s, the suburb was considered a wonder of modernism, with its towering apartment blocks and a central building in the shape of a horseshoe. But just a decade later, the picture changed entirely. Rågsved was suddenly described as a "problem area" associated with drugs and alienated youth.

Toward the end of the 1970s, the Swedish punk band Ebba Grön put the area on the map. In just a few years, the band's brooding lead singer, Joakim Thåström, became a national sensation. The band played to packed houses at Oasen, the local club next to the youth center.

Punk rockers from all over Stockholm came there to see Ebba Grön and suddenly Rågsved—or "Råggan," as it was called—became the heart of the whole punk rock movement in Sweden. The music united a generation that wanted to rebel with the clamor of Ebba Grön's politically charged hit "Staten och kapitalet" ("The State and the Capital") as their anthem.

When the local politicians announced that Oasen was to be rebuilt, the punk rockers responded by occupying the building. They painted protest signs and barricaded themselves for ten days until they were dragged out by police.

When Daniel Ek was born, in February 1983, the local punk scene had all but died out. His generation would rally around another call to arms against authorities trying to silence their music. Instead of punk rock, they were captivated by file-sharing, a culture that was deemed illegal and would spawn its own political movement.

SCHOOL DAZE

In 1996, Daniel Ek started middle school in Rågsvedsskolan, a short walk from the youth center. It had already earned a reputation as a rowdy school. Former students would describe how some kids fought, took drugs, and drank on the weekends. But for most, Rågsvedsskolan felt fairly normal. Many were proud, both of their school, and of the area they grew up in.

Daniel was not one of the bad kids who boozed and fought after the youth center's disco nights. He stood out as a clever and talented student with a wide range of interests. A former classmate would attest to his excelling during his guitar lessons. He would play lead roles in the school's musicals, befriending both boys and girls. He was, however, even by his own account, somewhat precocious, eager to talk to his teachers and to adults in general. He was top of the class in computer studies, but didn't put in more effort than he had to. Outside of school, his confidence grew as he helped classmates and acquaintances with computer problems that seemed difficult to them, but easy to him.

Word traveled quickly, and when locals needed homepages, they began to turn to Daniel. He would often retell how he started to build websites and make money at the age of fourteen. A few years later, he would teach HTML and programming to his classmates, turning them into teenage subcontractors. As his skills grew, Daniel started forming new friendships online, interacting on various chat forums. He would share hacker tips and exchange pirated files.

At one point, Daniel built his own virtual counter for his homepage. The counter would tally the number of visits to the homepage and show the number to each viewer. Soon, others on the Internet began to embed Daniel's counter on their homepages, teaching him an early lesson in online virality.

"I began to understand that, hang on a minute, it's all connected," he would explain. "If something is good, it will spread on its own."

Daniel graduated from middle school in June of 1999, with top grades in English, music, history, the history of religion, social studies, and computer studies. His strong report card got him admitted to IT-Gymnasiet, a technical high school in the suburb of Sundbyberg, across the city.

BREAKING THE LAW

That August, Daniel Ek began to commute to high school. Every morning he would take the green subway line to T-Centralen, the node of Stockholm's metro system in the middle of the city. Then he would switch to the blue line toward Hjulsta. Sweden was in the middle of an internet boom and the hallways of his new school were full of optimism. Every student was provided with their own personal computer, which was practically unheard of at the time. They were inspired to dream big and filled with the promise of lucrative careers in IT.

"All we did was toss ideas around. We were thinking that we were going to be the world's greatest," as Daniel would describe it.

During his first year of high school, Napster had just launched. Suddenly, Daniel could download all the world's music for free. For a music-loving hacker in his teens, it was almost a religious experience.

"Napster is probably the internet service which has changed my life more than anything else," he would say.

For Daniel, and many in his generation, file-sharing was a way of life. At school, Daniel and his classmates started broadening their tastes and listening to a greater range of music than when they bought CDs. Young people would no longer wrap their entire identity around a single genre of music. The influence of Napster, and the countless services that followed, was profound.

Later, when piracy came under fire, Daniel's generation banded together and demonstrated for the right to file-share without fear of prosecution. Daniel never ended up on the barricades. Instead, he would try to make peace between the pirates and the music industry. And he would get Sean Parker, one of Napster's two founders, to join him.

SCHOOL'S OUT

At school, Daniel Ek and his fellow students were taught how to program in C++ and build homepages using software such as Dreamweaver. Some of their classes took place in Kista, a high-tech office park north of Stockholm, where both Ericsson and IBM had offices. There, the students learned to disassemble and reassemble computers.

Daniel's ambitions already stretched far beyond what he was learning in class. At the age of sixteen, he sent a job application to Google. The search engine, started by Stanford students Larry Page and Sergey Brin, had only been around for about a year. A representative from Google wrote back to thank him for his interest and encouraged him to get back to them when he had a college degree. Irked by the setback, Daniel eventually tried to build his own search engine. He invested his own money in the project, which turned out to be more difficult than expected. Eventually, when he published the source code online, thousands of developers started contributing to it. The product lived on for many years and would eventually receive attention from companies such as Yahoo!.

In high school, Daniel matured into a young man. In the school's annual photo catalogue, Sweden's version of the yearbook, his blond bob cut had been replaced by dark bangs, combed casually to the side.

Daniel Ek, 16 years old, at his high school, IT-Gymnasiet, in Sundbyberg, a suburb of Stockholm. (*Jonas Leijonhufvud*)

When school was over, Daniel and his classmates would stick around and toy with their computers, using the school's LAN connection to play the computer game *Half-Life* and a subsequent version called *Counter-Strike*.

Former classmates would describe Daniel as shy around the school's few female students. He would avoid their gaze in the hallways but come alive when he interacted using the popular chat program ICQ. His online persona was confident and charming, but he wasn't known to have landed many dates, something Daniel himself would later attest to. He did, however, find that learning to play "Iris," a heartbreak anthem by the Goo Goo Dolls, on his guitar eventually charmed some of the girls around him.

Several former classmates would describe Daniel as ambitious, smart, and imaginative. He was also one of a select few students who had consultancy gigs on the side. During his last year at school, he worked almost full-time on various projects, fueled by a diet of Red Bull and coffee. He worked for a hot internet consultancy firm called Spray, and would guest star as acting CTO at Tradera, an auction website that would later be acquired by eBay, helping them improve their search engine optimization. He even hooked up some of his classmates with paid work, building websites and doing customer service. Some would suspect that Daniel took a far higher cut from some of these gigs than they did.

While in school, Daniel Ek began to realize that he was never going to be the best coder, even among his peers, as he would later recall in interviews. But he clearly had a knack for coming up with new ideas, motivating people, and getting stuff done.

In his final year, Daniel often cut class in favor of his entrepreneurial gigs and side projects. His grades suffered and he irritated many of his classmates by missing group assignments and giving perplexing excuses. One former student would describe how Daniel claimed that he was due to go on tour with some well-known band, something the classmate wrote off as nonsense.

His tendency to employ wishful thinking made some students doubt Daniel's intentions. Behind his back, some of them would refer to him as "Mytoman-Danne," or "Lying Danny," in English.

"What's Lying Danny cooked up now?" one former student would recall the teenagers at school saying.

Few could recall specific examples, but Daniel would often engage his friends with talk of business ventures, money, and musical feats that seemed fanciful. He wasn't exactly braggadocious, another source said, he just seemed to get caught up in the moment somehow.

These early accounts of Daniel Ek's entrepreneurial hustle stand out as an unvarnished, schoolyard version of traits that would follow him going forward. Speaking off the record, people close to him would, in later years, often describe Daniel as a determined ideas man who would sometimes embellish and distort the present reality so that he could instill belief in his vision. The trait is not uncommon among entrepreneurs in the tech sector. These descriptions bear a certain resemblance to the "reality distortion field" attributed to Daniel's future rival Steve Jobs, who would employ a blend of charisma, hyperbole, and conviction to inspire himself and others to believe in ideas that, when considered rationally, defied reality.

Just like Jobs, Daniel would eventually get away with skirting the facts while selling people on a grander vision. As a high school student, though, he was still finding his voice. Sometimes his enthusiasm got the best of him, and his friends and schoolmates pushed back.

"It's like he had clear visions inside him that came out as words before they actually happened," one of his former peers would explain.

Daniel would recall that his last year of high school was rough. He devoted his final few months to retaking tests and working to save his grades. By the time he graduated in 2002, the job market had cooled considerably. For the next few years, he would divide his time between working at tech companies and developing his own projects. He'd be on top of the world one moment, and tormented by self-doubt the next, uncertain of where he was headed.

PARTY LIKE IT'S 1999

WHILE DANIEL EK WAS STILL living with his mother and downloading music in his boyhood bedroom, his future partner had already founded a company that would be worth hundreds of millions of dollars.

In April 1999, Martin Lorentzon had just turned thirty. He was a rising star on the Stockholm tech scene, sporting a cheeky smile, a fiery gaze, and thick brown, slicked-back hair. He had a mind full of ideas and a belly bursting with the kind of confidence that only newly printed money can bring. By day, he worked at one of the city's leading venture capital firms, and by night he was an eligible bachelor about town.

Stockholm was now one of Europe's hottest tech clusters. Internet consultancies with names like Icon Medialab and Framtidsfabriken (The Future Factory) went public and used their soaring stock to buy up competitors at a dizzying pace. In newspaper and television interviews, the founders of these companies were treated as emissaries from an exciting future that was said to be just around the corner.

In the posh restaurants and bars around the Stureplan square, the city's new tech entrepreneurs would mix with fashion designers, film directors, pop stars, and captains of industry. The music business was experiencing its best year ever. The Cardigans were touring all over the world and Swedish producer Max Martin was working with superstars such as Britney Spears. Politicians, eager to take credit for the country's cultural successes, would talk about "the Swedish music sensation."

In London, the Swedish trio Ernst Malmsten, Kajsa Leander, and Patrik Hedelin added to the hype by raising $125 million with incredible speed to build Boo.com, an online fashion store for the international market. Upon launching in November 1999, Boo.com was immediately bogged down by technical problems. A few months later, when the dot-com bubble burst, it became one of the first spectacular bankruptcies. But in 1999, talk of a market crash was still theoretical. If anything, people with money to spare were anxious over the reverse outcome. They were scared to miss out on big returns.

One businessman who took a chance was Jan Stenbeck. He had spent the past decade using his family's fortune, and his investment firm Kinnevik, to challenge old state monopolies with his telecoms firm, Tele2, and the broadcasting company MTG. In this new era, he was quick to start an online music store called CDON. He also invested in a web portal called Everyday.com, which for a brief period had Niklas Zennström as CEO.

The web portal failed, but Niklas Zennström would move on to join forces with Janus Friis and found Kazaa, a file-sharing platform that succeeded Napster, in 2001. Kazaa would become a worldwide sensation for a few years before being struck down by the record industry. Zennström and Friis's greatest success, however, was Skype, which let its users make international calls for free, using only a computer connected to the internet. The company eventually turned Niklas Zennström into one of Sweden's first tech billionaires. He would later invest some of his money in the online music sector, co-founding the music service Rdio. But that lay almost ten years into the future.

Before the turn of the millennium, Sweden's premier industrial family, the Wallenbergs, also wanted in on the "new economy." Their company, Investor, bet more than $100 million on the Swedish web portal Spray, which doubled as an internet consulting company. Spray would turn into a huge disappointment for the family and make the Wallenberg sphere wary of the Swedish tech sector for years to come.

TWO PRINCES

In this whirlwind of technological optimism and fast money, Martin Lorentzon and Felix Hagnö were itching to start their own business. Both had moved to Stockholm from Gothenburg, Sweden's second-largest city, on the west coast. They were relatively junior employees at the investment firm Cell Ventures, where they had been tasked with improving a neglected e-commerce platform. They spent most of their time at the office, located in one of the five identical high rises in the center of the Swedish capital. After regular hours, they would devise plans to build their own company, one that would automate the purchase and placement of internet ads.

Martin had what it took to sell investors on the idea. He was outgoing, creative, and energetic, bordering on hyperactive. He would turn on the charm when he needed to and if things got technical, he could lighten the mood with a lowbrow joke. Some found him a bit brash, but he wasn't afraid to own the room, and that kind of behavior paid off handsomely in the bustling dot-com scene—even in Sweden, where bragging was frowned upon and most people avoided conflict. Felix was the sober yin to Martin's impulsive yang. He came from a wealthy family that had started Joy, a chain of women's clothing stores, in the 1970s. But Felix was more interested in computers than in fashion.

Martin Lorentzon had grown up in a suburban neighborhood in Borås, a textile town near Gothenburg. His mother was a teacher, his father an accountant. Both parents had been top-level athletes when they were young and Martin was sporty as well, with a strong competitive streak. As a teenager, he graduated from Sven Eriksonsgymnasiet in Borås with good grades. His school catalogue photo shows him looking like a young Patrick Swayze, with a blond-streaked mullet.

After high school, Martin enrolled at the prestigious Chalmers University of Technology in Gothenburg. He liked to party and was involved in the committee that planned the school's annual carnival. People would remember him as boisterous and impatient. An old story about Martin claims that he once broke up with a girl because she had broken her leg. But he was also an ambitious student. While at Chalmers, he took a few classes at the Gothenburg School of Economics. He also worked part-time as a cleaner at the Volvo factory in the nearby district of Torslanda.

In 1995, Martin was accepted as a trainee at Sweden's main telecoms firm, Telia. As part of the program, he was able to spend some time working at the search company Alta Vista in Silicon Valley. There, he learned early lessons in internet advertising, but also in how technological ecosystems could connect the academic world with founders and investors.

Martin did not formally graduate from Chalmers until 1997. His grades were high but not spotless. At some point, he ditched the more common spelling of "Lorentsson" found on his diploma for "Lorentzon," joining the growing number of Swedes who thought a "z" would add a touch of worldliness to their names. Soon, Martin Lorentzon had moved to Stockholm and started working at Cell Ventures.

His new boss was Pär-Jörgen Pärson, a man who would become an important figure in his career. Pär-Jörgen was a confident thirty-five-year-old with dark blond wavy hair and a gap between his front teeth. He spoke the colorful vernacular of a venture capitalist and would pepper his stories with American business terms. He noticed how Martin and Felix often stayed behind to work on their secret project. He let this minor transgression slide, hoping to be first in line to invest if the project showed promise.

The sprawling portfolio of Cell Ventures kept Pär-Jörgen busy. One of the investments was a company called PriceRunner, which would later evolve into a successful price comparison website. Another was DX3, which offered a tool to help record companies distribute music digitally. A third company was Tradera, the auction website that would employ Daniel Ek as acting CTO a few years later.

START ME UP

In the summer of 1999, Martin Lorentzon and Felix Hagnö started building their own company. They sat in Felix's apartment in the posh area of Östermalm in central Stockholm and cobbled together a business plan for something they called ClickCab. While Felix developed the technology, Martin would put on a suit and stroll down to Stureplan to have lunch with potential investors. He was surprised by their lack of understanding for his idea. The principle, after all, was simple: ClickCab was an advertising system that connected sellers and buyers on the Internet.

After a few frustrating months, the duo finally had a breakthrough when they presented their idea to Magnus Emilson, Felix's college buddy from the Gothenburg School of Economics. Magnus Emilson had made a small fortune by founding and listing the internet consultancy firm Mind on the Stockholm Stock Exchange, and was now looking to invest. One late Friday evening in August, he agreed to pay around $600,000 for 30 percent of the new company. The deal would, in time, make all three of them wealthy.

Martin and Felix started to hire staff and moved into an office on Grev Turegatan 21 in Östermalm. Their online ad service, which they soon renamed Tradedoubler, was launched in November 1999, and took off immediately.

While building Tradedoubler, Martin developed a habit of working late and sleeping in. He would start his days at a local Chinese restaurant, ordering the standard "four small dishes" main course accompanied by a glass of milk, and vanilla ice cream for dessert. He was now a thirty-something tech founder who enjoyed running his company the way he saw fit.

Pär-Jörgen Pärson missed his chance to invest in Tradedoubler. By the time the company was on its feet, Cell Ventures was about to be sold to a British company, and then the market tanked. But he would follow the founders' careers and get his chance seven years later, when Martin had moved on to a new project.

99 LUFTBALLONS

In early 2000, the internet boom in Stockholm reached its peak. In February, a picture of central Stockholm was featured on the cover of *Newsweek*. The headline read: "Hot IPOs and Cool Clubs in Europe's Internet Capital."

Within a few months, it all came crashing down. Shares in technology companies fell in Stockholm, and on the Nasdaq in New York. Boo.com went belly up in May and was soon followed by American peers such as Pets.com and Webvan. In the public eye, the celebrity tech founders went from being emissaries from the future to a thing of the past.

Martin Lorentzon and Felix Hagnö were lucky. In March 2000, they were looking to fill Tradedoubler's coffers with $10 million. They had a handshake agreement with none other than Soros Private Equity Partners, the investment vehicle of George Soros. His company was looking to invest alongside the Swedish VC firm Arctic Ventures. But time was running out. Tradedoubler's US competitors had already begun to slide in the public markets.

The finance team in Stockholm hurried to close the deal and by April the press release had gone out. With time, the Tradedoubler founders would clash with George Soros's firm over the size of their stock returns, eventually taking the battle to court and winning. But that tussle lay far in the future. All that mattered now was that the young adtech company had secured funding in the nick of time.

As valuations came crashing down, the capital markets dried up. One by one, Tradedoubler's European competitors started folding, unable to secure the funding they needed to grow. Suddenly, the job market was full of programmers looking for work. Competition for new deals in the ad space faded.

In the years to come, Tradedoubler's valuation would rise significantly, making the company worth hundreds of millions of dollars.

LIVIN' ON A PRAYER

When Daniel Ek graduated from high school in 2002, the hype had dissipated from the internet sector. He wanted to build something like Google, but had to make do with a job at Jajja, a local search engine optimization firm. Daniel did not love the work, but he was good at it and eventually became the company's CTO.

In his spare time, he toyed with several pet projects in his family's old apartment in Rågsved. Daniel would describe how he recorded and indexed tons of live TV broadcasts, and tried to figure out how to make use of the material. He was fascinated by how quickly file-sharing could spread content online.

In media interviews, Daniel would later claim that he was accepted to the KTH Royal Institute of Technology. In his telling, he started to take classes at the prestigious university, but opted to drop out after less than two months. The story is hard to confirm. KTH has no records of Daniel being admitted to the school, nor of his registering for any classes.

In 2005, when Daniel was twenty-two years old, he got a call from London. On the other end of the line was an investor who had taken note of the Swede's open-source search engine project. The investor wanted to know if Daniel was interested in working for a hot new website. Perhaps he could take a meeting with the CEO of Stardoll?

CANDY SHOP

During the seven years that passed between the launch of Napster in 1999 and Spotify's founding in 2006, the music industry underwent a dramatic transformation. Plummeting CD sales had put the record companies on the defensive. Their focus was less on technical innovation and more on legal action against file-sharing websites and services.

The first man to bridge this digital divide was Apple's CEO and co-founder, Steve Jobs. In 2001, he launched the music player iTunes, which was used to organize tracks and play music locally on a Macintosh computer. The technology was an instant hit, but the record companies were not amused. They felt that Jobs's digital jukebox went hand in hand with pirating music. Music executives also criticized Apple's ads for iTunes for making illegal practices appear acceptable, even cool.

Later the same year, when Jobs launched the iPod, his portable music player, CDs started becoming less relevant. Users could now collect and organize all their music in the iTunes player on their Mac and transfer the tracks straight to their iPod, which could be carried around like a Walkman or hooked up to a stereo system. Apple's influence over the music business was increasing, and it was beginning to hurt the record companies' own attempts at selling music online.

By this time, Universal and Sony Music had banded together to launch a digital music service called PressPlay, while EMI, BMG, and AOL Time Warner had built their own service, MusicNet. The major labels seemed to be on a collision course with Apple. But that was about to change.

Throughout 2002 and early 2003, Steve Jobs devoted a great deal of time and energy to signing new, secret deals with the heads of the music industry. One by one, he received visitors from the five biggest record companies at Apple's headquarters in Cupertino, Silicon Valley.

The Apple CEO's vision appeared to go beyond signing the labels up to his new music store. Around this time, Steve Jobs is said to have expressed his desire to acquire Universal Music outright, which would have been a major foray into the business of owning content.

"Steve said he wanted to buy the business, but was only going to pay some very low price," as Edgar Bronfman Jr., then the vice chairman of Universal owner Vivendi, would recall in an interview for this book.

During the call, Jobs indicated that he was willing to buy Universal Music for "around $3 billion," Bronfman said. That was around half of what the Vivendi vice chairman thought the label was worth at the time.

"I don't think anything close to that price will fly," Bronfman told Jobs, who was undeterred and continued to make progress on his music store.

Warner Music was first to sign a licensing deal with Apple. When it was time for Universal to come onboard, its CEO, Doug Morris, sent his trusted West Coast executive Jimmy Iovine to take the meeting. Gregarious and business minded, Iovine had once founded Interscope Records. He was captivated by Jobs's vision, and quickly gave the deal his wholehearted support.

During this time, Thomas Hesse, BMG's Chief Strategic Officer, flew from New York to San Francisco to meet the Apple leadership. He sat down with Steve Jobs and Eddy Cue, who was head of iTunes.

"I know that our iPods are full of pirated tracks, but I have an idea," Jobs told Hesse during the meeting, as the German would recall.

Apple's co-founder explained that he wanted to build a music store where the tracks were sold individually, for around a dollar each. As the negotiations continued, the five major record companies pushed back against the notion of letting customers cherry-pick songs, fearing it would hurt album sales. But they also saw several advantages in Jobs's approach. They found the share of revenue going to the labels—70 percent—especially compelling. That was a much better deal than what they were getting from physical CD sales.

In the end, all the major labels signed on: Warner, Universal, BMG, EMI, and Sony. Within a few years, Apple had become the record industry's most important digital business partner.

THE MESSAGE

On April 28, 2003, Steve Jobs stepped on stage for an Apple Special Event, wearing his signature blue jeans, a black turtleneck, and a pair of New Balance running shoes. The audience was hoping the visionary founder would once again surprise them with new products that would send shockwaves through Silicon Valley.

Jobs started by showing Apple's first television commercial for iTunes, which ended with the words "Rip. Mix. Burn." Then he moved on to talk about how iTunes, which was already being used by twenty million Mac owners, had spawned the iPod, which in turn was the world's most popular portable music player. He then attempted to clear up some controversy by translating the youthful expressions "Rip. Mix. Burn." into a more adult version: "Acquire. Manage. Listen." The updated phrase was perhaps less catchy, but it was more likely to sit well with the music industry.

"We acquire our music off of CDs, right?" the Apple CEO said, pausing to suppress a smile.

Pirating music had been standard practice in the tech world for years. Many members of the audience had likely file-shared music themselves.

"But we all know that starting in 1999, there was this phenomenon called Napster. It was shut down in 2001, but it demonstrated a few things for us. It demonstrated that the internet was made for music delivery. And its offspring, Kazaa, is still alive and well today," Jobs said.

The reference to Kazaa was timely. By now, Niklas Zennström's creation had become the world's biggest file-sharing service. Steve Jobs went on to praise the "near instant gratification" it brought.

"But the downside is, it's stealing," he added. "It. Is. Stealing."

The Apple CEO explained that people steal largely because of the lack of legal alternatives. Audience members nodded thoughtfully as the words "No legal alternative" popped up on the screen behind him. What he was saying wasn't quite true. Over the past few years, several legal music services had been launched in the US. A year prior, Rhapsody had begun offering unlimited access to an extensive music library for ten dollars per month. As usual, Jobs had the answer.

"But what about Rhapsody and PressPlay? What about these things? Well, they're subscription services. You can't just go get a song and pay a little."

What followed was a rant in which Jobs took aim at music subscription services, emphasizing how they would charge extra for downloads that vanished once you stopped paying the monthly fee.

"These services treat you like a criminal," he said, showing a slide of a man dressed in a black-and-white striped prison uniform. The audience broke out in laughter.

"People have bought their music for as long as we can remember," Jobs declared as images of LPs, cassettes, and CDs appeared on the screen behind him. "We think people want to buy their music on the internet by buying downloads, just like they bought LPs, just like they bought cassettes, just like they bought CDs," he sputtered.

"When you own your music it never goes away, when you own your music you have a broad set of personal use rights, you can listen to it however you want."

By now, he was all riled up, ready to drop his big news.

"We started about a year and a half ago to create a music store. Music downloads done right."

Jobs said he had met with the big five record companies, whose logos appeared behind him. Then he paused again.

"Before we did this, I was reminded of a quote by Hunter S Thompson," he said with a wry smile.

The quote appeared on the screen, and Jobs read it aloud:

"The music business is a cruel and shallow money trench, a long plastic hallway where thieves and pimps run free, and good men die like dogs . . . There's also a negative side."

The audience roared with laughter, even breaking out in applause. Jobs made jokes about the war that had been raging for years between the content companies and the music industry. He explained how he hadn't known what to expect, but that he'd met some great people in the industry over the past year and a half.

Apple, he explained, had made landmark deals with all the major record companies and built the iTunes Music Store. It contained two hundred thousand tracks from day one, and let users download them on an unlimited number of iPods and up to three Mac computers. The tracks could also be burnt onto an unlimited number of CDs. However, the music was for personal use only, so there was a limit of ten CDs per playlist to prevent large-scale copying.

"All this music, with all of these rights, you can buy for ninety-nine cents per song, with no subscription fees," he explained, over the din of loud applause that lasted for a full ten seconds.

Apple's new music store became an instant hit. Six months later, when Steve Jobs launched iTunes for the PC, he held another live demonstration, during which he held brief video chats with Mick Jagger, Dr. Dre, and Bono.

Bono signed off by shouting out a record company boss who had once produced U2's album *Rattle and Hum*: "Jimmy Iovine! Universal!"

His words would eventually seem prophetic. Both Jimmy Iovine and Universal Music would play central roles as Spotify challenged Apple for the throne of the music industry.

BETTER THAN PIRACY

T HREE YEARS AFTER STEVE JOBS launched the iTunes Music Store, Daniel Ek and Martin Lorentzon started Spotify. The economy was picking up steam and venture capitalists were feeling more optimistic about tech startups.

During Spotify's first two years, the founders oversaw the launch of a beta version of their music player. Meanwhile, they were trying to secure licenses to launch the service internationally. For them, persuading the major labels would prove much harder than it had for Steve Jobs a few years prior.

Martin mainly presided over the finances, while Daniel flew to London, New York, and Los Angeles to meet executives at the major labels. In the early days, Martin would accompany him. Several people in their orbit would recall them as polar opposites. Where Martin's handshake was firm, Daniel's was weak and clammy. While Martin had a piercing gaze, Daniel's eyes would often drop to the floor. Martin was the impulsive investor, Daniel the low-key innovator. But Daniel was the patient one who would wear down his skeptics and eventually win them over.

The industry was still in crisis. Every week, executives at the major record companies would hold meetings with young tech entrepreneurs who claimed to be able save them. Their efforts would invariably fail. Apple was still the dominant force, having sold two billion songs through iTunes by January 2007, but music sales were still decreasing by about a billion dollars every year. Meanwhile, the labels were still trying to stomp out piracy. Their lawyers sued file-sharing services—such as LimeWire and iMesh—but also tens of thousands of private individuals. The goal was to scare young people away from pirating music. In Sweden, prosecutors were preparing an indictment against the founders of The Pirate Bay.

At Spotify, the engineers viewed the bittorrent world not as enemies, but as competitors. Daniel would often declare that they needed to build a product experience that was stronger than downloading music files of mixed quality off the web. Spotify needed to offer all the world's music in a manner that was easy, legal, and free to the user. The company's revenue would come from advertising and be shared with the record companies and music publishers. One of Daniel's early advisers was Fred Davis, a music lawyer from New York who acted as outside counsel for Spotify in the early years. He would describe how Daniel wanted to "build something that was better than piracy."

This pitch would often fall flat when Daniel presented it to people in the music industry. At times it provoked anger. On an early trip to Los Angeles, the two founders are said to have visited the office of Tom Whalley, then CEO of Warner Bros Records in Burbank. According to this account, the meeting ended with Tom Whalley raising his voice, lecturing the Swedes about how free music would never save his industry. Despite frequent setbacks, Daniel Ek stuck to his vision. Eventually, the record label executives began taking him seriously.

LONDON CALLING

When Fred Davis first heard about Spotify, the company was in its infancy. He was an accomplished music rights lawyer with his own team, and digital clients such as Myspace and MOG. He visited Stockholm regularly, since he sat on the board of Stardoll, where Daniel Ek had previously served as CTO. Davis called the Stardoll alum to offer his firm's services. Soon enough he was paying visits to Spotify's first office, on Riddargatan 20.

Daniel quickly took to the American lawyer with the receding hairline and the no-nonsense East Coast accent. Fred seemed to know a lot about the industry, perhaps because he had grown up around it. His father was the legendary producer Clive Davis, who became CEO of Columbia Records in the late 1960s and later signed artists such as Bruce Springsteen and Whitney Houston.

At an early meeting in the upscale London area of Kensington, Fred met with Rob Wells, who was head of digital at Universal's international arm, UMGI. A jovial former rugby player with curly dark-blond hair and a Cockney accent, Rob Wells had hammered out licensing agreements with Fred Davis in the past. They sat in a conference room with Daniel, who briefly explained how his new service could change the industry. Rob Wells had heard a lot of pitches over the years, but this one was different. He would recall thinking that Spotify really could become a billion-dollar idea.

"Do you think we have a shot at getting licenses?" Daniel asked.

"Yes," Rob Wells would recall answering. "But I'd really like to try out a prototype."

Spotify's music player wasn't quite ready, but within a few months, Rob Wells would become one of the company's early beta testers. Eventually, he would prove to be one of Daniel's most loyal supporters in the music industry.

I'M A BELIEVER

Early on, Daniel Ek estimated that it would take around six months to secure the rights to a full music catalogue. He had Googled the topic and found indications that music licenses should cost around five percent of a company's annual revenue. However, that estimate was way off. There were several other lessons he needed to learn. For example, how to distinguish between linear licenses—which he needed—and the non-linear music rights that enabled internet radio services such as LastFM and Pandora.

Fred Davis did his best to enlighten Daniel and help him navigate the waters. The industry was changing quickly, and ad-based solutions were both gaining ground and becoming controversial. Record labels that licensed their music to new digital services would sometimes end up feeling short-changed. In September 2006, Warner Music had astonished onlookers by signing a licensing agreement with the nascent video platform YouTube. The deal gave YouTube the right to stream Warner's music videos in exchange for part of the advertising revenues. A few weeks later, Google bought YouTube for the record sum of $1.7 billion.

"This left the record labels feeling screwed, Warner in particular. There was bad blood between Warner and YouTube for years because of that," as one industry lawyer would recall.

Daniel was a fast learner, and he was aiming high. During some of his early meetings with record companies, he claimed that Spotify could bring the industry back to its heyday in the late 1990s. He would describe his product as the link between a declining industry and hundreds of millions of digital consumers. Some label executives found the young Swede conceited and would describe unbearable meetings during which he droned on about the future of their industry. But he also made a few convincing points—the industry couldn't win in the long term by playing whack-a-mole with individual file-sharers.

Daniel was perseverant, coming back for meeting after meeting. Many of them took place at EMI's head offices in London, in a sandstone building just off of Kensington High Street.

"He had a sort of force field around him. He was convincing, and seemed to be getting good advice from somewhere," a former label executive would recall.

An appealing aspect of Daniel's pitch was that he seemed to be backed by real money. Unlike many music startups, he wanted to launch with commercial licenses from the very start. Daniel offered to pay proper advances and, in time, even showed a certain willingness to compromise.

"He had a big head," another source would recall, noting that the Swede was "smart, but also a bit full of himself."

In his travels, the Spotify founder made new connections, sometimes recruiting them to join his company. In the summer of 2007, he was introduced to Ken Parks, an affable, straight-talking music-industry lawyer in his early forties with a slender build and a mischievous smile. Parks had previously handled digital business development at EMI, where he, among other things, negotiated strategic deals with Apple.

At a meeting in New York, Ken and Daniel struck up a conversation that quickly evolved into a friendship. Daniel had a beta version of the service with a trial license from the Swedish collection society, but he had little idea of how to get the linear music rights he needed for a commercial launch.

Ken was already a veteran of the digital music industry. He had been general counsel of a startup called GetMusic that had, among other things, built one of the world's first online karaoke applications. Now he was open to new ideas and would soon join Spotify as a consultant. Together with Spotify's negotiating duo in Stockholm—Niklas Ivarsson and Petra Hansson—he began to tinker with the business plan, figuring out how to secure the music licenses that would get the service off the ground. In time, he would become one of Daniel Ek's closest advisors.

PARTNER IN CRIME

In February 2007, at a dinner with friends in London, Daniel Ek met a tech entrepreneur who would become both an important Spotify ally and one of his closest friends. Shakil Khan had raven-black hair, a disarming smile, and, at thirty-three, was already a well-known figure in London's tech community. Within a few years, Shak, as he was widely known, would invest in Spotify and become Daniel's envoy in areas beyond the Swede's reach.

Just like the Spotify founders, Shak had done business in search engine optimization and online advertising. At this time, cunning entrepreneurs could exploit flaws in Google's search infrastructure for quick profits. Shak's company, Lightstate, collected personal information online and sold it to companies in the financial industry.

Over dinner, Shak told Daniel about his recent experiences in Shanghai. China already had a booming tech sector, full of venture capitalists ready to take risky bets.

With time, Spotify's young founder would understand that the self-made Brit had a rocky past. Shak had a history of homelessness and at least one court conviction in the 1990s. Since then, Shak had modernized his schemes, selling search words and domains, and marketing erectile dysfunction pills online. Slowly, he had climbed the ladder into more respectable areas of business.

"What are you up to right now?" Daniel asked him at the dinner.

As Shak would recall, he explained that he was close to selling Lightstate. A bond was beginning to be forged between the two. Barely a year had passed since Daniel had sold Advertigo to Tradedoubler. His money was now largely tied up in Spotify.

During his business trips to London, Daniel would stay at cheap hotels to keep his company's costs down. Hearing this, Shak offered him to stay in his apartment, adjacent to a train station in East London. Daniel accepted.

When Daniel showed him an early version of Spotify's music player, Shak knew his Swedish friend was onto something big. Shak would recall one night when Daniel was staying over at his place. Having gotten up to get a glass of water from the kitchen, Shak caught a glimpse of Daniel sitting in bed, staring into a glowing laptop screen. A few hours later, when the sun had risen, Daniel had fallen asleep with his computer on his lap.

Looking back, Shak would comment, "This guy is either going to be really successful—or die trying."

BOOM CLAP

Spotify wasn't the only Swedish startup hoping to transform the music industry. In 2007, two former KTH students started SoundCloud, and quickly moved the office to Berlin. One of the founders was Eric Wahlforss, who had spent a few years in the German capital working at a tech company and making electronic music. His co-founder was Alexander Ljung, a half Swedish, half British sound designer who had run a media agency alongside his studies in Stockholm. Their first office in the German capital was located in a refurbished attic on Auguststrasse 5, above a nightclub in a historic building that had once belonged to the German post office. From their rooftop terrace, they had a splendid view of the gilded dome belonging to Berlin's Neue Synagoge, and the spear-shaped television tower shooting up from Alexanderplatz.

The duo saw the need for a website where musicians could share their work and interact with each other. Until recently, the American company Myspace had served this purpose, and was still one of the world's largest websites. But now, the company—which had been acquired by the media mogul Rupert Murdoch—wanted to do everything at once: e-commerce, social networking, online dating, and so on.

SoundCloud's founders envisioned something more like YouTube, but for audio. They considered the name Clap.com, but reconsidered when they realized that "the clap" was slang for gonorrhea in the US. They finally decided on SoundCloud, a digital platform for audio stored in the cloud.

Daniel Ek heard of the project early on and was quick to meet with Eric Wahlforss at a café in Stockholm. The SoundCloud founder explained his vision to Daniel, who seemed to like it.

"This is perfect," he said. "You're building something for creators, and we're taking care of the listeners."

There were also cultural differences between the two companies. The circle around SoundCloud tended to be music nerds, while the Spotify team consisted mainly of engineers.

In the summer of 2007, the SoundCloud founders released a closed trial version of their website. Alexander Ljung and Eric Wahlforss had dreamt of building something as big as Flickr, which had been sold to Yahoo! in 2005 for around $25 million. With time, SoundCloud would grow much bigger than that.

ONE IN A MILLION

In April 2007, Spotify CTO Andreas Ehn spoke publicly about the music service for the first time. The 27-year-old engineer had returned to the KTH campus to partake in a tech conference called "Hey! 2007." Other speakers at the event included SoundCloud's co-founders and Henrik Torstensson, Ehn's former colleague from Stardoll.

Andreas stepped onto the stage dressed in dark blue jeans, a white collared shirt, and shiny black shoes that matched the belt around his waist.

"We're trying to make music fun again," he said.

The audience perked their ears. Andreas Ehn was a respected figure at KTH, and his new company was clearly up to something exciting. Andreas spoke of how a future with broader bandwidth was paving the way for new possibilities in the music industry.

"It is only a question of time before someone gathers all the music in one place. The users expect as much," he said.

The students were now eating out of his hand. When he mentioned that Spotify's client only weighed 700 kilobytes, whispers began to spread through the room. At one point, an audience member asked where Spotify was getting its money.

"The people funding the company already have several successes behind them. And they are very brave," Andreas said.

The guests at the conference received some of Spotify's early beta invites. The same day, rumors of the new service spread through blogs and various Swedish tech forums. Fredrik Cassel, a young investor at the venture capital firm Creandum, had missed the conference, but he read up on it and called Daniel Ek the following Monday.

"We haven't really started looking for capital yet," the Spotify CEO said, sounding reassured.

Daniel knew that his partner, Martin Lorentzon, had already shown the client to Pär-Jörgen Pärson at the competing venture firm Northzone. And he had no idea who Fredrik Cassel was.

"What did you say you guys are called? Creandum?" the young founder reportedly said.

A slim thirty-three-year-old with brown eyes, Fredrik Cassel was new to the business of venture capital. At this point, his only previous investment was in a Finnish startup company that would later go bankrupt. He promised himself not to let Spotify slip out of his grip.

THE HEAT IS ON

In the spring of 2007, Spotify had outgrown its first office. The heat from the servers was making the air thick and muggy. The engineers were getting restless. Fredrik Niemelä, the head of product, was dealing with endless arguments over product design. At one point, he put his foot down on a controversial issue, approving a feature that let the listener queue the next song without interrupting the listening experience.

Ideological discussions were frequent, particularly on the subject of immaterial rights. Hailing from the north of Sweden, Niemelä had grown up with traditional, Social Democratic values. He tended to take the side of the little guy, favoring a system that would assure the artists' right to be paid for their music. Andreas Ehn, ever the prep school type, was more laissez-faire and believed in the principle of free and open platforms. His vision was always that Spotify should evolve into a free service in the style of Skype, and quickly reach hundreds of millions of users across the world. With a little luck, a percentage of them might be convinced to pay.

The engineers generally saw the music industry as hopelessly backward. Many felt a stronger kinship with the founders of The Pirate Bay, whom they would run into in various social situations. None of them thought file-sharing was a serious crime, but they generally recognized the need for a legal alternative.

The label negotiations now devoured most of Daniel Ek's time. At Spotify's monthly employee meetings, he would often claim that a breakthrough was close. The more honest conversations were reserved for the negotiating team, or for Martin Lorentzon, whose incurable optimism was an important asset.

"Martin saw the brilliance in Daniel, but also that he lacked resolve early on, and tended to overthink things," as one source would recall.

Where Daniel might get bogged down in details, Martin shunned complicated arrangements. He encouraged the young CEO to keep things simple and avoid straying from their original plan.

TIGHTROPE

The Spotify client remained in beta in 2007 and for most of 2008, but the engineers treated it as if it had been commercially launched. They tinkered with product updates until they were blocked by Petra Hansson. Sensitive to the needs of the music industry, she had a reputation for being a hard-ass, corporate-style lawyer who would clamp down on their impulsive ideas, like letting users import their own downloaded MP3 files into the Spotify client.

In late June 2007, Spotify's staff were finally able to move into a real office, located a few blocks west on Humlegårdsgatan. They ordered food from a Thai restaurant and drank beer to inaugurate the new space. Martin saw to it that the new office was equipped with a foosball table and a pool table. In the entrance, guests were met by a large, three-dimensional logo with the word Spotify in big white letters against a pea green wall above a dark gray sofa. Soon, the little *TM* symbol above the "y" in Spotify fell down. The office administrator, Martin Birkeldh, had to order a new one.

The new office was a huge step up, but Spotify still had no revenue and no outside investors on the cap table.

"WEALTH-TYPE
MONEY"

I N THE EARLY SUMMER OF 2007, Daniel Ek returned
to London to pitch investors at the Essential Web conference. He entered the BFI Imax cinema, a large glass building near Waterloo Station, which on this day was draped in colorful ads for Apple's iPod and
trademark white headphones.

Inside the movie theater, representatives from Europe's top venture capital
companies had gathered, hoping to find new investments. Startups like Garlik
and Wonga.com took turns vying for the investors' attention on the big stage.

The Lehman Brothers financial crisis was still a year off, but some experts
were already talking about a new tech bubble. Many of the founders pitching their startups lacked clear business plans and had no idea how they
would actually make money. Daniel had complete faith in his product, but
the chubby, balding twenty-four-year-old looked far from convincing as he
stepped up on stage in a bunchy black pullover with a large white collar
sticking out of it at random angles. His name tag was slanted and pinned
below his chest.

"We will give you all the world's music—for free," Daniel told the
roughly one hundred people in the audience.

He proceeded to explain how Spotify would make money from advertisers.
He did not demo his music player. All that was shown on the screen was

Spotify's bright green logo. The presentation could hardly be described as a success. Still, Daniel showed a conviction that impressed Joe Cohen, an American entrepreneur who had previously worked on the dating site Match.com.

"To him, it was like Spotify and streaming had already happened. Like it was a settled fact of future history," Joe Cohen would recall.

Daniel got off the stage to scattered applause. He still hadn't managed to sign any deals with any of the big record companies.

Two days after the conference, Apple's first iPhone model hit stores. The device would soon spawn an app revolution and turn the Cupertino giant into one of the most valuable public companies in the world. Spotify was still in beta mode, and only available on desktop.

I NEED A DOLLAR

Back in Stockholm, Martin Lorentzon was working out a deal that would fund the company. He got back in touch with Pär-Jörgen Pärson, saying he was ready to start negotiating. Pär-Jörgen was elated by the news but balked at Martin's asking price. The Spotify chairman wanted around $22 million, or 150 million Swedish crowns, for 20 percent of his company.

To the Northzone partner, it was an absurdly aggressive starting bid. That price tag would value Spotify—a company that still had no deals with the labels and no commercially available product—at more than $100 million. Pär-Jörgen was torn. After all, Martin had a proven track record and seemed to be prepared to invest a large part of his personal fortune. Pär-Jörgen said he needed to discuss things with his associates at Northzone.

Other investors, like Tradedoubler's first investor Magnus Emilson, were far more skeptical. Emilson rejected Martin's proposal, noting that Spotify lacked music licenses and feeling the valuation was way too high. Sonali De Rycker, a partner at Atlas Ventures in London, was impressed by the beta version of Spotify, but found Martin's valuation laughable.

"I thought he was crazy," she would recall.

In Stockholm, it fell on Pär-Jörgen Pärson to piece together a group of investors that would be willing to share the risk. But with so few interested in betting on music technology, he didn't even have the wholehearted support of his own firm. His partners said they had seen too many "road kills" in the sector.

The music industry was infamous for bleeding VC-funded startups dry, almost as their only form of digital strategy. Money would flow from investors straight to the labels through companies that would have done well to survive for more than a couple of years. Pär-Jörgen, who still believed Spotify could dominate the space, was growing frustrated.

He wasn't the only suitor fretting over the deal. Fredrik Cassel at Creandum had cultivated his relationship with Daniel Ek over Skype for months. Daniel had tipped him off about a promising video-based adtech company called Videoplaza, which Fredrik would go on to make a successful investment in. But the young venture capitalist had his eyes on a bigger prize. His main objective was to get in on Spotify's A-round of funding, alongside Creandum's rival, Northzone.

HANGIN' TOUGH

For most of 2007, Daniel Ek is said to have held firm on his vision that Spotify would be a global service, free to all of its users. This is also the way would-be investors Creandum described the service in a written document dated June 2007.

The young Spotify CEO felt his pitch had a good chance of succeeding. He entered meetings with the labels with a strong product and a track record in monetizing ads online.

"That was unique. But the labels were already skeptical of anything ad-funded. They felt the money wasn't really there," as one source would describe it.

Daniel's approach clashed with the conventional wisdom of the music industry. The young Swede would offer labels a share of Spotify's revenue which would hopefully grow significantly over time. But the labels generally wanted to be paid per stream, regardless of Spotify's ability to sell ads. In short, Daniel wanted a structure that rewarded growth and didn't punish Spotify for users who streamed a lot of music. To the Spotify team, payouts per stream risked running up costs that would kill the business.

Toward the end of the year, Spotify's finances were strained. On their many business trips to the US, Daniel and his top managers flew coach and held back on expenses. For years, employees would love to tell the story of how Daniel and his main negotiator, Niklas Ivarsson, were forced to share a bed in "the cheapest hotel in Manhattan." Niklas, who had a bad cold, spent the night coughing and sniffling next to his CEO.

One source would recall that in late 2007, Daniel and Niklas visited Universal Music's headquarters in New York, where their pitch failed to impress. With them was the attorney Fred Davis and his coworker Elizabeth Moody. The Spotify quartet struggled. Universal's team thought an ad-based model would never generate enough revenue. The main stumbling block was that the label wanted a high per-stream payment of around 0.5–1.0 cents on a sliding scale, while Spotify wanted the deal to mainly be based on sharing ad revenues, according to two sources.

Eventually, Daniel had to compromise by adding a paid service. Three people at Spotify drove him to that shift in strategy: Spotify's "dynamic duo"—Niklas Ivarsson and Petra Hansson—and the New York-based advisor Ken Parks. After scores of meetings with labels and legal consultants, they are said to have convinced Daniel that a paid version was the only way forward. The alternative would simply cost too much, in both cash and company shares, and never lead to a sustainable business.

The freemium model that would define Spotify was thus born out of a tit-for-tat dialogue with the labels, with Niklas and Petra painstakingly hammering out the details of a new template. The industry hated the free service, but was prepared to put up with it as a means to an end, with Spotify vowing to convert free users to an ad-free, premium version.

Daniel's global ambitions remained intact, but launching in the United States was a tall order. His focus thus shifted toward signing licenses in Europe. The talks with Universal, for example, would now take place in London, where the Spotify team dealt with its head of digital, Rob Wells.

TAKE A CHANCE ON ME

Toward the end of 2007, Spotify's potential financier was struggling to get co-investors on board. Pär-Jörgen Pärson was beginning to feel like the awkward kid at the school dance. The investment company Kinnevik—at which the young Cristina Stenbeck had succeeded her late father, Jan—passed. The same went for international venture firms like Index Ventures and Balderton Capital. Finally, Pär-Jörgen managed to put together a consortium of investors consisting of the Stockholm firm Creandum and Innovationskapital, based in Gothenburg. Together, the trio would put up $15 million for a piece of Spotify.

It was a risky deal, but the investors lauded the constant improvements to Spotify's software. In September 2007, the growing company released its seventh beta version. This time, the group photo pictured twenty coworkers.

In the photo, Andreas Ehn is seated in the front row. The key programmer, Ludvig Strigeus, is smiling from his wheelchair in the second row, two spots down from a nearly obscured Daniel Ek. In the far back are Sophia Bendz and Petra Hansson, surrounded by male engineers. Many in the Spotify team continued to believe that the commercial launch was just weeks off.

A few blocks away, at the Northzone offices, a frustrated Pär-Jörgen knew that wasn't the case. But he was reassured by his contacts in the music business, who appeared to believe in the service. He had several phone conversations with Per Sundin at Sony BMG. The record executive was a beta tester and claimed to love the product.

"It's only a matter of time before Spotify will have licenses," Sundin said over the phone.

Pledges from music executives shouldn't be taken literally, Pär-Jörgen thought. He knew they were desperate to find new revenue sources, particularly if they came with no financial risk to their own business. Besides, the labels were said to be "thick as thieves," colluding with each other at every turn. It was hard to know when they were actually being forthright.

By the summer of 2008, it finally looked as if Northzone's joint investment was ready to go. But then the third investor, Innovationskapital, suddenly backed out.

HAIR

Daniel Ek was at this time still flying frantically between Stockholm, London, and New York, trying to close deals with the four major labels.

In July 2008, the young Swede hit a major roadblock. He would, four years later, describe the incident on Swedish public radio, retelling how he stepped out onto the hot pavement near Rockefeller Plaza, feeling nauseous and jetlagged, with a splitting headache. A hectic week had ended in a catastrophic meeting with one of the labels, and Daniel felt it might all be over.

"I've just been told that my baby, Spotify, the music company I've worked on day and night over the past two years, won't work out," he said. "It's July 2008, I'm twenty-five years old and it feels like my life is about to end."

After the failed meeting, Daniel said, he called co-founder Martin Lorentzon and told him that "the man who looks like a hairdresser" had changed his mind. The label was no longer on board.

During his radio appearance, Daniel did not name the label or the man with the funny hairdo. But, looking back, it was most likely Warner Music, with its offices by Rockefeller Plaza. The "hairdresser" would have been Michael Nash, Warner's head of strategy and business development, who was known for his frosty highlights.

During the call, Martin did his best to calm his protégé.

"Problems aren't problems. We'll solve this, we'll think of something," Martin said, in Daniel's retelling.

At this point, Daniel was still hoping to gain global licenses for Spotify, according to one source with knowledge of the matter.

"This may have been the moment that Daniel realized that a single deal for both North America and Europe was going to be impossible," the source said.

ANTE UP

Daniel Ek was now acutely aware that Spotify's money was running out. The company struggled to pay rent at their new offices on Humlegårdsgatan. According to one person familiar with the finances, Daniel lent the company tens of thousands of dollars so that salaries could be paid.

Pär-Jörgen Pärson had become desperate, wondering if there would ever be a funding round with the support of other outside investors. But then Daniel started making some real progress with the record companies.

By now, the five major record labels had become four. During the summer, two of them shook hands with Spotify for licenses that covered the

A meeting at Spotify's office, eight months ahead of the launch. From left: Ludvig Strigeus, Andreas Ehn, Andreas Mattsson, Mattias Arrelid, and Emil Fredriksson. *(Rasmus Andersson)*

Nordic countries and a few additional European markets. Suddenly, the Spotify investment was looking much less risky. Northzone vowed to cover Innovationskapital's share of the funding, with Creandum taking the remaining third. But now, with things already delicately poised, Martin Lorentzon decided to ante up.

"We're changing the investment to euros," he told Pär-Jörgen over the phone in late summer.

At first, Martin's former boss didn't know what he meant.

"Absolutely, we can convert the round to euros," he said.

But Martin didn't want to change the figure, just the currency. The dollar had been falling against the euro, and Martin felt he simply needed more money.

"Martin, you must be joking."

"No. We want it in euros. Take it or leave it," he said.

The stubborn founder would eventually get his way. According to one person involved, Martin was able to talk up the valuation by around 20 percent.

In late August 2008, Spotify's first external funding round was registered in Luxembourg. Northzone invested more than $12 million and became the company's third-largest owner, after the founders. Creandum came in fourth on the cap table, followed by Martin's former Tradedoubler buddy, Felix Hagnö.

Spotify was now valued at $86 million. Both Pär-Jörgen Pärson and Fredrik Cassel were elected to the board of directors. After prolonged and shaky negotiations, Northzone had made what would become its best-ever investment by a long stretch. Pär-Jörgen would remain a board member at Spotify for nine years.

At the Spotify office, around forty employees toasted to the news with glasses of sparkling wine. Daniel was visibly relieved, according to one account.

"That was lucky. If we hadn't gotten funded, you guys wouldn't have received your salaries," he reportedly told his colleagues afterward.

In fact, the timing was immaculate. A few months later, the investment bank Lehman Brothers filed for bankruptcy, setting off the worst financial crisis in more than seventy years.

EYE OF THE TIGER

In 2008, Daniel Ek's man in London, Shakil Khan, finally got the exit he had been seeking. It came when AOL bought Buy.at, of which his company, Lightstate, was now a part. Only a few people know exactly how rich the deal made him. But Shak has stated that it made him serious cash or, in his words, "wealth-type money." Daniel reached out to his nouveau riche friend in London.

"Are you depressed yet?" Daniel said, according to Shak's subsequent account.

"Yes, a bit," he answered.

"Have you bought a new car?"

"I was actually just looking at one today."

"You'll be fed up with all that in a week," Daniel said.

Daniel had probably tightened his bond with Shak by learning the details of his troubled past. Like Daniel, Shak had come from humble beginnings and made money through online advertising. But the odds stacked against the Brit had been even greater.

Shak's parents were immigrants from a small village in Pakistan who moved to the UK in the 1970s. As a teenager, Shak found himself in the working-class area of Dagenham in London, where he had to contend with local skinheads who would spit in his direction and call him a "paki." He would fight and smoke weed. When his parents found out about the drugs, they confronted him, according to Shak, which led to a blowout.

Later in life, Shak would describe how he left home in March of 1989, the same day he turned sixteen. In his late teens, Shak stole cars and was forced to sleep rough at times. He eventually started selling drugs, which led to two years of confinement.

"I'm probably the man I am today because of these trials," Shak would admit.

In the mid-1990s, he started buying and selling used cell phones, exploiting the price discrepancy between local phone shops in Dublin and the second-hand market in London. Shak would look through the Yellow Pages and then drive around the British capital buying used phones, polishing them up before flying to Dublin to peddle them to shop owners. Before returning to London, he'd lock himself inside one of the airport restrooms and count his billfold.

Eventually, Shak would use computer technology to escape a life of poverty and crime. He did not use a computer until 1995, when he was twenty-two years old. Yet around the turn of the millennium, he founded the company Smsboy.com, a website that let users send text messages online. Shak would go on to sell domain names and market off-brand Viagra pills online through a company called Activemed.

By the spring of 2008, Shak had turned thirty-four. The deal with AOL had made him independently wealthy, and he was looking for a new project to invest in. His friends in London warned him against it, but he decided to trust his instincts and invest half of his fortune in Spotify.

"I wasn't backing a music product. I was backing an entrepreneur named Daniel Ek," Shak would explain.

But Shak did not rest on his laurels. Soon, he was back on the grind, doing what he does best. He would network and schmooze with rich, powerful figures in the international tech world. Gradually, he became Daniel's special envoy, his "eyes and ears" in the secret circles where decisions are made.

It was Shak who would eventually provide Sean Parker, the co-founder of Napster, with an early version of Spotify, long before the service was legally available in the US.

ALL MUSIC FOR FREE

O N SEPTEMBER 27, 2008, SPOTIFY threw a huge launch party at Berns, a classic nightclub and concert venue originally built in the late 1800s to accommodate a rowdy variety theater crowd. The lofty salons and ornate galleries were decorated with oversized helium balloons in Spotify green, and guests were invited to play *Guitar Hero*. The financial crisis was raging, but Spotify had already secured its funding. Now the coworkers wanted to celebrate their launch in style. The only problem was that it hadn't quite happened yet. A few licensing details remained unresolved.

"Daniel and Martin were nervous," as one source would recall.

News of Spotify's funding round had leaked before the negotiations were done. Suddenly, knowing that Spotify had the money, the labels had started demanding better terms, according to one source.

During the party, though, Daniel and Martin held straight faces in their black suits. The group photo, taken in front of the main stage in the Grand Salon, shows just over forty employees, dressed to party. The head of marketing, Sophia Bendz, wore a beige dress. The programmer Gunnar Kreitz, however, saluted his alma mater by wearing his usual KTH t-shirt.

Sophia had seen to it that the party was sponsored by a beer brand and Xanté, a French brand of pear cognac. The drinks flowed all night as the staff mingled with friends, investors, and people from the music business. Shakil Khan worked the room, shaking hands with Spotify employees, but few understood what his role was at the company.

Spotify's negotiators, Petra Hansson and Niklas Ivarsson, had been in final talks with the labels for months. The secret blueprint that had emerged centered largely around revenue sharing, creating an incentive for growth. Around 55 percent of Spotify's revenue would go to the record companies, who own the recordings. Another 15 percent would go to the music publishers, who administer the rights of the songwriters. In theory, around 30 percent would be left over to finance Spotify's operations.

But in practice, Spotify risked running up costs that would eat away at their 30 percent. In order to protect themselves against lost revenue, the record companies had negotiated all kinds of extra measures. For instance, they had demanded that a minimum charge per stream be met if Spotify's revenues from ads and subscriptions dipped below a certain level. Spotify's negotiators had also agreed to making advance payments on their expected payouts. If Spotify missed its targets, the labels would keep any unearned advance. The labels had also secured a significant amount of shares in the company, for which they paid next to nothing. It was a complex arrangement. In short, Spotify would be punished harshly if the service didn't take off quickly, but the major labels would get paid either way.

During Spotify's first few years of operation, the payments to the music industry would exceed the company's total earnings. This meant that Spotify was turning a loss before they even started counting the expense of running the actual business. For years to come, a long line of investors would question if Spotify was a viable business.

Everything surrounding the deals with the music industry was top secret. Only a few of Daniel's trusted officers knew the details. It certainly wasn't a conversation starter during a festive launch party at Berns. The short answer was that the deals were basically done, and could you please pass me another shot of Xanté?

Spotify's launch party became a boozy affair. One employee reportedly drank so much Xanté that he lost his keys, forcing him to break into his own apartment in the middle of the night, ending with a police interrogation.

ROCKIN' IN THE FREE WORLD

The deals with the labels were signed a few weeks later and on October 7, Spotify's head of marketing, Sophia Bendz, sent out a press release. It stated that the streaming service had now officially launched in Sweden and that a premium, ad-free version was available for ninety-nine Swedish crowns (around twelve US dollars) per month, but only to customers of the broadband provider Bredbandsbolaget. This was essentially a soft launch. Free subscriptions were still invite-only, and the premium deal with Bredbandsbolaget was a limited promotional offer.

The Spotify team gather to witness the commercial launch in October 2008. *(Rasmus Andersson)*

Around the same time, Sophia started calling the many journalists who had wanted to interview Spotify's founders during the beta period. A few weeks later, near the end of October, one of us interviewed Daniel Ek and Martin Lorentzon while on assignment for Sweden's biggest morning newspaper, *Dagens Nyheter*. Martin, who was more experienced in dealing with journalists, took charge of the interview. It was held on the sofa underneath the big Spotify sign in the lobby.

"This could become huge," said the thirty-nine-year-old chairman, dressed informally in a white sweatshirt, with an intensity about his person. He then proceeded to describe Spotify's mission.

"We want to be the best music player on the market. I think that within two to three years, we will have twenty million users," he said.

At the time, those figures seemed outlandishly optimistic—but he wasn't too far off. It would take Spotify around four years to reach twenty million users. Martin also explained that Spotify's free tier was the key to rapid growth.

"We believe that 2–15 percent of our users will be paying subscribers. The rest will use the free version," he said.

Again, his prediction wasn't far off. Spotify would grow quickly, but it would take many years before the level of paying users was high enough to appease skeptics in the music industry.

According to its chairman, Spotify would initially launch in eight countries. The number would later be dialed back to six, due to delays in Germany and Italy. Sweden was the first country to launch. In the UK, Spotify was rolled out gradually during 2009, closely monitored by various music industry bosses. The other early launches took place in Finland, Norway, France, and Spain.

The article in *Dagens Nyheter* was published on October 31 with the headline, "Swedes are Apple's Nightmare."

Spotify's founders Martin Lorentzon and Daniel Ek
around the time of the launch in October 2008. *(Niklas Larsson)*

CALIFORNIA LOVE

The founders of Spotify and SoundCloud built their visions on software, but there were also Swedes who believed they could revolutionize the music industry through innovative hardware.

In the summer of 2008, one of them landed at the LAX airport in Los Angeles. His name was Ola Sars, and he was one of the founders of Pacemaker, a pocket-sized DJ gadget that could be used to share playlists and MP3 mixes online.

Ola Sars was a former management consultant who hung around some of the people who would form the DJ collective, Swedish House Mafia. He had traveled to Los Angeles to pitch his vision of a new community in which "tastemakers" shared music with "taste takers."

"I'm here to see Jimmy Iovine," he said at the reception of Universal Music in Santa Monica.

Jimmy Iovine was a big deal. He had founded Interscope Records, which had spawned the pop sensation Gwen Stefani, as well as Dr. Dre's two celebrated albums, *The Chronic* and *2001*. Recently, he and Dr. Dre had started a company, Beats Electronics, that would soon introduce its headphone brand, Beats by Dre. Their products would be a huge success, but they hadn't reached the market yet and Jimmy was still open to new ideas. So, Ola found himself waiting outside the label boss's office, nervously stroking the Pacemaker that sat in his lap. The AC was on full blast and the thirty-five-year-old Swede was freezing in his black t-shirt. Finally, he was called into Iovine's office.

"The future of the industry will be all about lifestyle products," Ola would recall the fifty-five-year-old Iovine saying in a thick Brooklyn accent.

Ola briefly demonstrated how the Pacemaker worked, but Iovine didn't need to be convinced. He'd been thinking about digital music distribution for years and explained that he and Dre would love to be partners in Tonium, the company behind Pacemaker. Ola liked what he heard, but soon realized that Iovine wasn't willing to invest actual money in his company. Any deal was essentially going to boil down to trading shares for promotional value. Still, Iovine was a master at promotion. He had helped Steve Jobs market Apple's products with artists such U2 and 50 Cent. He could, Ola thought, have a decisive impact on the future of the Pacemaker.

Back in Stockholm, the investors in Ola Sars's company weren't seeing it. Why would they let the head of an American label become a shareholder at a bargain price? After a bit of back and forth, the negotiations fizzled out.

A few months later, when Jimmy Iovine and Dr. Dre launched their first products, the Beats by Dre brand became an instant phenomenon. Iovine used his connections to get artists and sports stars to pose with the fat headphones that sold for around three hundred dollars apiece. In 2009 alone, the company sold headphones for $180 million, which was about a third of the entire US market.

The Pacemaker never became a hit, but Ola Sars would be reunited with Jimmy Iovine three years later, when the Beats co-founder decided to take on Spotify.

HUNG UP

Spotify's launch with Bredbandsbolaget started on a small scale. But in early December 2008, Daniel Ek raised the bar in order to kickstart the company's growth. He let the provider run Christmas ads promising half a million free accounts to its broadband customers. In a country with only nine million inhabitants, that was a high number.

It was only a matter of time before Spotify opened up its free version to all of Sweden. Still, the ad campaign caused a stir in the music industry. A business developer at Warner Music named Jacob Key was astonished to see the ads in the Stockholm subway.

"You can't do this," he yelled over the phone to his contact at Spotify, as he would recall.

"You can't make money off of Bredbandsbolaget while letting them market Spotify as a free service. If you do that, we need to get paid as well," he said.

Representatives from Universal and Sony also complained. They all resented that music was ostensibly being given away for free—and was marketing the very broadband subscriptions that were killing their industry.

Soon, their criticism had reached Andreas Liffgarden, the business developer behind the deal with Bredbandsbolaget. He quickly learned to be careful when using words like "free" or "free of charge" in ad campaigns with telcos and broadband providers.

Yet it was clear to Andreas and Daniel that the larger telcos of Europe could play an important role for Spotify. To most customers, they offered services that looked the same. These companies urgently needed to differentiate themselves and partnering with Spotify could be the perfect way to do so.

The labels would soon push for Spotify to prioritize growing the number of paid customers. At Warner Music, Jacob Key demanded that Spotify's promotional deals with broadband companies result in paying customers. He also pushed for those subscriptions to be renewed automatically at the end of a promotional period in which Spotify's monthly fee may have been bundled into some sort of package deal.

These principles would prove important as Spotify approached an even bigger broadband provider.

EVERYBODY'S TALKIN'

In February 2009, Spotify became broadly available in the UK, gaining a million British users in just over two months. The founders soon opened a London office located on the fifteenth floor of Centre Point, a skyscraper on the eastern end of Oxford Street, adjacent to Soho. Daniel Ek would also introduce himself to the British public.

"I've created things that millions of people have used before," the twenty-six-year-old CEO said in an interview with *The Independent* in Stockholm, "but this is the first time people have started to recognize me in the street."

The article describes Daniel's early years at Stardoll and lets him pontificate about the future of the music business. In it, the founder describes Spotify as a potential tool for launching artists in new markets. He mentions that the Scottish rock band Glasvegas started being played on the radio in Sweden as a result of their music being on Spotify.

"Record companies need to think about the way they break artists internationally. Why not just make the music free everywhere and see where it gets picked up?" Daniel is quoted as saying, airing an idea often used to defend file-sharing that must have irked people in the music industry.

In London, the Spotify CEO would often hang out with Shakil Khan, whose role ranged from friend to investor to fixer to paid consultant. Shak liked to do people favors, knowing that he might be able to ask for something in return.

Daniel and Shak would eat and work late in Spotify's office, with views over the river Thames and the Tower Bridge.

By now, Spotify had risen to become one of Europe's hottest startups.

"The user experience is beyond even the best web based streaming services like LaLa, MySpace Music, and Imeem," the website TechCrunch wrote in early 2009, explaining in detail, how to access Spotify via proxy servers. That way, listeners based where the service wasn't available could cheat the system and gain access.

"It acts like a fully stocked iTunes, with everything hyperlinked to easily find related music. Creating playlists is a snap," the article read.

One evening in their near-empty office, Daniel and Shak received a visit from someone looking to partner with Spotify— Joe Cohen, who had encountered a then-unknown Daniel Ek at the Essential Web conference a few years back.

The trio sat down and Daniel began to wax lyrical about the challenges ahead for Spotify. They casually exchanged business ideas before Cohen got to the point. He wanted Spotify to partner with his company, Seatwave, an online marketplace for concert tickets.

As he argued his case, Cohen noticed the interaction between Daniel, the introverted boss, and Shak, the extroverted dealmaker. The two appeared to be acting almost in unison, as if they were two parts of the same person. Finally, Daniel put his foot down.

"Listen, the thing is, you guys are selling tickets on the secondary market and that would just piss off artists and labels. I can't be in the business of pissing off artists and labels," Daniel said, sounding assured.

Spotify had launched in the UK using the words "instant, simple, and free." But the blowback from the labels was severe, and Daniel was now carefully avoiding anything that could be seen as his succeeding at the expense of the industry. It was important for Spotify's operations, but also for raising much-needed capital.

Back in Stockholm, Spotify's developers had done their part to clean up the company's act. They had just carried out what was internally known as "The Big Clean," a purge of the last pirated files from the Spotify catalogue.

TAXI

In February 2009, the entertainment industry was set for a decisive victory against the piracy movement. The founders of The Pirate Bay were brought before the Stockholm district court.

During the seventh day of trial, representatives from the creative industries were due to testify. Per Sundin, now head of Universal Music Sweden, hopped in a cab and headed to the court. On his way there, he noticed that the driver had a small plastic case of what looked like blank CDs stuck in the sun visor of his car. After a polite inquiry, the driver admitted that he often listened to pirated music.

"I figure it's OK. I've bought so many CDs in my life," he said.

Once again, Sundin felt the indignation rise within him. When the taxi pulled up outside the court building, he told the driver that he wouldn't be paying the fare.

"You know, I've paid for so many cab journeys in my life," he said, getting out of the car.

Outside, the hordes of journalists and young protesters with Pirate Bay flags made him reassess. Grudgingly, he paid the driver and made his way through the crowd.

In his testimony, Per Sundin said that file-sharing had essentially cut the record industry's sales in half. The trial made front-page news, and many Swedes were sympathetic to the young hackers that appeared to be bullied by "Hollywood lawyers." Swedish artists, like the rapper Timbuktu, grabbed headlines by praising the technology behind The Pirate Bay. Some experts questioned the whole premise of the case, claiming that file-sharing could not be blamed for declining CD sales.

But attitudes would soon be shifting. On the same day that Sundin testified in court, the Swedish parliament passed the so-called IPRED law. Authorities would now have a broader mandate to take action against the unlawful sharing of music and video files.

The four defendants in The Pirate Bay case lost in the district court, and later in the court of appeals. In the election to the European Parliament, in June 2009, many young voters showed their dissatisfaction by voting for the Pirate Party. But soon, the prevalence of streaming services like Spotify would mollify the public debate. Five years later, when the

Pirate Party was voted out of the European Parliament, the issue had been all but forgotten.

WHENEVER, WHEREVER

With the launch behind him, Daniel Ek started focusing his attention on building a mobile app. Many of Spotify's competitors were already offering music on handheld devices. The Finnish mobile giant Nokia had just launched a massive marketing campaign for its service, Nokia Comes With Music. Its Swedish competitor, Sony Ericsson, had a music service called Play Now Arena, and Sweden's biggest telco, Telia, had the Telia Music Player.

But Daniel didn't want to compete with regional players. He wanted to challenge Apple's iPod head on, and he felt he had found the right man for the job: Gustav Söderström, an athletic KTH alum with blond hair, blue eyes, and a chiseled jawline. At thirty-two, he had already amassed some personal wealth by founding and selling a mobile internet company to Yahoo!. He was up for a new challenge and, short of moving to Silicon Valley, Spotify seemed like the coolest job around.

Daniel wanted Gustav Söderström to build an app that worked wherever the iPod worked. The Spotify CEO explained that it needed to have an "offline mode" so that it would work on airplanes and without access to 3G. His theory was that users would pay not only for music, but for access and ease of use. The app needed to sync automatically with Spotify's desktop client. If you put a track into a Spotify playlist on your computer, it needed to appear on the phone as well.

The app would require new licenses from the music industry, but Daniel had reason to believe they would cooperate. He was leaning toward making the app a premium feature, thus creating a new incentive for users to pay for the service. The math was simple: Paying users generated almost all of Spotify's revenue, and more revenue meant higher payouts to the industry.

Gustav signed up as Spotify's new head of mobile, insisting on handpicking his own team, which would include some of Spotify's best engineers. Daniel gave him his blessing.

Gustav Söderström was used to getting what he wanted. While doing his mandatory military service as a young man, he led a ski battalion in the northern municipality of Arvidsjaur. The soldiers were loyal, following his every lead. Leading a new project at Spotify would, however, turn out to be more like herding cats.

Spotify's engineers had good reason to be proud of their work. They had built the world's best streaming player from scratch and felt that their indie spirit had paid off. They had pulled off some impressive feats with mobile apps, such as hacking into Nokia's Series 60 operating system and Apple's first rendition of the iPhone. So, when Gustav started poaching engineers to build a new mobile team, he was met with resistance.

In a podcast interview, Gustav would recall how he was forced to hold endless email conversations with some of the more stubborn engineers. Eventually, he managed to wear down his critics. The experience seems to have shaped his outlook as a manager. For years to come, he would send long emails to the staff, at all hours of the day, about where Spotify was heading and what they needed to do to get there.

Within a few months, the mobile team had built an app that met Daniel's specifications. Gustav had flown to London with Niklas Ivarsson to negotiate with Sony and Universal. Daniel had been right; the app was approved without too many questions. After all, a strong premium service meant more revenue for the music industry, and higher personal bonuses for its executives.

In July 2009, Daniel stepped into Soho House on Greek Street in London, a dimly lit members' club full of designer furniture. He approached a familiar journalist named Rory Cellan-Jones, who was a tech correspondent for the BBC.

"I have something to show you," the Swedish CEO said, with a wry smile and an iPhone in his hand.

Rory Cellan-Jones was used to getting daily news tips from startups, but Daniel's pitch was special. It was the hot Spotify music client, inside an iPhone. The app was still in beta and would crash occasionally, but it carried several impressive features. For one, you could download your playlists to the phone and listen to them on the subway, where the 3G signal was crap.

The BBC journalist tried the app over the course of a few days, concluding that it would prove the Swedish's company's big breakthrough. Soon, he had broken the news of Spotify's forthcoming mobile product.

Toward the end of July, Gustav's team submitted the app to Apple's App Store. Many staffers were afraid that Apple would find an excuse to block it. After all, they were asking Steve Jobs to open the door to a competitor.

TICKET TO RIDE

In early 2009, Spotify resumed negotiations to launch in the United States. Fred Davis and his team were gradually becoming less involved, with Daniel Ek relying more on Ken Parks, Petra Hansson, and Niklas Ivarsson.

Late in the summer of 2009, Daniel received a long email that gave him renewed hope. It came from Napster's co-founder Sean Parker, who had made a killing off of his shares in Facebook and would soon become a billionaire.

"You've built an amazing experience," Sean wrote. "Ever since Napster I've dreamt of building a product similar to Spotify."

Daniel could hardly believe his eyes.

Sean Parker had moved on from Napster, becoming Facebook's first president at the age of twenty-four. But in 2005, police found cocaine in a vacation home he was renting. He wasn't charged, but the arrest rattled investors and led to his resigning from Facebook. Now, Spotify had become his new obsession.

Sean had recently met Daniel's personal envoy, Shakil Khan, at a private barbecue in New York City. The American had asked about the music coming out of the speakers. It turned out that Shak could offer him a private demo of a service that had yet to be launched in the US. Shak gave Sean one of Daniel Ek's secret, prepaid invites.

In his email, Sean waxed lyrical about the service, which he felt was completely superior to iTunes.

"You've distilled the product down to its core essence," he wrote, before he opened the door to Facebook's founder and CEO.

"Zuck and I have been talking about what this partnership should look like," he wrote.

To Daniel, the email was a gift from above. At the very least, it could help his company launch and grow in the US.

PICK UP THE PHONE

During the spring and summer of 2009, the global economy was suffering. Just a few months earlier, America's new president, Barack Obama, had pushed through a gigantic stimulus package, but the markets were still reeling from the financial crisis as Spotify started preparing its next round of funding.

The music service was adding tens of thousands of users daily, but the business itself was very risky. Spotify was paying more for its music than it was pulling in revenues, the company still had no US licenses, and the app had not yet been included in the App Store.

Daniel Ek now had seventy-five employees on his payroll. The finance team had been told to fetch a valuation of $250 million, a level that few investors found reasonable. Once again, Spotify had to raise capital based on an optimistic projection of their future growth. Their pitch centered around the famous hockey-stick graph, the idea that the company's modest growth would shoot up once they had more money to hire staff, enter new markets, and keep growing.

Several high-profile US funds passed on the deal, but the finance team— led by the CFO, Daniel Ekberger—found a willing trio of investors from Europe and Asia. The group consisted of London's Wellington Partners, German investor Klaus Hommels's firm Lakestar, and Li Ka-shing, one of Asia's top business magnates. Together, they invested around $25 million in a deal that valued Spotify at $270 million.

One summer night, Daniel Ek was awakened by a loud buzz in Vasastan in Stockholm. He grabbed his phone and tried to make out the number on the display. It appeared to be a call from Asia.

"Our chairman would like to speak with you," a voice said at the other end, as Daniel would recall.

"Yes, okay," the Spotify CEO said.

The chairman in question was the eighty-one-year-old Li Ka-shing himself. He was on Spotify, struggling to find his favorite song. Daniel Ek had to perform customer service duties over the phone to please his new investor.

THE TIMES THEY ARE A-CHANGIN'

Soon, the financial press reported on Spotify's new valuation and a user total of two million. The label bosses followed the progress closely. At the same time, many artists were skeptical of the streaming service, some even refusing to take part. Music by Metallica, Pink Floyd, and The Beatles was notably lacking in Spotify's otherwise steadily growing catalogue.

In early August, a tall, slender man entered the Sony Music offices on Derry Street in London. It was Bob Dylan's legendary manager, Jeff Rosen, who had come to learn more about this new European streaming service. His job was to ensure that his client was getting a fair share of the company's revenues.

Jeff Rosen was an astute businessman. He had masterminded Bob Dylan's *Biograph*, one of the record industry's first CD box collections from the mid-1980s. Later, he convinced artists like Eric Clapton, Stevie Wonder, and Sinéad O'Connor to perform at a tribute concert for Bob Dylan in Madison Square Garden. The concert was broadcast live on pay-per-view, and was later released as a double disk DVD. In short, Rosen had made a ton of money for Columbia Records, which was now owned by Sony, and he demanded to be treated accordingly.

After the usual introductions, he ended up in a meeting room with glass walls and thick drapes, across from three mid-level managers at Sony's digital division.

"So, tell me about Spotify," Rosen said.

The heads turned to the only Swede in the room, Samuel Arvidsson, who did his best to describe how the service worked on a technical level. He explained the difference between Spotify's free tier and its premium subscription service. He said that the record companies were paid a share of this revenue that they would then use to compensate artists. After a few minutes, Rosen cut in.

"How many shares in Spotify does Bob Dylan own?"

The room fell silent. The three label managers glanced nervously at each other. A widely quoted Swedish newspaper article had recently reported that the record companies, in secret, had been allowed to buy shares amounting to 17 percent of the company for next to nothing.

"Sony owns shares in Spotify, right? Now I'd like to know how many of those belong to my client," Rosen said, as Arvidsson would recall.

The Sony Music trio knew that their label owned shares in Spotify, and they strongly suspected that Bob Dylan wasn't entitled to a single one of them. But they promised to make inquiries. According to one account, one of the managers sent an email to Thomas Hesse, Sony's Chief Strategic Officer in New York. He would not recall receiving a clear answer.

A few days later, Bob Dylan withdrew all of his music from Spotify. The news sent a wave of fear through Spotify's office on Humlegårdsgatan. Having a legendary singer-songwriter like Bob Dylan leave the service was bad enough. But what would happen if Bob Dylan got Eric Clapton, Stevie Wonder, Sinéad O'Connor, and all his other buddies to do the same? If enough big names boycotted Spotify, the service could quickly become irrelevant.

FULA GUBBAR

The press broke the story of Bob Dylan's boycott in mid-August 2009. Reporters at the Swedish tabloid *Expressen* made calls and reported that several other musicians were considering the same move. The well-known Swedish pop star Magnus Uggla, signed to the same label as Bob Dylan, wondered aloud why Sony Music would be allowed to buy several percent of Spotify for the paltry sum of a few thousand dollars.

"It's because Sony has sold out their artists," Magnus Uggla wrote on his blog before launching into a colorful attack on his own label and its Swedish managing director, Hasse Breitholtz.

"One thing is certain. I'd rather be raped by The Pirate Bay than fucked in the ass by Hasse Breitholtz and Sony Music. I will therefore remove all my tracks from Spotify and wait for an honest internet service," the artist declared.

The reporters at *Expressen* tried to reach Spotify for comment, to no avail. They then paid a visit to Spotify's office on Humlegårdsgatan, where they were denied entrance. Finally, Spotify's press people sent out a short statement where Daniel Ek described his company as "a significant digital revenue source" for the industry. The reporters also reached Hasse Breitholtz at Sony Music.

"Both Spotify and the record companies pay royalties to the authors— Pirate Bay pays nothing," the label head was quoted as saying.

The tabloid reporters also reached out to Per Sundin at Universal Music. They asked how much artists were paid each time someone streamed a song. It was a straightforward question. But Spotify's secret deals with the record companies were so complicated that it was impossible to answer in kind. Therefore, Sundin couldn't offer a clear explanation.

This chain of events would repeat itself many times over the coming years. An artist would make a public statement about Spotify ripping off creators, and Daniel would react by stating how much Spotify was paying the industry as a whole. But neither Spotify nor the record companies would go further than that. One reason was that Spotify's revenue sharing agreements with the industry, while pegged at around 70 percent, would fluctuate wildly depending on a variety of variables. Another was that the labels had their own agreements with artists that they wouldn't discuss in public. There wasn't a neat figure to sum up the payout for every stream.

The artists had many legitimate reasons to complain. In 2009, Spotify's payouts were still relatively small—and would continue to be as long as the overwhelming majority used the free version. The artists could argue that Spotify was growing at their expense, while the record labels had a vested interest in the success of the service. After all, they owned shares. Another complicating factor was that streaming services had a much longer payout cycle. Customers paid for CDs and downloads upfront, while streaming revenues trickled in gradually over many years.

Certain artists now started demanding that their music only be available to Spotify's paid subscribers, but Daniel refused. He made it clear to the record companies, and to his staff, that every artist would join Spotify on the same terms. The full catalogue had to be available both to free users and paying subscribers. Otherwise the whole business model would fall apart.

While the commercial launch had made Spotify's communications more open, the spat with Bob Dylan made the company pull back. One former employee would recall how, around this time, Spotify's head of marketing, Sophia Bendz, began to demand that they conduct themselves more like an American tech giant. The company would communicate on its own terms when it had something to say, and make few comments beyond that.

Over the years, Spotify's founders would often feel that they were misunderstood and mistreated by the media and the outside world. Martin Lorentzon generally felt that journalists were out to get him and often got the facts wrong. Daniel—known to buy thick stacks of magazines before boarding a flight—appreciated a good read, but saw much of the coverage of Spotify as sloppy. He would try to limit his appearances to reputable news outlets where he could deliver strategic talking points.

As a result, Spotify adopted an "us against the world" culture. The employees were told not to speak to the media without explicit approval. Among journalists, Spotify would become known as an exceptionally opaque company. At parties and gatherings, Spotify employees would clam up at the mere mention of a journalist being in the room.

In the months after Bob Dylan's defection, Daniel and his team carefully examined Spotify's user data. The boycott didn't affect the figures to any great extent. Users did not appear to abandon the service, and new ones continued to join at an undiminished rate. Nor was there a major string of boycotts from other artists following the singer-songwriter's lead.

Many famous artists would abandon Spotify over the years, but the record companies would generally succeed in luring them back. As much as they disliked the business model, abstaining from the service didn't do them much good either. Their CD and download sales largely did not increase when they left Spotify; they just missed out on a revenue stream that was growing in importance. Bob Dylan was no exception. Less than three years later, his music was back on Spotify.

Whether artists would share any of the profits from Spotify shares, however, would remain hotly debated for many years to come. It would resurface with a vengeance ahead of Spotify's IPO, nine years after Bob Dylan's original boycott.

I GOTTA FEELING

In late August 2009, a few dozen Spotify employees met up by Nybrokajen, a small dock lined by boats in central Stockholm. They boarded small recreational motorboats and headed out for an evening in the archipelago. Martin Lorentzon, who loves Swedish traditions, was laughing in the back of one of the boats and fiddling with his phone.

"What do you think, is Apple going to let us into that goddamn App Store?" he said, grinning. "Who wants to bet a thousand crowns?"

They anchored the boats in an inlet called Skurusundet. The coworkers unloaded picnic food, beer, sausages, and disposable grills and held a simple barbecue together by the water in the evening sunshine.

When the sun finally started setting, they returned to the city for a night on the town. They anchored their boats in the canal by Djurgården and made their way to Utecompagniet, an open-air restaurant on the Stureplan square. Martin ordered drinks and champagne and suddenly, made an announcement.

"We got it!" he shouted.

The Spotify employees exploded with joy and started toasting and congratulating each other. The drinks kept coming and emotions ran high.

The evening is said to have ended abruptly after one employee emptied a champagne bucket of ice water over Martin's head. The Spotify co-founder lost his temper. The employees finished their drinks and parted ways.

For the rest of the world, the news became official on August 27. Daniel Ek confirmed it in a tweet.

"We're happy but have had a great dialogue with Apple all the way. They've been great!" he wrote.

Behind the scenes, the atmosphere between the two companies had been less than perfect. For years, Spotify would have a hard time getting new versions of their app approved by the App Store. The developers would often complain about how Apple was making things more difficult by changing or reinterpreting their own guidelines.

The conflict over Apple's outsized power over the app economy had only begun.

BRIDGE TO AMERICA

POTIFY'S BUSINESS MODEL RELIED ON volume. In order to succeed, Daniel Ek had to outgrow his competitors, enter the US market, and become one of the world's biggest music-streaming providers. If investors didn't see constant breakneck growth, they would stop pumping in the cash that fueled the company and Spotify would likely spiral to its death. Daniel knew it, the heads of the record companies knew it, and Steve Jobs knew it, too.

The Apple CEO had seen enough streaming companies fail and falter to understand the importance of momentum. Apple had allowed Spotify to be part of the App Store and keep growing in Europe. But, when its founder heard that Daniel was looking for music licenses in the US, he pushed back, as several people would recall.

Some saw Jobs's behavior as a whisper campaign intended to stop, or at least delay, Spotify's entry in the US. Apple's chief executive had, after all, spent years building and marketing iTunes together with his allies at the major labels. It had become the world's largest music store, and an integral part of Apple's ecosystem, driving the sale of Macs, iPods, and iPhones. Spotify was like a foreign vermin threatening to invade Apple's walled garden.

Many music executives shared Jobs's perspective. Sure, Apple was dominant, but the company was selling downloads for billions of dollars, giving around 70 percent back to the industry. Spotify's growth was based on giving music away for pennies on the dollar, with a vague promise of changing digital distribution down the line.

If Daniel wanted the keys to their market, he needed to make them an offer they couldn't refuse.

CALIFORNIA DREAMIN'

On a sunny day in September 2009, one of America's best-known tech journalists stepped into Centre Point in London. The sound of her heels hitting the marble floors echoed through the lobby. Kara Swisher had covered the industry for more than ten years, interviewing names like Bill Gates and Steve Jobs. Today, she had an appointment to see Daniel Ek.

Swisher took the elevator up to Spotify's offices, set up her video camera, and opened the interview with a bit of flattery.

"You're *it* in Silicon Valley," she said, as the camera started recording.

Daniel smiled cautiously.

"We're quite big here in London," he said. "Hopefully we can make our leap over to the US quite soon."

He then launched into his usual pitch: Spotify was going to beat the pirates and save the music industry. When asked about the company's future direction, he was clear.

"I want to grow and become an independent company. I don't want to sell to anyone."

Daniel did not want Spotify to be acquired by a US tech giant.

"What I hope to do is build a good, independent company that hopefully can start acquiring US businesses," he said.

The Spotify CEO had now adopted a more polished style. His disheveled combover had been shaved off, and at times he'd throw a suit jacket over his usual garb of polo shirts or t-shirts.

Daniel had recently relocated to London with his Swedish girlfriend, Charlotte Ågren, whom he had been dating for more than six months. A few years younger than Daniel, Charlotte was a charming and outgoing Stockholmer who loved to organize dinners and was often the life of the party. She would later acquire and develop an online community for Swedes based in London.

When they met at a poker night for entrepreneurs in Stockholm, Charlotte had been saving money to study in Australia. Instead, she settled for Marylebone, a picturesque area of central London known for its quaint high street with cafés and book shops. She and Daniel moved into an apartment with a large balcony and hardwood floors, within walking distance of the Spotify UK office.

The young Swedish couple lived on Great Portland Street, just a few buildings down from Shakil Khan. In fact, Shak had been the one who found their rented condo apartment and welcomed them with membership cards at trendy members' clubs like Soho House. He would also introduce Daniel to restaurants like Nobu in the posh, nearby area of Mayfair.

"Shak took Daniel's life to a whole new level," as one person familiar with their interactions would recall.

Like Daniel, Shak was a self-made entrepreneur who had spent years hustling on the startup scene. Charlotte was a self-starter, too. In the years to come, Daniel would often be drawn to people—whether colleagues, friends, or lovers—who were bold in character and in their achievements.

When the CEO made public appearances, the charismatic Shak would work the room, using the buzz around Spotify to make new connections and keep building what his friends called his "global favor bank."

When they weren't working, Daniel and Shak would binge-watch the HBO series *Entourage*, which chronicled a young actor's ascent in Hollywood alongside his crew of male friends and his over-the-top agent, Ari Gold.

One day, Shak returned from a trip to Los Angeles, where he had visited the *Entourage* set. He brought back a t-shirt with a bulging "Suits Suck" print on the front, a version of which had been worn in several scenes in the series. It quickly became one of Daniel's favorite items of clothing.

In London, there were constant demands for Daniel's time. He would frequently dine with celebrities and tech millionaires eager to get to know him in an informal setting. He'd often bring Charlotte, who would join him at dinners, events, and even business trips to the United States. The couple would show up casually dressed, comfortable with each other and their surroundings. Daniel would also give keynote interviews and once traveled northwest for an appearance at the University of Oxford, one of the few occasions for which he slipped on a button-up shirt.

Once he had moved to the UK, the life that Daniel would describe as "a fairytale" appeared to have begun.

But his calendar was demanding, and constantly shifting. Most of the time, the twenty-six-year-old only had a firm itinerary for the upcoming week. And at any moment, his personal assistant could throw in yet another cross-Atlantic flight.

UP WHERE WE BELONG

Around the time of Daniel Ek's interview with Kara Swisher, the Spotify founders flew to New York to meet Sean Parker.

When he was in New York, the Napster co-founder would live and work out of a luxuriously renovated townhouse in the West Village. It was called "the Bacchus House," after the Roman god of wine and intoxication. The place was famous for its parties and its unapologetic mixing of business with pleasure. The basement featured a gym and a pool, and the rooftop terrace offered a view of the Manhattan skyline.

The Swedes rang the doorbell and were let into a hallway filled with people who were also there to see Sean. After a bit of confusion, Daniel and Martin were finally approached by the wide-eyed, curly-haired entrepreneur who, without knowing it, had inspired Daniel to start Spotify.

As they settled into the meeting, Daniel and Sean were quick to find common ground. They reminisced about their teenage years as file-sharing computer nerds, and Daniel got the impression that Sean, four years his senior, may even have been a part of the same online hacker forum. In yet another hard-to-confirm story, the Swede would faintly recall chatting with "Napshon," an alias he assumed had belonged to Sean Parker.

The meeting's fourth participant was Peter Thiel, one of PayPal's founders and Facebook's first outside investor. He ran the Founders Fund, where Sean was now a partner. Daniel would recall how the meeting lasted for hours, during which the Americans expressed an interest in investing in Spotify. Having recently secured new funding from other investors, the Swedish duo didn't exactly need the money, but the offer felt like a breakthrough, nonetheless. Having the energetic Sean Parker on board could prove strategically valuable, not least because he could get them closer to Facebook, which was about to surpass 300 million monthly users.

In late December 2009, the Founders Fund invested $16.5 million in Spotify in exchange for five percent of the company. According to public records, the deal valued Spotify at $330 million. It was a fraction of Facebook's $10 billion price tag, but Sean sensed that Spotify had upward momentum. He joined the board and would quickly surpass Shakil Khan as the company's ambassador and informal dealmaker in the US. At this point, the Napster co-founder was still a rising star. (He would soon be portrayed by Justin Timberlake as a tech billionaire in the hit movie *The Social Network*.)

The primary objective was now to bring Spotify to the US market. All that stood in their way were the very same record companies that had brought Napster to its knees. Daniel would recall saying that he thought Spotify could obtain the necessary music licenses within six weeks, a goal Sean thought sounded unrealistic.

"Daniel, it's going to take twelve weeks," he said, as Daniel would recall.

By the end of 2009, Daniel returned to New York City, where he would remain for several months. He was also booked to appear at South by Southwest, a music and technology festival in Austin, Texas.

Among tech reporters, the forthcoming appearance was taken as a sure sign that Spotify would soon hit the US.

I WANT IT ALL

To ensure broad appeal in Sweden, Daniel Ek wanted Spotify to abandon its deal with Bredbandsbolaget and start working with the country's biggest telecoms firm, Telia. Representatives of the telco appeared willing to switch from offering their own clunky streaming service, Telia Music Player, to Spotify. They did, however, make a few requests.

As the meetings wore on, it became clear that Telia essentially wanted to "skin" the Spotify player, adding their own colors and design. As the business developer Andreas Liffgarden started going through Telia's ballooning list of demands, Daniel made it clear that he would not compromise.

"We'll let them put their logo on it, but nothing else. Otherwise forget about it," he said.

The gambit paid off. In October 2009, a year after Spotify's first commercial launch, the startup presented a two-year deal with Telia. For an extra monthly fee, customers were offered the ad-free version of Spotify on their computers, mobile phones, and Telia's set-top boxes.

The deal was Spotify's biggest sale to date, and an important milestone for both companies. It is said that Telia bought Spotify subscriptions at a wholesale discount for around $7 million.

The bundle had given Telia a "hero product," something they had been without ever since they partnered temporarily with Apple as exclusive distributor of the iPhone in Sweden. For Daniel Ek, it was an opportunity to reach Swedish households en masse. The bundle promised a stable source of income and free marketing, beginning with a broad Christmas campaign.

The local record labels generally approved. Telia had been given a hefty discount on its Spotify subscriptions, but the "sticker price" in the promotional campaigns was in line with Spotify's full price of around ten dollars per month. Crucially, the messaging did not dilute the perceived value of music. Telia also promised that the subscriptions would be renewed automatically at full price when the promotional period ran out.

Most importantly, the partnership with Telia gave Daniel Ek a blueprint for telco bundles down the line, one of his best arguments when he needed to convince music executives that Spotify could convert free listeners to paid subscribers. In the coming years, Spotify's paid service was bundled with Virgin Media in the UK, Telefonica in Spain, KPN in Holland, SFR in France, and Deutsche Telekom in Germany. Spotify would often enter a new market by partnering with a telco and expanding from there.

Spotify's competitors—from the Swedish-Norwegian service WiMP to Deezer in France—would follow suit. Many years later, WiMP's parent company, Aspiro, would be purchased by the hip-hop mogul Jay-Z and change its name to Tidal.

EVERYBODY'S CHANGING

As Spotify turned into a commercial service, major changes were in store for its engineers. Many of the original programmers would complain that the company was becoming too corporate and too concerned with pleasing the music industry. For more than two years, they had ruled the roost. Now, business developers and marketing people were starting to call the shots.

When CTO Andreas Ehn heard that Spotify was going to procure a certain type of enterprise software, he strongly objected.

"We can build something better ourselves," a former colleague recalled Andreas saying.

This do-it-yourself attitude made no sense to his new, business-oriented colleagues. Spotify was clearly too big to be cobbling together its own software. Surely the engineers had better things to do. Frustrated by his dwindling authority, Andreas Ehn started feeling estranged from his own company. He missed the early days of dreaming big and solving problems with his team on the whiteboard.

Toward the end of 2009, Andreas Ehn resigned from the company he had helped build from the ground up. In the following months, several early engineers followed him out the door. One of them was Spotify's first head of product, Fredrik Niemelä. To him, the final straw was when his colleagues introduced Spotify Unlimited, a later-discontinued subscription option which offered an ad-free experience, only without access to the mobile app. The head of product found the name to be misleading. He felt the whole idea ran counter to Spotify's core value of inclusiveness. Spotify's head of mobile, the rising star Gustav Söderström, took Fredrik's place and within a year, he had assumed the title of CPO.

Spotify was now growing in leaps and bounds, with new challenges cropping up every day. In lieu of a clear organizational plan, colleagues would compete over who should do what. Some quit while others stayed on, honing their skills as Spotify grew bigger and became more international.

Outgoing employees were often given a chance to sell their stock options, rights that were worth hundreds of thousands of dollars or more. Despite his frustration, Andreas Ehn held onto his shares, a decision that would, in time, make him very rich.

WHAT YOU WAITING FOR?

In mid-March 2010, Daniel Ek sat down in a tall director's chair on a stage in Austin, Texas. The twenty-seven-year-old looked like he'd been through a rough winter. He was heavyset and pasty, dressed in a pullover with white and blue horizontal stripes. The spotlight made his head shine. He was about to be interviewed by a reporter from *Wired* magazine during a keynote appearance at South by Southwest.

Many in the audience hoped that Daniel Ek would announce when Spotify was going to enter the US. On that, he would disappoint. Talks with the labels, particularly Universal and Warner, had ground to a near halt in the six months that had followed his first meeting with Sean Parker in New York.

Universal Music's long-serving CEO, Doug Morris, is said to have told one of his staff members that the label "should hitch its ride to Apple's train." In early 2010, Morris even told his digital team to "stop talking to Spotify," according to one source, although the silent treatment would only last for about a month.

One reason for Morris's skepticism may have been a rumor that Google was poised to buy Spotify once the service had gained access to the US. Two sources would recall him expressing this suspicion.

"And if there is one thing label executives don't like, it's making *other* people rich," as one source would describe it.

Another source would point out that the heads of Universal would have been uneasy about Google, another tech giant, wielding even more influence over their industry, having already acquired YouTube and its music rights in 2006.

The Google rumor was not unfounded. One well-placed source would confirm that Daniel Ek was indeed talking to Google representatives about selling his company, perhaps as early as 2009. By the following year, Google's co-founder, Larry Page, its CEO, Eric Schmidt, and their legal counsel, Zahavah Levine, were all said to be involved. According to the source, the price tag grew from a figure in the hundreds of millions to, at one point, a billion dollars. For Google, the choice stood between buying Spotify and building their own service. The following year, the search giant would launch the cloud-based Google Play Music.

Daniel's true intentions would remain hotly debated among people who were close to him. Many sources would claim that his wish was never to sell, but that he would use the negotiations to see what kind of strategic value Spotify had in the world of tech and entertainment. The talks also served as leverage in Spotify's negotiations with investors. Others claim that Google simply never offered enough money and that Larry Page didn't prioritize music highly enough. Regardless, the Google rumor would impact Spotify's negotiations with Universal for years to come.

Around early 2010, Warner Music wasn't cooperating with Spotify either. A month before Daniel's appearance in Austin, Edgar Bronfman Jr.—now CEO of Warner—had publicly attacked the business model that powered

Spotify. Bronfman declared that the label would not license its music to any free, ad-supported streaming services in the future. Daniel had responded by saying that Spotify was taking on music piracy and was on its way to becoming one of the industry's "top four" sources of revenue.

During the interview in Austin, Daniel made no mention of the drama with the labels or his meetings with Google. He limited the interview to a demo of Spotify's desktop client and mobile app, which were both projected on the big screen behind him.

"One of my personal favorites, that I think will be very big, is our collaborative playlists," Daniel said in his fluent, carefully articulated English.

On stage, the Spotify founder hardly mentioned his main rival, Apple. When he pulled up the Spotify mobile app, it was on an Android-based Sony Ericsson X10 mini, not an iPhone. At one point, he remarked that many users found Spotify to be faster than iTunes.

As Spotify struggled to gain access to the US market, Apple appeared to be making strides. A few months earlier, Steve Jobs had acquired a streaming service called Lala for what was believed to be $80 million. The deal led some in the music world to speculate that the Apple CEO was about to make the shift to streaming, or at least to a cloud-based version of iTunes.

Daniel also had to worry about other competitors. Niklas Zennström's streaming service, Rdio, was gearing up to go live in the US in a few months' time. But the Skype founder's Spotify rival did not have a free service.

In some ways, Spotify was making progress. A few weeks after Daniel's appearance in Austin, he presented a Facebook integration that let users browse their friends' playlists. Ever aware of trends in the online space, the Swede would now begin to describe Spotify as a "social" music service more frequently.

Yet Daniel Ek still lacked what his company needed most: a date when Spotify would enter the US.

LEARNING TO FLY

What Spotify lacked in firm launch dates, it made up for in buzz and hype. Throughout 2010, Shakil Khan continued to spread the word among the many rich and famous people he met.

The British smooth talker had managed to impress Chris Sacca, an early investor in Twitter, and would soon ask his friends in Stockholm to set up a free account for the R&B star Frank Ocean. Spotify was an increasingly hot topic among the pop-culture elite.

"Spotify is the sh*t!" actress Demi Moore tweeted in August 2010, having been fed an account by Shak.

Later the same year, she and then-husband Ashton Kutcher held a Christmas party in Los Angeles. Their guests all received dedicated Spotify invites prepared by the staff in Stockholm.

Daniel Ek welcomed the attention. He appreciated the value of hype and would make use of his increasing base of supporters. Two years after Spotify's launch in Sweden, the young CEO had met many of the most powerful people in the American tech and entertainment industry. But there was one exception.

"I've met all of them—except Steve Jobs," he said, according to one person he spoke to. Many others believe that Daniel never got to meet Steve Jobs.

His underlying suspicion appeared to be that Apple's CEO was conspiring against the vision he had for his company.

"I'm sure he wanted to know why Jobs was fucking with us," a source who worked closely with Daniel at the time would put it.

Daniel articulated his mission to upset the iTunes order during one of his trips to Los Angeles in 2010. At a meeting in Beverly Hills, the Swede met with several executives at Myspace, who wondered whether he might be willing to sell his company.

The social network, having already squandered their lead over Facebook, was looking to return to its roots in digital music. Myspace had recently acquired several music startups, but Spotify was the hottest of them all. As one person familiar with the talks would recall, one of Myspace's assets was exceptionally cheap and long-running licensing deals with the record companies. But the Spotify founder did not take the bait.

"If you're going to help me kill iTunes, we can keep talking," Daniel said, according to one person who was close to the Myspace leadership at the time.

"Otherwise, I'm not interested."

WIND OF CHANGE

In 2010, Spotify's burn rate was becoming a cause for concern. The company now had nearly 200 employees and around five million users, but no profits in sight. In June, the company moved out of its head office on Humlegårdsgatan and into a bigger space on Birger Jarlsgatan 6, next to Riche, a well-known, upscale bistro where bankers would rub elbows with entrepreneurs and creatives.

Spotify also had offices in London and New York, where a small team had recently moved into a massive brick building on 8th Avenue in Chelsea. The New York team was led by Ken Parks, Spotify's Chief Content Officer.

Spotify's costs kept swelling and the company was, once again, in need of funding. And, despite there having been no US launch, its valuation needed to increase substantially. It was the only way to ensure that the newly issued shares would not overly dilute the company's investors and founders, threatening their continued control over the company.

By the spring, Spotify's funding had become such an urgent problem that Martin Lorentzon had to put the company's new CFO to work earlier than expected.

"I'd like a valuation of a billion dollars. That's a nice, round figure," he told Peter Sterky, who wasn't due to start as finance chief until later in the year.

By Swedish standards, the number was staggering. It would be another three years before the expression "unicorn" was coined to describe companies with billion-dollar valuations. At this point, Facebook and Twitter were among the few tech startups that had reached that level.

Peter Sterky was used to Martin's boundless ambition. They had worked together at Tradedoubler, which Peter had joined as one of the first hires. He knew that many investors would balk at the Spotify chairman's aggressive asking price.

But the new CFO found that there was one influential investor willing to pay that high a price: a Russian backed by Alisher Usmanov, an oligarch with ties to the Kremlin and the Chinese tech giant Tencent.

And if that didn't pan out, the Spotify founders had other options.

MAN IN BLACK

One cloudy day in October 2010, dozens of students and hordes of journalists squeezed into a packed lecture hall at the KTH Royal Institute of Technology. Daniel Ek was about to take the stage, but right now, the cameras were pointed at a six-foot-five man pacing back and forth in front of the podium.

The man in the white collared shirt with the rolled-up sleeves was Microsoft's energetic CEO, Steve Ballmer, whom Bill Gates had personally selected as his successor twelve years earlier.

"The cloud drives advances that drive the cloud," Microsoft's CEO roared in a well-rehearsed routine about the software giant's cloud services.

Then he looked across the sea faces and welcomed a special guest.

"Danyelek," he exclaimed, compressing all the syllables into one loud burst of sound.

The audience exploded in applause for the man who had employed countless KTH engineers and built one of Europe's hottest startups. The Spotify CEO looked tanned and in good shape, dressed in a black shirt and suit jacket. Steve Ballmer shook Daniel's hand and gave him a double back pat before yielding the stage.

As the applause carried on, Daniel let an anxious gaze drift over the room. For an instant it looked as if he were going to start clapping, too, as if to honor Steve Ballmer, but instead, he brushed his hands against each other. Perhaps he didn't want to appear to be clapping for himself. Finally, the auditorium settled down.

"It's great to be here, back in Sweden, which is always nice. I don't get the chance to be back that often," he said, in English, assuming the stance of a returning rock star. "As Steve said, I'm Daniel Ek, the CEO and founder of Spotify."

He used the opportunity to introduce a new partnership between Spotify and Microsoft, explaining how the service would be integrated into the Windows Phone. News of the collaboration would soon make headlines in a dozen Swedish media outlets.

After he was done, Daniel stepped to the side and received four more slaps on the back from the towering Microsoft CEO.

"I've heard a lot about Daniel through the years. It's the first time we've met personally," Steve Ballmer said. "We have a lot to talk about between us."

The exact contents of their conversation would remain a secret. But several people familiar with the discussions would recall that Microsoft was willing to invest in Spotify, or possibly buy the company outright. On one occasion, Daniel is said to have been offered a billion dollars for his company, the very valuation his CFO was trying to fetch in the capital markets.

Daniel traveled to Microsoft's head office in Redmond, outside Seattle, to meet Steve Ballmer again, several people would recall. Even Bill Gates, the Microsoft founder whom Daniel looked up to as a child, is said to have shown an interest. The idea was that Microsoft would integrate Spotify in its portable media player, Zune, whose own music software had failed to catch on.

At the time, Microsoft was known for its deep pockets and willingness to make bold bets. A few years earlier, Ballmer had managed to talk his way into investing in Facebook. But the software behemoth was hardly seen as cutting edge when it came to building new consumer applications or products.

Microsoft had missed the search-engine revolution, which had become Google's domain, and Ballmer completely misjudged the potential of the iPhone when it launched in 2007.

Microsoft would later purchase Skype, another Swedish innovation, and for years be criticized for stifling the company's development.

Daniel Ek took Steve Ballmer seriously, but he was never truly out to sell his company to Microsoft. Besides, he didn't want Spotify to become just another play in a game of catch-up with Apple.

IT'S NOT RIGHT BUT IT'S OKAY

Despite negotiating with tech giants, Daniel Ek's core focus remained to stay independent, keep growing with the aid of venture capital, and launch in the US as soon as he could.

His best bet was now Yuri Milner and his firm DST Global, with whom Spotify's CFO, Peter Sterky, was negotiating. The Russian billionaire was best known as the founder of the internet company Mail.ru, which had recently gone public on the stock market in London.

Since the financial crisis, DST, which stood for Digital Sky Technologies, had been making waves in Silicon Valley. In 2009, it famously spent $200 million buying 2 percent of Facebook's shares, an investment that valued the company at $10 billion. Mark Zuckerberg had not been able to find any other investors willing to purchase shares at that price.

"We have started to actively expand abroad," Yuri Milner said of DST's future plans in connection with the Facebook deal.

A former physicist, Yuri Milner's investment strategy was both simple and profound. He saw large swaths of the internet as underdeveloped territory and believed that the companies that dominated their specific verticals—be it e-commerce, social networking, or home rental—would emerge victorious.

The scale of these companies, he reasoned, would guarantee them considerably more revenue than their competitors, and they would eventually become extremely profitable. Milner, therefore, did not fear fast burn rates and high valuations.

He had built internet companies himself, but as an investor he operated in the background, seldom claiming a board seat. It was with this attitude that he, by the end of 2010, was willing to invest $50 million in Spotify, tripling its valuation in the process.

For Spotify, the DST money was necessary but controversial. One of the fund's largest shareholders was the oligarch Alisher Usmanov, who would often praise the Russian president, Vladimir Putin. Another major shareholder was Tencent, an internet conglomerate dependent on the approval of the Chinese government.

Spotify's board realized that taking Russian money might cause problems. The directors would ask each other who the "ultimate backer" behind DST might be, well aware of the likely ties to the Russian government.

Martin Lorentzon, who had always stood for freedom and open markets, found Putin's authoritarian regime deplorable. Yet his ultimate goal was to make sure that Spotify had the cash it needed to break into the US market. Besides, Yuri Milner was an established, clever investor who was sure to prove himself useful. Toward the end of 2010, Spotify therefore signed a preliminary agreement with DST. The VC firms Accel and Kleiner Perkins, both based in Silicon Valley, were brought onboard as well.

The valuation was high, but it came with strings attached. One condition was that Spotify's board guarantee that discussions of an IPO be initiated by 2014 at the latest.

The investors also placed three specific demands on the CEO: Daniel Ek needed to renew the music licenses in Europe; grow by partnering with Facebook; and secure the necessary music licenses for a US launch. The final point would become one of his most difficult challenges to date.

9

"SCHMUCK INSURANCE"

T HROUGHOUT 2010, DANIEL EK AND his team would shuttle between the head offices of the three biggest labels in Midtown Manhattan. They were all based just south of Central Park. His goal was to sign with Universal and Sony, and then force the third-largest and most stubborn label, Warner, to fall in line. EMI, the smallest of the four, was basically a shoo-in, but the others were hard to convince.

ALLES NEU

Thomas Hesse, a worldly German with wavy, salt-and-pepper hair, oversaw Sony Music's digital division. He and Daniel would have lunch at the Sony Club, a private dining room on the thirty-fifth floor of the Sony Building on Madison Avenue. Daniel would tell him about his years as a teenage entrepreneur in Rågsved and expound on how music could be shared in social networks like Facebook, as Hesse would recall.

For the major labels, sales were still plummeting. Digital distribution had grown to almost 30 percent of global revenue, but that wasn't enough to compensate for the decline in physical sales. Hesse, who was also responsible for Sony's sales and distribution in the US, watched as CD revenues fell every month. Soon, music sales in the US would be exactly half of what they were in the golden year of 1999.

"We can return the industry to growth," Daniel would say during their encounters.

Hesse felt sympathetic toward the Swede. In Europe, Spotify's model was clearly working. Beyond that, he was impressed that Ek had the backing of Sean Parker, whom Hesse would also meet with on occasion.

The Napster co-founder claimed that Spotify was needed to counterbalance Apple's dominance over the music industry. Gradually, Hesse began to feel that it would be reasonable to let Spotify into the US.

But he needed to be certain. In the balance was Sony Music's CD business and its long-standing, fruitful relationship with Apple. Hesse knew Steve Jobs personally. He had negotiated the iTunes deal with the Apple CEO in 2003, before the merger between Sony and BMG. Now, Steve Jobs was expressing skepticism about Spotify.

"I don't understand why you would want to give your music away for free," Jobs told Hesse, the German would recall.

The words weighed heavily on the label executive's shoulders. After all, iTunes stood for the lion's share of Sony's digital sales in the US. And criticism of Spotify's free tier was not without merit. At this point, the vast majority of the company's users were still on the ad-funded side.

Daniel made a decent argument, showing how Spotify was converting free users to paying users, particularly in Sweden. But the equation was complicated, even to a former McKinsey management consultant like Hesse. It was far from a given that what worked over fast broadband connections in Sweden would be a success in the US. He wondered how Spotify's free tier might impact Sony Music's long-term revenue per customer, and its CD sales as a whole.

Usually, Hesse would let the numbers do the talking, but this one was tricky. Perhaps it would come down to the concessions Spotify were willing to make.

FAME

"What do you do about the iPod monopoly? That's the interesting question," Sean Parker said, riled up by his new favorite subject.

It was October 2010, and Daniel Ek's most outspoken board member was taking part in a panel discussion in New Orleans, sporting a beige vest, striped tie, and gray silk scarf.

The movie *The Social Network* had just premiered, raising Sean's public profile. He was famous for Justin Timberlake's portrayal of him as the suave mentor to Mark Zuckerberg. But on stage, Sean was more interested in talking about Apple than about the movie. He stated that the iPod now had an 85 percent market share and that Apple's closed ecosystem was shutting out every streaming provider in the US.

"They can't move content on the iPod," he said.

A few days after the debate, *The Daily Beast* senior correspondent Peter Lauria published a commentary describing a "war" between Sean Parker and Steve Jobs ahead of Spotify's US launch.

"With Spotify, I want to finish what I started with Napster," Sean is quoted saying in the article, which also states that the only man who can stop him is the CEO of Apple.

The piece would echo many of Sean's own arguments. It praised iTunes for its "elegant design" but lambasted the service for selling music that could "only be played on PCs or devices manufactured by Apple."

According to the article, the music industry had made a "devil's bargain" with Steve Jobs, only to turn around and stifle alternative services by demanding upfront payments so large that their business models would be doomed. The list of startups to "flame out or fail to gain traction" was long, the article stated, listing Lala.com, Qtrax, Spiral Frog, Imeem, iLike, Project Playlist, Grooveshark, Rhapsody, and Napster as examples.

Lauria argued that Spotify could break the cycle, with seven million users in Europe—a figure that now included around half a million paying subscribers. But its launch in the United States had been blocked twice because of delays in signing deals with the major record labels, Lauria wrote, before delivering a final zinger: "A major cause of the delays has been Jobs himself, who is known for frequent calls to industry executives arguing that Spotify will cause them even more business pain."

To the reader, it was unclear where exactly the information about Jobs's behavior had come from.

KILLING IN THE NAME

Behind the scenes, the previous month had been a dramatic one for Spotify. In September 2010, Warner Music threatened to pull its entire catalogue if Spotify didn't kill its free service, according to one source involved in the process.

The threat is said to have been delivered by Warner CEO Edgar Bronfman Jr., an imposing business magnate in his mid-fifties, who had become something of a nemesis for Spotify's negotiating team. Bronfman made the statement in a conference room at Warner Music's headquarters by Rockefeller Center, with Daniel Ek and his lead negotiator, Ken Parks, in attendance. Bronfman was backed up by his head of digital strategy, Michael Nash, along with several other lieutenants.

Visibly agitated, Bronfman repeated that he would not renew the European licenses if the free tier wasn't scrapped, or at least severely limited. Daniel hid his emotions during the meeting but is said to have been taken aback by the display.

"He hated the idea of asking permission from anyone, for anything," as one source would describe Daniel.

In an interview, Bronfman would deny ever asking Spotify to scrap its free tier, but he did admit to being one of the free service's staunchest critics. His goal, he said, was to put a time limit on the free service instead of letting listeners use Spotify for free indefinitely.

"It's unreasonable for us to continue to subsidize a free tier forever, and we're not going to do it," Edgar Bronfman Jr. recalled telling Daniel.

To the Spotify team, that demand was tantamount to killing its business model, reducing their product to yet another subscription service with a free trial period. The whole point of the free tier was that it had no time limit. That's what made Spotify better than piracy.

It had only been two years since Spotify launched as a commercial service. While amounting to tens of millions of dollars a year, its payouts to the industry were still modest, especially compared to Apple's. It wasn't unthinkable that one of the major labels would suddenly object on a matter of principle. Yet the Spotify executives regrouped after the meeting and quickly regained their composure.

An outer time limit on the free service was unthinkable not just to Daniel, but to his whole negotiating team. They felt that such a fundamental revamp would be tantamount to killing the company. The question was if Bronfman really had a strong enough hand, or if he was bluffing.

Spotify's two-year renewals in Europe had already been cleared with Sony and Universal. If Warner pulled out, they would risk looking like the only label unwilling to bet on a promising digital service whose payouts to the industry were growing. Besides, Warner's owners were rumored to be negotiating a sale of the entire company, a process during which turbulence would be unwelcome. Sure, Bronfman hated Spotify's free service with a passion—all the record labels did—but if he was truly ready to pull the plug, why did he seem so flustered about it? It seemed clear to the Spotify team that Warner's chief executive was bluffing.

What followed was a month-long game of poker. Daniel met with Edgar Bronfman in London, while Ken Parks worked his magic in New York. Petra Hansson, Niklas Ivarsson, and Spotify's new CFO, Peter Sterky, were also involved.

Finally, they worked out a deal that let Bronfman back down without losing face. The terms lowered Spotify's costs of running the free tier, and let the company keep more of its revenues from paid subscribers. Warner's catalogue would continue to be available on Spotify in Europe. The license was renewed for another two years.

"It felt like we'd won an existential battle," as one person from Spotify would recall.

The terms were "not great, but at least they were sustainable," as another source described it.

In one particular feat of financial engineering, the Spotify team managed to extend the amount of time they would have to make payments. The longer window of 45 days would prove a crucial resource for at least another decade. It meant that as long as Spotify's revenues kept growing, the company would have more cash on hand than it needed to pay out at any given time. The negotiating team essentially had given their company extra cash flow to run their operations. As Spotify grew, so would the pile of available cash.

Daniel was relieved, having escaped yet another brush with death. But the new European licenses also came with concessions, said to have been made on the insistence of Universal Music. In certain markets, Spotify's free users could now only listen for twenty hours per month, and only stream any given song a maximum of five times total. After six months of use, the time limit was lowered to ten hours per month.

While the new European deals were largely an improvement, the streaming caps would soon do serious damage to Spotify's metrics. The company's growth curve—its most important tool for attracting more capital—was in fact headed toward a downward slump.

THINGS THAT MAKE YOU GO HMMMM . . .

Securing US licenses was a matter of survival for Daniel Ek. Without them, the new round of funding would fall apart, and he could kiss that one-billion-dollar valuation goodbye.

The problem with a phrase like "a billion" was that it stuck in people's minds and tended to travel. At this point, details of Spotify's soaring valuation had reached Doug Morris, several sources would claim.

The buzz around the Swedish startup reminded the Universal CEO and many of his label heads of other companies that had profited from their industry over the years. Skeptics would point to examples that stretched even further back than Google's purchase of YouTube, or the wave of file-sharing services.

"It was a psychological problem dating all the way back to MTV, which made money off of videos that we had to beg them to play," as one source described it.

Whether Spotify was headed for an exit by selling to a tech giant, like Google or Microsoft, or by securing its own funding, Universal had plenty of reasons to be skeptical. A deal with Spotify could cannibalize the label's revenues from iTunes and upset their friend and collaborator Steve Jobs.

"All of that to help some little Swedish startup flip their company and get rich. Morris had no interest or incentive to do the deal," as one source would explain it.

Universal Music was well known for having close ties to Apple—Steve Jobs had even floated the idea of buying the label outright on at least one occasion. Such a deal would likely have benefited many of its label heads. Jobs had also spent years cultivating powerful allies by means of Apple's enormous marketing budget.

One source would recall that Jobs, as early as 2003, paid $150,000 to Jimmy Iovine for putting a new version of the iPod in the video for 50 Cent's "P.I.M.P." At the time, the rapper was represented by Jimmy Iovine's Interscope Records.

The following year, Iovine spearheaded U2's long-standing partnership with Apple, starting with the cross-promotion of the album *How to Dismantle an Atomic Bomb* involving a special U2 edition of the iPod. The arrangement, in which Steve Jobs was personally involved, culminated ten years later, in a deal involving the album *Songs of Innocence*—worth a reported $100 million. Iovine's ties to the Irish superband spanned decades. He had produced their albums *Rattle and Hum* and *Under a Blood Red Sky* in the 1980s, and later signed them to Interscope, although U2 also had contracts with other Universal labels over the years.

Apple presents the U2 Special Edition iPod in October of 2004.
From left: Jimmy Iovine, co-chair of Interscope Records, Apple's CEO
Steve Jobs, Bono and The Edge from U2. *(ZUMA Press, Inc. / Alamy Stock Photo)*

According to four sources, Jobs was now using his sway over Universal to try to block or delay Spotify's arrival in the US. He appeared to do so by discrediting the Swedish company's free service.

The Apple CEO was in frequent contact with Universal's top executives in 2010, as the sources would recall. Two of them claimed that Jobs implied that Apple could withhold marketing money, or even shut the entire iTunes Store down.

"If the monopolist in the marketplace is subtly threatening you, you're going to have to listen," as one well-placed source would describe it.

One source claims that representatives from Apple also considered, in 2010, launching their own streaming service. The idea was to undercut Spotify's price with a subscription that would cost six or seven dollars per month, instead of the going rate of $9.99. Another source would suggest Apple planned to launch a radio service, similar to Pandora, that would coexist with downloads in the iTunes Store.

The idea of revamping iTunes may partly have been the result of lobbying by the music industry. Edgar Bronfman Jr. would recall how he, as Warner Music's CEO, flew to Silicon Valley to meet with Steve Jobs in the years after iTunes launched. He wanted the Apple CEO to incorporate a subscription service into iTunes, and he said that his counterpart at Universal, Doug Morris, had a similar agenda. Alas, Steve Jobs was not having it.

"He said people want to own their music. They don't want to rent their music," Edgar Bronfman Jr. would recall.

In 2010, the talks between Universal and Spotify were slowed down by constant chatter and gossip. One theory suggests that Steve Jobs wanted to buy time, at least until he had moved iTunes into the cloud. Others would claim that Spotify was but a blip on Steve Jobs's radar and that he was simply looking after his own interests.

The subject matter would remain sensitive for years to come. The legal aspects are thorny. If a dominant distributor like Apple would have tried to counteract a competitor by colluding with one or several major labels, it could amount to a violation of federal antitrust laws. A similar situation was playing out with the iBooks Store. Apple would later be found to have conspired with five book publishers in 2009 and 2010, in an attempt to challenge Amazon's dominant position in the e-book market. That case would go all the way to the Supreme Court, where Apple was smacked with a $450 million price-fixing fine as part of an antitrust settlement. (Apple would deny that it had conspired to fix prices.)

The topic would also remain sensitive because of Steve Jobs's failing health. In January 2011, the Apple co-founder went on sick leave without stepping down as CEO.

Beyond the intrigue, Jobs's worldview was aligned with Universal's American executives. Jimmy Iovine would, for example, openly voice his opposition to any streaming service with an unlimited free tier, as a source would recall. The freewheeling founder of Interscope and Beats Electronics had, at least in his own mind, been fighting piracy through innovation for more than a decade.

As Iovine would recall in interviews, he and the Universal CEO, Doug Morris, had created a talent show with digital ambitions on late-night TV as early as the year 2000. It was called *Farmclub*, and it aired on the USA Network. The venture was backed with $25 million from Edgar Bronfman Jr., then CEO of Seagram, which owned Universal Music and 43 percent of the USA Network.

Posing for pictures on the Universal Studios soundstage, the two formed a comical duo—the thin, boisterous Jimmy Iovine, with his baseball cap and flamboyant streetwear, next to the heavyset Doug Morris, in his pinstripe suit and boardroom tie. The show—which featured former Miss USA Ali Landry and MTV personality Matt Pinfield as hosts, with Eminem in the green room—set out to challenge Napster by letting viewers vote for unsigned bands on a website called Farmclub.com. Later, they could watch the most popular acts perform on air in the hope of getting signed. It was a haphazard production, but Iovine, Morris, and the others ultimately wanted to turn it into a digital music service, and maybe even IPO the whole thing. But the slowly bursting tech bubble put an end to the duo's ambitions. The venture left an indelible impression on Iovine, however, convincing him that he could innovate in the digital age.

In the years to come, Iovine would hitch his star to the promise of combining digital music with physical hardware. When Apple started building the iTunes Music Store in 2002, Steve Jobs's main motivation was to bolster the sale of iPods and Macs. Iovine was quick to seize the opportunity and make money by using his artists to help with the marketing. In 2006, he founded his own hardware company, Beats Electronics, once again using artists to market the headphones. By the time Spotify came knocking in 2010, Iovine felt that a distribution platform with free music as its selling point, had little to offer the industry—an opinion he wasn't afraid to share.

There were plenty of Spotify critics at the very top of the Universal camp. From Daniel Ek's point of view, the tide needed to turn. Toward the end of 2010, it seemed as though it might.

Universal's leadership was about to change. The French owner, Vivendi, had recently tapped Lucian Grainge, the fifty-year-old chairman of Universal Music Group International, to leave London and take the reins from Doug Morris in the US. The operations were set to become more globally integrated.

The two appeared to be embroiled in what several sources would describe as a personal feud. The long-serving Morris, now into his seventies, is said to have wanted Grainge to move to New York, where he was based, so they could run things together for a while. But Grainge would instead assert his power by choosing to move to Universal's Santa Monica offices in Los Angeles.

Along for the ride was Universal's head of digital, Rob Wells, who had first met Daniel Ek in London a few years prior. Wells, who was now known as a vocal Spotify proponent, was promoted and given the title President of Global Digital Business in October 2010. His main task would be to create a unified digital strategy within Universal. That meant bringing Spotify to the US, while keeping Apple happy at the same time.

In a written statement, now-co-CEO Lucian Grainge hailed Rob Wells, saying that no one was better equipped for the new position.

"And he's the best surfer I know," he added.

Wells would have to navigate some pretty gnarly waves in the months to come.

THORN IN MY SIDE

As Lucian Grainge was taking over the reins in the fall of 2010, it looked as though Spotify had finally reached a landmark US deal with Universal. By the end of the year a contract was drawn up and ready. But, suddenly, Universal refused to sign. The label simply didn't return their signature page of the contract, as one source would recall.

"They took the deal and sat on it," as another source familiar with Spotify's end of the process would express it.

The Spotify headquarters was now rife with rumors and speculation. Its various teams had been looking forward to launching in the United States by the end of 2010, but now they were being told that everything was on hold. They were not told why. Some began to whisper that Warner was the problem, while others blamed Universal.

At the Consumer Electronics Show (CES) in Las Vegas in the early days of the new year, Universal executive Rob Wells told a Spotify employee that a deal would soon be done, according to two sources. One of them would recall him saying that Universal couldn't be first. Spotify needed to sign with another label first, and they would follow.

FINE PRINT

Spotify's first major breakthrough in the US came later the same month, in January 2011, when they signed a licensing deal with Sony Music. The terms looked much like the deal they had recently agreed to in Europe. But it also came at a hefty price for Spotify's shareholders.

Secret internal documents, which would not emerge until the publication of the Swedish edition of this book, reveal that Sony had negotiated an option—triggered four years down the line—to purchase what would amount to 2.5 percent of Spotify at a heavy discount. The label's payoff came in the spring of 2015, when Sony paid just under $8 million for shares that, a few months later, would become worth twenty-five times more. Largely as a result of this deal, Sony would become the label with the largest Spotify holdings by the time the company went public in 2018.

The actual license agreement with Sony Music was forty-two pages long and would eventually leak to The Verge. The details show how complex Spotify's deals can be, and why some would argue that the system favored labels over artists. For readers with a special interest in this kind of fine print, here are some highlights and analysis:

- For the right to stream Sony's music catalogue in the US, Spotify agrees to pay a $25 million advance for the two-year duration of the contract: $9 million the first year, and $16 million the second. The advance is to be paid in installments every three months, and Spotify can only recoup this money if it meets or beats its revenue targets. The contract, however, does not stipulate how Sony Music can use the advance money. Some industry insiders claim that advance money is generally spent on things other than payouts to artists. Others wonder what happens to the "breakage," or the part of the advance that is left with the label, when Spotify fails to reach its revenue goals. Is it attributed to streams and distributed to artists, or kept entirely by the label?

- The contract also includes a standard "Most Favored Nation" clause that ensures that Sony Music's various percentages won't fall behind those of other music labels. The arrangement stops labels from waiting each other out in the negotiation process, in hope of getting the best deal. The labels are not allowed to see each other's contracts, so independent auditors are employed to check and compare them.

- Another muddy, yet interesting, section of the contract deals with the advertising revenue from Spotify's free tier. As a general rule, Spotify will give 70 percent of its gross revenue to labels and publishers. But here, Sony allows Spotify to keep up to 15 percent "off the top" of all advertising revenues generated by third parties. Spotify might need this money to cover the commissions they pay to external ad companies, or they might just keep it. On that point, the contract is unclear. At any rate, the money is not accounted for in Spotify's gross revenue total.

- The contract also stipulates that Spotify give Sony free ad space worth $9 million over three years. Sony can use that space to promote its own artists or resell it at any price they want. Spotify also promises to make a further $15 million of ads available for purchase by Sony at a discounted rate. On top of this, Spotify must also offer Sony a portion of its unsold ad inventory for free, to allow the label to promote its artists.

- The contract also states that Spotify's smallest payout per stream will be 0.2 cents. But this measure can't be used to calculate how much Spotify pays for the artists' streams. It's only used when it results in a larger payout than the label's regular cut of Spotify's total revenue. In essence, it's a type of minimum guarantee. If too many users get stuck in the free tier, and Spotify's average revenue per user falls below a certain level, Sony Music can ask to be paid per stream instead.

The complexity of the deal shows why Daniel Ek would always prefer to talk about Spotify's total payouts to the music industry, rather than get into the details.

How much are artists paid? It depends.

FAIRYTALE OF NEW YORK

Although a deal was reached with Sony Music, negotiations remained at a standstill with Universal. It seemed as if Lucian Grainge, having installed himself in Santa Monica, was getting cold feet.

"Lucian didn't want to become global head of Universal and piss off his largest digital retailer, Apple, as his first official act," as a source would describe it.

The chatter at Universal's headquarters was still that the Swedes were hoping to launch in the United States and then sell their company to the highest bidder—and Universal Music wanted its fair share.

"If they flipped it quickly, it would not be a fair exchange," as a different source would recall.

For this reason, Universal had demanded that a secret side deal be drafted. It stipulated that Martin Lorentzon, Daniel Ek, and several other major Spotify shareholders would pay Universal tens of millions of dollars if they sold their company, or went public, within a certain time frame. Two sources would recall that the agreement was in place for two years, and could be extended after that.

"They called it 'schmuck insurance,'" as a third source described it.

The deal would remain extra sensitive since it wasn't struck between the two companies, but rather between Universal and most of Spotify's shareholders. This may have been a way of sidestepping the "Most Favored Nation" clause that assured that no one label could get a better deal than the others.

One source would claim that Spotify and Lucian Grainge struck this deal as early as the fall of 2010. By early 2011, it had been signed. Documents registered with Daniel Ek's holding company in Cyprus would confirm the details. An "Exit Payment Agreement"—signed on January 25, 2011—stated that Universal had the right to two percent of the total purchase price if Spotify was sold or listed.

With Spotify's valuation about to hit a billion dollars, that extra payment would have amounted to $20 million at the time of signing. Two years later, the same share of Spotify's valuation had risen to $80 million. It would only be paid out, however, if Spotify was sold or taken public.

For the music industry, there was an upside in letting Spotify remain independent. A dedicated music service in which the major labels held equity would be easier to control and might be used as a counterweight to Apple or Google.

The "schmuck insurance" deal was seen as a win for Universal, but it may also have served the interests of Steve Jobs. After all, it reduced Daniel Ek's incentive to sell Spotify to one of his competitors, like Microsoft or Google. At this point, the Swede had held acquisition talks with both of them.

The prospect of Google acquiring Spotify would have been especially irritating to Jobs. A leaked email from this period, written by the Apple CEO, would show that he viewed music as a weapon in a "holy war" with the search giant. When it came to music, his main plan seems to have been to strengthen iTunes and keep it out of Google's Android phones.

DEVIL INSIDE

Despite having secured a potentially lucrative side deal, Universal kept stalling throughout the spring of 2011. Spotify's recently imposed streaming caps caused the number of monthly active users—still hovering around seven million—to decline for the first time in Spotify's history.

"Very few companies get to stare negative growth in the face and live to talk about it," as the CPO, Gustav Söderström, would recall.

The growth scare made gaining access to the United States even more urgent. Daniel Ek's company was shrinking in Europe, running out of money, and still didn't have its US licenses. Yuri Milner and the other investors remained on the sidelines. Spotify's founders had to ask their shareholders for a bridge loan to cover salaries and keep the money flowing to the music labels.

Then, after months of silence, Universal Music dropped a bombshell on the Spotify leadership.

Sometime in late May or early June, the world's largest record label informed them that Lucian Grainge wanted ten percent of the company in exchange for granting it licenses in the US, as two sources on either side of the negotiations would recall. It was an extraordinary ask. Universal was effectively demanding to receive additional shares worth $100 million before handing over the keys to the world's largest music market.

The message is said to have been delivered to Spotify over the phone by Rob Wells, Universal's head of digital. Privately, Wells was embarrassed by his boss's audacity, as were several other members of his team at Universal, three sources would recall. One of them described the process as "humiliating."

The next day, Ken Parks showed up at the Universal complex on Colorado Avenue in Santa Monica, for a long, emotional meeting with Rob Wells. Somehow, two sources said, the two of them hashed out a deal. The talks were held in Wells's office right next door to Lucian Grainge, and the Universal CEO is said to have been involved as well.

Universal did not end up getting ten percent of Spotify's shares. They received licensing terms that they could live with and the Exit Payment Agreement. The cherry on top was a lump of cash, as several sources would recall.

What additional sweetener was worked out in Santa Monica would remain a secret. One source, however, would describe a second "schmuck insurance," in which Universal was promised an additional cash payment if the founders sold Spotify within a shorter time frame.

Lucian Grainge is said to have signed off on the deal at the end of the day. And with that, a crucial part of the Spotify catalogue was cleared and ready to stream in the US.

CLOUD NINE

On June 6, 2011, Steve Jobs stepped up on stage for Apple's Worldwide Developers Conference. As usual, he was wearing blue jeans and a black

turtleneck, but the clothes hung from his body like sheets. He looked frag-
ile, thinner than ever before.

"You like everything so far?" the CEO said.

The audience cheered encouragingly.

"Good. Well, I'll try not to blow it."

Steve Jobs's health was failing, yet he was still delivering the most important presentation of the day.

"So, I get to talk about iCloud," he said with a smile.

He explained how a new, overarching cloud infrastructure would replace
the Mac as the core of Apple's ecosystem, uniting all its products—including its music service.

"Last but not least, iTunes in the cloud," he said.

Jobs then described how all the songs customers bought on iTunes would
now be available on all devices, from the Mac to the iPhone to the iPad.

"This is the first time we've seen this in the music industry."

Apple's CEO had just taken iTunes halfway into the age of streaming.
And he'd done it before Spotify had had the chance to launch in the US.

Steve Jobs gazed triumphantly over the sea of faces that had gathered for
what would be his last keynote.

NEVER GONNA GIVE YOU UP

All that remained for Spotify was a deal with Warner, who had been playing
hardball with them all year.

In January, at the Consumer Electronics Show in Las Vegas, Warner's
Michael Nash had told two Spotify staffers that the label would never let
the company into the US with its free service intact, according to two
sources.

"Never is a long time," Ken Parks is said to have replied, before cutting
the meeting short.

Throughout the spring, Spotify and Warner were at a standstill, unable
to agree on the future of the free tier. Spotify had deals with Sony and Universal by summer. Then, the negotiating team had enough confidence to
turn the tables on Warner. They relayed that Spotify would love to have
them onboard, but that they now had a launch date and would enter the

US even without the Warner catalogue. By this time, Warner had too much to lose by not signing on.

Besides, the label had recently been acquired by Access Industries, whose billionaire owner, Len Blavatnik, was expected to modernize Warner's business. The deal meant that the influence of its long-serving CEO, Edgar Bronfman Jr., was waning. In late June or early July, Warner agreed to the terms and cleared Spotify's path to the United States.

Spotify now had fulfilled all three of their promises to the new investors. They had renewed the licenses in Europe and finally gained access to the US market. The partnership with Facebook was coming along, too.

During the summer, Spotify re-upped on venture capital. The three new shareholders—Yuri Milner's DST, Accel, and Kleiner Perkins—transferred around $100 million to Spotify's parent company in Luxembourg.

Doggedness, dedication and chaotic music-industry dealmaking had gotten the Swedish startup over the line.

"And boom, we're a billion-dollar company," one Spotify executive would recall.

2 PHONES

A few weeks later, Spotify had all but entered the US market—but Spotify's communications director, Angela Watts, still wasn't taking calls from reporters. There were a few final details to iron out in the Warner contract.

On a Tuesday afternoon in July, Daniel Ek found himself pacing around the Spotify offices on Eighth Avenue, his two cell phones vibrating constantly.

"People are prepared to pay for convenience," the twenty-eight-year-old CEO told a reporter from the *New York Times*.

"If you want to take your music with you, you shouldn't have to worry about fifteen different sync programs or anything else. It ought to be as simple as pressing play and it works."

The following afternoon, Warner signed the final deal. Spotify's press team did not waste any time getting the news out, beginning with a select number of influencers.

"So excited Spotify is FINALLY coming to the US tomorrow!" Britney Spears wrote on Twitter.

Users in the United States were offered an ad-free version with unlimited desktop listening for five dollars per month. For twice that, they could save songs offline and listen on their cell phones. As with previous launches, free users initially needed an invitation to get started.

"New Service Offers Music by Quantity, Not by Song," read the headline in the *New York Times*. The article outlined the differences between iTunes, Spotify, and file-sharing.

EUPHORIA

The following week was a victory lap for Daniel Ek. He traveled across the United States with Shakil Khan at breakneck speed. They went from New York to San Francisco and on to Los Angeles. They stayed at a boutique hotel in West Hollywood and dined at the celebrity chef Nobuyuki Matsuhisa's restaurant in Beverly Hills. Then they went to San Jose and to the Aspen ski resort in Colorado.

Shak's trail of tweets indicates a kind of giddy anticipation. At one airport, he joked that Daniel had pretended not to know him while passing through security.

"Me: Daniel, where are we going? He: Sssssh, pretend you don't know me, I don't want to be strip-searched like you," Shak wrote on Twitter.

Spotify's PR team in New York had kicked into high gear, supplying certain celebrities with invites. Shakira and 50 Cent were just two of the many artists that would spray the public with free accounts. When The Verge held a raffle with a hundred invites, the "giveaways" were gone inside nine minutes. The PR team was pushing up demand by creating a feeling of scarcity.

"I tried to pull some strings, this is the best I can do," wrote Ashton Kutcher, sending out a link with invites.

Whether the supply was really that limited is another matter. Angela Watts had, for example, given Motorola and Sprite one hundred thousand invites each to pass on to their customers. Spotify proved, once again, that it knew how to leverage its exclusivity and generate buzz.

Even before the US launch, Spotify had more paying subscribers than rivals like Rhapsody, MOG, and Rdio. With eight million users and 1.6

million paid subscribers, Daniel Ek was about to strengthen his position in music streaming.

The Spotify CEO celebrated his company's arrival in the US at a party in a huge, faux Louis XVI-style mansion overlooking the San Francisco Bay. It had marble pillars, pools, its own cinema, and belonged to Spotify's new investor, an absent Yuri Milner.

One of Daniel's old friends attended the party. Unaccustomed to valet parking, he left his car outside the gates, and would have to walk hundreds of yards to reach the house.

Daniel's first triumph on American soil was celebrated in one of the most expensive private homes in the country. Fifteen minutes away, in Palo Alto, lay Steve Jobs's modest brick home. His challenger from Stockholm had finally arrived.

SEAN & ZUCK

MUSIC LICENSES FROM THE MAJOR record companies had now given Daniel Ek the keys to the US market, where tech press—from *TechCrunch* to *AllThingsD* to the *New York Times*—frequently reported on the new streaming service. Yet bicoastal hype was far from enough to ensure success in the United States. Spotify needed to reach college campuses around the country and desktop computers in the homes of teenagers. Luckily, Daniel Ek had a newfound friend who could expose his music service to around half of the US population. During a meeting in early 2011, five months before Spotify's US launch, this ally—another t-shirt-clad entrepreneur in his mid-twenties—offered his thoughts on how music might spread online.

"I absolutely believe that you want to share music with your friends," Mark Zuckerberg told a small group of Facebook and Spotify employees.

The Facebook CEO was holding court in his office on the company's Palo Alto campus. Its transparent walls made it look like a fish tank in the middle of Facebook's bustling workspace. The company headquarters were five minutes away from Stanford University, where Zuckerberg and his many competitors would turn to recruit technologically savvy graduates. For this meeting, he had gathered a handful of his closest co-workers, among them his trusted Chief Product Officer, Chris Cox. Other attendees included Spotify's VP of Product, Gustav Söderström, and his head of product development, Michelle Kadir.

"I don't think you care that much about what music your friends are playing," Gustav disagreed. "I think you'd rather see what people with the same taste as you are listening to."

The tall, blond Swede—whose chiseled jawline had given him the nickname "The Viking" among Spotify staffers—usually had a crystal-clear vision for his company. Like his boss Daniel Ek, he enjoyed waxing lyrical about the future of the internet. Colleagues rarely witnessed him abandon an opinion. But he was now talking to the man who had founded Facebook, making him more prone to compromise.

Zuckerberg held firm. One attendee from the Spotify side would recall how the Facebook founder tended to interrupt others and ignore counterarguments. He appeared to have made up his mind, and Spotify's prize for agreement was a chance to impress his base of around 150 million monthly active users.

"I don't believe in the idea of tastemakers. You want to share the music with your friends," Zuckerberg concluded.

The conversation set the framework for Spotify's landmark integration with Facebook. Daniel's coworkers soon began to call the project "Hulken," or "The Hulk," since it would give the small Swedish company new and oversized muscles. Expectations at Spotify ran high. The company had fewer than ten million total users. At the high end of internal estimates, employees in Stockholm noted that a successful partnership with Facebook could send that number to half a billion.

RAW LIKE SUSHI

Mark Zuckerberg had long been interested in digital music. Before the move from the Harvard University campus to Palo Alto, when his site was still called Thefacebook.com, he ran a parallel project called Wirehog, where users could send photos, documents, and MP3 files to each other. The file-sharing service was shuttered in 2006 after Sean Parker, serving as chairman of Facebook, anticipated trouble from the music industry. Mark Zuckerberg now had a chance to combine his old idea with that of a globally spanning social network.

By early 2011, Daniel and Mark had become friends. Both were self-made, confident tech entrepreneurs born in the early 1980s. They had much to talk about during their walks around the Facebook campus whenever Daniel visited Silicon Valley. People in Daniel's orbit would describe how he looked up to Mark, who had built a globally thriving tech business without apologizing for it.

Their companionship developed at an opportune time for the twenty-seven-year-old Swede. For a brief period, Facebook ran two parallel business models: one was to open up the network's "social graph" to partner companies, allow them to build third-party apps, and become a platform central to all kinds of online activity; the other was to amass as much user data as possible and charge advertisers for the opportunity to target the user base. The latter would eventually prove far more lucrative and become Facebook's dominant business model in the years following its IPO in 2012. But before then, the idea of becoming a connective node on the internet lived on. With its superior product, unparalleled buzz in media circles, and a CEO similar to Zuckerberg, Spotify managed to slot right into a golden window of opportunity for companies looking for global exposure through Facebook.

In February 2011, a handful of key Spotify personnel were greeted with open arms on the Facebook campus. Product designers from both companies spent several days in a designated meeting room, attempting to deepen how Facebook users interacted with the Swedish music service. They created individual tags for artists and songs. A tab on the right side of the homepage would broadcast what music each user was listening to in real time. A user who clicked on a song would be redirected to register for a Spotify account, install the client on their computer, and start using the service.

One evening, a group of fifteen higher-ups had a teambuilding dinner at Fuki Sushi in Palo Alto, one of Mark's favorite haunts. The Facebook CEO was seated across from Martin Lorentzon, who was surrounded by staff from both companies, as well as Priscilla Chan, Mark's fiancée. At the head of the table, in a Spotify-green polo shirt, was Daniel, seated next to a quiet but highly influential guest: Russian investor Yuri Milner, who had invested heavily in Facebook after the financial crisis and had now promised to do the same with Spotify. From the corner of the table, Yuri rarely joined the group discussion and spoke mostly with Daniel, one attendee would recall. But he seemed pleased to see employees from two of his portfolio companies bond. The party ordered hundreds of pieces of sushi, which arrived at the table on miniature wooden boats.

In another part of the world, the Arab Spring was beginning to culminate. Protesters had flooded Tahrir Square in Cairo, while also spreading their messages through social media. In a few days, Hosni Mubarak, Egypt's authoritarian president, would resign, ousted by a popular movement that some would call the Facebook Revolution.

In the months that followed, Facebook and Twitter were celebrated as champions of democratic causes in autocratic countries. But by the end of 2011, political groups in Egypt would reportedly begin to use Facebook to spread propaganda, misinformation, and hate speech, in some cases resulting in physical violence. The trend would spread to other countries and, many years later, cause many to question whether Mark Zuckerberg was fit to control one of the most powerful digital tools ever created. But for now, at the outset of 2011, boundless optimism surrounded the dinner table. The twenty-six-year-old Harvard dropout was a visionary helping the citizens of the world connect, and Daniel was his European counterpart, on a quest to make music easily accessible throughout the world.

A few weeks later, an email arrived. It outlined the specific demands Facebook wished to place on Spotify. As the product team in Stockholm scrolled through the fine print, they found one detail especially worrisome. Mark Zuckerberg required everyone who registered for Spotify to do so via Facebook, effectively shutting out people who might find the streaming service through other channels. Several employees would recall how this issue was sensitive for Daniel. It would shut out listeners in a number of European countries where Facebook had not yet taken hold. Even in Sweden, where Facebook was popular, only around half of all internet users had joined the network. One of Daniel's core principles had always been that Spotify should be available to everyone. In order to let the world's largest social network supercharge Spotify's growth, he, too, needed to compromise.

MY WAY

For some, like Sean Parker, the marriage between Facebook and Spotify was especially significant. Sean served both as one of Mark Zuckerberg's trusted mentors and as a board member of Spotify, giving him the chance to achieve what he never could with Napster: a boundless, global digital music experience with the backing of the music establishment.

"This is actually very similar to what I dreamt of ten years ago," as he would describe it. "We never wanted to create a service to destroy the record business or hurt artists in any way. The goal was always to create a more open and frictionless system."

In August 2011, the Napster veteran flew to Stockholm to monitor the team working on "The Hulk." A photograph shows him perched over a desk at Spotify's headquarters, pointing at a screen and offering detailed instructions. Many of Spotify's top designers and engineers saw him as a jet-setting, independently wealthy entrepreneur who was frequently out of his depth. He seemed bent on moving pixels around on the screen, as one employee would later quip. The product team found Sean overbearing, at times pedantic, but there wasn't much they could do. After all, he had Daniel's ear. Even when his input directly contradicted the core principles of what they were doing, they would comply. One example was the download store that Sean had instructed the product team to build during the spring of 2011. The feature let Spotify users download music files, just like on iTunes, and sync them with their iPod. Suddenly, the very business model that Daniel had spent years fighting against had become a part of his own service. Spotify employees would dub this rebuild "The Beauty and the Beast."

Not all of Sean's ideas came to fruition. His attempt to create a tab in Spotify where listeners could burn mp3-files onto CDs—another concept copied directly from iTunes—fell on deaf ears, especially when it reached Gustav Söderström. However, the Spotify download shop was pushed out as part of a Spotify update in May 2011. Within a few months, it became clear that the store hardly attracted any users, rendering the project short lived.

Sean would remain active on Spotify's board and serve as one of its most prominent advocates in Silicon Valley. His loyalty to the Swedish startup would eventually grow so strong that Mark Zuckerberg began to consider it a problem.

WHO AM I?

On September 22, 2011, a few months after Spotify's US launch, a nervous group of employees gathered at Spotify's headquarters on Birger Jarlsgatan 6 around eight p.m. The product team was fully focused on what was about to happen at the San Francisco Design Center, where the audience was still finishing its morning coffee. During this edition of F8, Facebook's recurring conference for developers and the epicenter of its product roll-outs, Mark Zuckerberg was due to introduce collaborations with video companies such as Netflix and Hulu, news sites like the *Washington Post*, and music apps such as Spotify. The Facebook CEO walked on stage in his signature gray t-shirt, proclaiming that half a billion users recently visited Facebook on the same day. What truly excited him, he said, was what his company could do with all those new users.

"The next era is going to be defined by the apps and the depth of engagement that is now possible," he said.

About halfway through the keynote presentation, it was time for him to demo a purpose-built version of Spotify. The product team in Stockholm was on the edge of their seats. The plan was for Mark to click once on a song and have it start streaming instantly, without installing Spotify or even opening the player in a new window. The underlying technology had been carefully constructed, but the Spotify team wasn't certain that it would work during the live presentation.

On the right side of Mark's real-time Facebook feed, beamed onto a massive screen behind him on stage, the company's CTO Mike Schroepfer appeared. He was listening to "Welcome to the Jungle," a new and energetic rap song by Jay-Z and Kanye West.

"I like Jay-Z", Mark said, clicking on the song. "Here we go!"

As the room in San Francisco fell silent, the Spotify team in Stockholm held their breath. The player seemed to be buffering. An interval of four seconds passed before the kick drums started thumping through the speakers. The audience in San Francisco cheered, and the Spotify staff breathed a sigh of relief. Facebook finally had a soundtrack, with Spotify as its favored provider.

Over the next few years, Mark Zuckerberg would go on to acquire companies such as Instagram and WhatsApp for billions of dollars. Whenever he failed to buy a competitor, such as Snapchat, he would typically offer them fierce competition. Yet he didn't appear to view Spotify as a rival. For the better part of a year, Facebook granted the streaming service free access to its feed, resulting in the kind of global exposure advertisers would ordinarily pay a fortune for.

Toward the latter stages of the F8 presentation, Daniel Ek walked on stage to the tune of his favorite song by the French dance music duo Daft Punk.

"Work it harder, make it better, do it faster, makes us stronger," a voice blared out over the sound system, filtered through a thick layer of autotune.

Sporting a gray suit jacket over a black t-shirt with a neon-green Spotify print, Daniel got four minutes of coveted stage time. At this point, Facebook was closing in on 800 million global users.

"Today is a big day for Facebook, and it's a big day for Spotify. But most importantly, it is a big day for everyone who loves music," Daniel told the crowd as Mark waited on the side of the stage.

Facebook users would now be able to digitally browse their friends' record collections, the Swede explained, adding that Mark had a soft spot for Taylor Swift while he himself enjoyed "really bad one-hit wonders from the 80s."

"Thanks, Daniel," the Facebook co-founder said as his partner exited the stage. "I really love the app that they've made and I think that millions of more people will enjoy using it."

But their partnership hadn't gone down as smoothly as it appeared. With only one day to go until the keynote, Daniel and Sean Parker had received word that Spotify was not Facebook's exclusive music partner at the launch. Another fifteen apps, among them Soundcloud, Deezer, the San Francisco-based MOG, and the streaming pioneer Rhapsody, would be along for the ride. However, Spotify was alone in offering a free service, complete with a full catalogue. And Daniel was the only music executive that would appear on stage during the presentation.

Sean figured out a way to ensure that Spotify stole the show. With 48 hours to go until the conference, he set out to throw an after-party that San Francisco would remember. He picked a venue in nearby Potrero Hill, a warehouse that was covered in graffiti tags in a rapid makeover. The maverick tech investor chartered jets to fly in musical guests such as The Killers, Jane's Addiction, DJ Kaskade, and Snoop Dogg. A large Spotify logo greeted attendees inside the building. Refreshments included spit-roasted pig, truffles imported from France, and a large bottle of dark tequila next to each of the roughly fifty seats reserved for members of the press.

"Thank you for being willing to put up with this completely manic and totally insane schedule," Sean told the crowd that had gathered as the event kicked off. "How we managed to convince four of the biggest artists in the world to participate in such a short time frame is a mystery to me," he added.

Next to him was Daniel, making his second stage appearance of the day. He had changed into a bright red t-shirt with "Suits Suck" printed on it, the same kind Shak had once brought back from the *Entourage* set in Los Angeles.

"This is so awesome. Thanks, Sean, and everyone else organizing this," the Swedish entrepreneur said. "Napster, for me, was probably the biggest event in my life when it comes to the internet. It really changed how I consumed music, my favorite artists, and how I shared music with my friends."

Among the crowd was music industry veteran Paul Rosenberg, longtime manager of the rapper Eminem; Napster co-founder Shawn Fanning; Daniel Ek's partner Martin Lorentzon; and Rasmus Andersson, who led Spotify's design team during the early years before he departed for a role at Facebook in Silicon Valley. For Sean, the party offered a shot at redemption.

"People say he destroyed the music business. He didn't want to destroy the music business. He loves the music business," one of his friends, the entrepreneur Sebastien de Halleux, told the *San Francisco Business Times* during the party.

The evening reached its crescendo when Snoop Dogg, dressed in a gray Adidas tracksuit, took the stage backed by a live band and three sidekicks ad libbing him.

"With so much drama in the LBC, it's kinda hard bein' Snoop D-O-double-G", he rapped as the party erupted. Later, he jumped off the stage to finish a verse in the middle of the cheering crowd.

After the show, Sean posed for a photo backstage alongside Snoop, who appears to have stuck a thin, unlit blunt between his lips. Mark and Daniel also made sure to be photographed next to the rap star, for a picture that would soon be published all over the internet.

"Sean Parker stole some of Facebook's thunder last night," *Business Insider* reported the day after the party.

Spotify's launch with Facebook in San Francisco in September 2011. From left:
Mark Zuckerberg, Daniel Ek, Snoop Dogg and Sean Parker. *(Kevin Mazur / Getty Images)*

Several weeks later, tensions appeared to flare up between Sean and Mark. After spending some time at a West Hollywood nightclub, the pair got into an argument over the terms of collaboration between Spotify and Facebook. Sean did not want new Spotify users to have to register through Facebook. Reports of the disagreement reached the *New York Post*, whose source described how the duo engaged in "a full on screaming match outside the club, but stopped short of coming to blows." A spokesperson for Sean confirmed that the two had had a discussion but denied that it was an argument.

Facebook had offered Spotify much-coveted visibility in the United States. For several months, users could barely log on to the site without being fed the name of the music service and what people were listening to. Between March and November of 2011, Spotify's number of paying subscribers would leap from one million to 2.5 million.

THE NEXT EPISODE

In the early fall of 2011, a private jet landed at Bromma Airport just outside of Stockholm. Out stepped the Universal Music executive Jimmy Iovine, co-founder of Beats Electronics, alongside a small entourage that included Beats' Head of Operations, Luke Wood. The team had traveled to Stockholm to recruit digital music experts for a new streaming project that remained a secret to the outside world.

The crew from Beats made their way to Stockholm's financial district and Nobis Hotel, where they had booked the largest suite. It offered a view over Norrmalmstorg and was located just a block away from Spotify's headquarters. Beats had become a pop culture sensation in the United States. The company was on track to sell headphones for a total of hundreds of millions of dollars that year. Jimmy Iovine's stature in the music business was growing. Now he wanted to ride the streaming wave and challenge Spotify, which had only just arrived in the US.

"We're gonna win," Iovine said repeatedly during his visit to Sweden.

For more than ten years, he had watched as Universal Music and a host of other companies had failed to build popular streaming services. He refused to roll over and concede to a bunch of engineering types from Sweden. Moreover, he saw a gap in the market. The streaming world needed something rooted in the music business—a service that didn't just offer sleek technology, but a whole lifestyle. Iovine envisioned a new cultural hub that could play the role that MTV had in the '90s. A company with that type of cultural relevance could be sold to Apple, where Tim Cook had recently taken over as CEO, or perhaps to Google or Microsoft.

The Beats team acquainted themselves with several key figures in Stockholm's music world. Iovine—who, despite pushing sixty, still dressed in leather jackets, hoodies, and baseball caps—found a local guide in Ola Sars, the man who three years prior had tried to talk him into partnering with the Swedish music hardware company Pacemaker. They were joined by amicable music industry veteran Luke Wood, who started out in the 1990s working for bands like Nirvana and Sonic Youth.

One of their business meetings was with the eternally boyish Andreas Ehn, Spotify's first CTO, who was now a co-founder of Wrapp, a local fintech startup. Iovine and Wood were eyeing him for the role of CTO in their new project, but Andreas Ehn—who still owned a sizable amount of Spotify stock—was not interested in a permanent role in what might become be his former company's main competitor.

Ola Sars tried to set up a meeting with Fredric Vinnå, a brilliant former colleague from Pacemaker, whom he deemed had the capacity to build a new streaming service from the ground up. But Vinnå was happy to be working at Propellerhead, a Swedish music tech company specializing in software synths. He thought the new Beats project sounded too vague and loose around the edges. It wasn't clear to him exactly what Iovine wanted to build. Sars himself, however, was keen to be involved, and joined the project as a consultant.

ANARCHY IN THE UK

A few weeks later, Ola Sars was in a crowd outside the Mandarin Oriental, a high-end hotel in London's Knightsbridge district. It was a cloudy afternoon, October 4th, 2011, and the Swede held his laptop in a tight grip under his arm. He was minutes away from pitching his ideas to the top brass at Beats. Yet hordes of reporters and paparazzi photographers stood in between him and the entrance to the five-star establishment, adorned with Roman columns. Someone must have tipped off the tabloids about the American pop stars currently staying there, he thought to himself.

Sars was able to convince the doormen to let him inside and find the conference room where Jimmy Iovine had gathered his inner circle. Luke Wood was there, as well as the streaming project's intended chief executive Jonas Tempel, co-founder of the DJ portal Beatport. Sars greeted the pop icon Gwen Stefani, one of the many stars that Iovine held close. Iovine's co-founder Andre Young, better known as Dr. Dre, was somewhere nearby, as was the star producer Will.i.am, another Beats shareholder.

Sars connected his laptop to the big screen and presented the "Beats Audio Network." The pitch was tailored to appeal to Jimmy Iovine. Sars said Beats would think like a media company when they built their service, offering channels, programs, star presenters, and a constant focus on "human curation." Iovine nodded, seemingly taking in those last two words. His face lit up when the Swede suggested collaborations with brands like

Pitchfork, *Wired*, *Rolling Stone*, and Chrysler. The founder of Interscope Records was a master of cross promotion. Iovine offered Sars a few encouraging words about the presentation. The goal was to quickly establish themselves as the main competitor to Spotify, he said.

The following evening, Iovine's son played records at one of London's exclusive night clubs. Security guards protected the entrance to the private room where Dr. Dre and a few others from the Beats crew had gathered. The drinks abounded and Sars was elated by his star-studded company. But later that evening, the news broke that Steve Jobs had passed away at the age of fifty-six. The cause of death would later be reported as complications from pancreatic cancer. Suddenly, everyone in the club began to hurry. Iovine and his crew had to fly home to California and pay their respects. They also had to establish how this tragic turn of events would affect their project. Sars's trip to London ended abruptly. The following day, Daniel Ek tweeted out a dedication to the man who had served both as his idol and his chief opponent.

"Thank you Steve. You were a true inspiration in so many parts of my life, both personal and professional. My hat off to our time's Da Vinci," he wrote.

11

"WINTER IS COMING"

D ANIEL EK'S PARTNERSHIP WITH FACEBOOK brought seven million new listeners to Spotify within a few months. But, knowing that only explosive growth could ensure his company's survival, the CEO was not content. The expression "Winter is coming," the signature line from HBO's *Game of Thrones*, began to spread among Spotify employees. The series constantly foretells the impending arrival of a long winter. The Stark family's ultimate fear is that hordes of "white walkers" will break through their wall of ice and unleash an epic war. Spotify didn't fear a humanoid invasion, but rather relentless attacks from the world's largest technology companies. A number of them were already encroaching on music streaming. Apple was shifting iTunes to the cloud, and Jeff Bezos continued to develop the Amazon Cloud Player. Google appeared to be planning to revamp their own store, Google Play Music.

While he assured everyone that his service remained technically superior, Daniel did worry about the sheer size of his rivals. In mid-2011, Apple's balance sheet carried funds of nearly $80 billion, a figure that was growing steadily. With that money, new CEO Tim Cook could buy Spotify forty or fifty times over. The nimble Swedish upstart opted to counter the threat by growing really fast. At scale, they might even be able to free themselves from the grip of the record labels. Artists might begin to come directly to Spotify to release their music. "Everything changes at scale," as Daniel would often remind his C-level executives.

PUSH IT

During the fall of 2011, many of Spotify's new users dropped off, while others began to criticize the partnership with Facebook. Swarms of listeners had become upset that their choice of music was suddenly being shared widely on the social network. Shutting off the feature required several seemingly complicated steps. Daniel Ek began to fill in as customer support on Twitter.

"We'll try lots of things, and probably screw up from time to time, but we value feedback and will make changes based on it," he wrote.

A new version of Spotify was on its way, where users would be offered a private listening mode that did not broadcast their taste to the world. Yet the feedback also noted that Spotify was so visible on Facebook that it appeared to have taken over the social network.

"Our intention is not to spam you," Daniel wrote in response to one of the complainants.

Another point of contention was that registering for Spotify now required a Facebook account. Many months would pass before Daniel budged on this point. His priority was to attract as many users as possible. Through Facebook, he saw an opportunity to make a dent in the US, and he felt it wasn't happening fast enough.

"Why aren't we growing faster?" he wrote in a one-line email to one of his associates as early results from the partnership began to appear.

His mantra at this time was "harder, better, faster, stronger," four words lifted from Daft Punk that he would often use to sign off his emails. The young Swede was a demanding CEO known for hounding his top executives, appearing to never run out of follow-up questions. He occasionally would tell off individual staff members in front of their peers, as if to demonstrate his power. One senior staff member would recall how a friendlier Daniel approached a colleague after a meeting, asking them not to take his public scolding personally.

Back in the spring of 2011, Daniel had head hunted a growth specialist who lived up to his exacting standards. Alex Norström was a thirty-three -year-old hip-hop and R&B fan who had previously helped the Swedish fashion brand Acne with their e-commerce. He had recently left a senior position at King.com, whose mobile games reached tens of millions of users each month. His former gaming studio would become known as the inventors of Candy Crush, an addictive game that would dominate the mobile gaming charts for years to come. Alex's new colleagues at Spotify saw him as a manager who both worked and played hard, was eager to rise through the ranks and sometimes made jokes at other people's expense. Some would describe his management style as "American." He would, at times, push people to greater heights and call out poor performance.

Daniel had given Alex a clear task: bring Spotify to one hundred million users. The figure was ten times what the company had at the end of 2011. Alex Norström became Spotify's Head of Growth, a title that came with its own team and, crucially, its own small squad of developers.

Obsessed with growing quickly, Daniel gave this new team free rein and rarely interfered in their work. His growth team was built on the same model Mark Zuckerberg had used at Facebook. They had three goals: acquire new users, get them to activate their accounts, and turn them into frequent users. Their work centered around three buzzwords—"acquisition," "activation," and "retention"—that, if successfully executed, could make Spotify a dominant force in the music world.

Alex and his team would constantly devise new growth hacks to reach their aggressively set goals. They prompted all users who had connected Spotify to Facebook to invite all of their friends to join the music service. Alex kept a constant eye on the numbers. Metrics such as "second-day retention"—the extent to which a new user returned to Spotify on day two— would prove especially important.

Above all, Alex fixated on the number of daily and monthly listeners. The higher the daily number, the more engaged the users had become, and the more likely it seemed that they would eventually become paying subscribers. Like thousands of other third-party apps, Spotify could now access slices of Facebook's user data. Several years would pass before that exchange became the subject of widespread criticism.

During the fall of 2011, Spotify was gaining tens of thousands of new users every day, but the intake from Facebook appeared to be of relatively low quality, including a large share of passive listeners. Alex and his team would eventually start recruiting in other ways. Their efforts centered around marketing campaigns through both Facebook and Google where Spotify would effectively pay a price for every new user. As long as the cost of attracting a new user was lower than the expected revenue from the same user over time—his or her "lifetime value"—Alex had no reason to take his foot off the gas.

Another way to grow was to expand into new territories. During 2011, Daniel brought Spotify to Austria, Belgium, and Switzerland. The following year, ahead of a much-anticipated launch in Germany, he finally scrapped the rule that required new users to sign up via Facebook. That requirement would have been a problem in the German market, where Facebook was nowhere near as popular as in Sweden or the UK.

By September 2012, Facebook had been removed as the sole entry point in all other markets too. That year, Spotify brought its services to Australia and New Zealand. The international expansion was led by the young business and marketing graduate Axel Bard Bringéus who, like Alex Norström, had spent a few years at King.com. During Spotify's rapid global rollout, he would often find himself waking up in a taxi, wondering whether he was on his way to or from an airport.

ROCKET MAN

By mid-2012, Spotify had reached twelve countries and fifteen million active users. Daniel Ek now split his time between Stockholm and New York, where he had a second home in lower Manhattan. While in Sweden, he would arrive at the office at ten a.m. and stay until at least seven p.m. "An early New York time zone," as he described his own schedule.

At home, about twenty minutes' walk from the office, he would log on to his computer again. Work would usually keep him busy until two or three in the morning, around the time his contacts in Silicon Valley were getting ready to call it a day.

Daniel was now fully focused on the bigger picture. His Chief Finance Officer, Peter Sterky, had stepped in as acting CEO. That allowed Daniel to focus on his strengths: the company's vision and matters that lay at least six months into the future. In Stockholm, he worked on product development;

in New York, on deals with the music industry. On average, Spotify was now hiring one new employee every day. Within their first week, newcomers might be expected to guide even fresher recruits around their new office. Neither Daniel nor Martin Lorentzon were early risers. On a typical day, the headquarters would clear out only after midnight, and not fill up until mid-morning the next day.

During the summer of 2012, Spotify's employees moved into the Jarla House, a few blocks down Birger Jarlsgatan. The music startup leased floors seven, eight, nine, and eleven in the recently renovated office building. Soon Spotify's main offices had all the attributes of a startup company, with colorful furniture, graffiti art on the walls, a video game corner, and a ping-pong room. The canteen on the eleventh floor overlooked the characteristic metal roofs of central Stockholm. Martin would joke that they needed to "smoke out" the neighbors so Spotify could take over the whole building.

Many employees were now having the time of their lives. For some, the trips abroad were becoming frequent. In New York, they would stay at boutique hotels like The Standard, a glittering building that rose up over the Meatpacking District on concrete suspensions. Others booked rooms at the Dream Downtown on West 16th Street. They worked hard, ate well, and partied at night. Some of them ended up in each other's rooms. There was no company policy against sleeping with coworkers. After all, this was a tech company in the music world, and Spotify's fresh venture funding had things looking pretty rock 'n' roll. Business and pleasure would frequently mix. Even the company's chairman, Martin Lorentzon, slept with several employees over the years, three sources would claim.

Spotify's travel budgets were generous. If a company offsite at a Soho House location was scheduled for Monday, it wasn't unheard of for employees to check in the Friday before, all on the company's dime. Some would even routinely upgrade their flights abroad to business class, and expense the cost. Eventually, the finance team mandated that business class would only be accepted for flights longer than eight hours, as one frequent traveler would recall.

The venture capital from Yuri Milner's DST Global had given Spotify a fresh range of options. For the first time, Daniel was able to recruit executives from some of the world's largest tech companies. Many Spotify employees would recall how a new layer of mid-level managers, often Americans, were ushered in far too quickly, and with decidedly mixed results.

Several early staff members recalled their new bosses fighting for months over territory instead of pursuing their goals. But with a billion-dollar valuation, Daniel now had to answer to new owners and transform his homespun Swedish startup into a competitive, international tech firm. He found he had to accept collateral damage within the organization.

Some of the new executives—such as the much-liked Chief Revenue Officer, Jeff Levick, who had previously spent time at AOL and Google—would remain at Spotify for years to come. Others did not stay as long. The company's new Chief Marketing Officer, Teymour Farman-Farmaian, another Google veteran, left after about a year. He had a management style that some staffers found overly confrontational, as three people would recall. Farman-Farmaian himself would later put any friction down to growing pains at a "hyperscaling" company. He had been placed, he said, between Daniel and staff members who had previously enjoyed direct access to their CEO.

For new employees, Spotify could feel like a free and spontaneous work environment, with no clear hierarchy. New recruits sometimes found room to push out their predecessors. Several sources point to the arrival of the new marketing VP Erin Clift as leading to the departure of the internally admired Sophia Bendz, who had built hype around Spotify's beta product in the early years and remained a key figure in marketing. To the dismay of several employees, Sophia returned after maternity leave only to find her role marginalized. (Such demotions are taboo in Sweden, which has one of the most generous parental-leave systems in the world.) Critics within the company accused Daniel of pandering to investors, too concerned about the optics to reprimand or fire high-profile recruits.

"With American money come American executives, and things are often never the same again," as one person who spent years in the Stockholm startup scene would put it.

Throughout the years, Spotify was a place ridden with intense internal rivalries. Some would describe the atmosphere as downright Darwinistic. Daniel Ek would rarely mediate in a conflict, opting instead to let his subordinates duke it out themselves. Instead, his focus was on the grand chessboard, where he would map out new ideas and growth targets wild enough to seem fanciful to some of his colleagues.

"When it comes to team leadership and deciding on specifics, he doesn't always deliver," as one employee would put it.

Perhaps Daniel lacked interest in office politics because he was always looking a few years ahead. One of his highest priorities was to keep recruiting the sharpest minds available. People with strong resumes needed to be headhunted, whether or not they slotted easily into the corporate culture. "Come join the band," as the company's HR department would put it. For Daniel, a little organized confusion did not cloud the bigger picture. His goal was to make Spotify huge.

"I am quite simply rather naïve. Maybe that is why I dare to try to achieve what is impossible," he said in an appearance on Swedish public radio in the summer of 2012. "Then—and this might not be very Swedish— I want to do something that can really change the world, even if it's in a very small way."

Those who had come to know Daniel Ek would rarely describe him as naïve. If anything, he might sometimes appear fairly calculated in his decision making. His friends and associates had become accustomed to his endless ambitions and would often praise his tendency to constantly challenge the status quo.

Eventually, the rest of the world would echo their praises. One of his many accolades hung framed on his office wall. It was a remake of the album art from Pink Floyd's classic *Dark Side of the Moon*, where rays of light travel through a prism and create a color spectrum on the other side. In this version, the light passes not through a prism, but through the bald head of Daniel Ek. The illustration had appeared in *Bloomberg Business Week*.

Daniel had seen how Facebook's mind-boggling growth had made Mark Zuckerberg virtually immortal. He was therefore focused solely on one thing: how many active users Spotify could rack up every month. As long as his streaming service became a global sensation, petty workplace conflicts and internal rivalries didn't matter.

I'M COMING OUT

In 2012, Daniel Ek began to properly introduce himself to the Swedish public. In March, he sat for a primetime talk show interview on Swedish

Television, charming the audience with stories of buzzing servers in his Rågsved apartment and his file-sharing habits as a young man. The host, Fredrik Skavlan, asked about his public appearances in the US, where the audience was used to Steve Jobs's immaculate performances.

"It doesn't come naturally to me. After all, I started as a programmer," Daniel Ek replied.

A few months later, the Spotify founder appeared on the beloved summertime radio show Sommar i P1, where celebrities and public figures play songs and speak openly about their lives for ninety minutes straight.

"I have my lows, just like everyone else, when I feel down and above all inadequate," he said during the show.

Before entering the studio, the staff had shown him around the massive record archive kept at Swedish Radio's colossal Broadcasting House, on the outskirts of central Stockholm. Its roughly four million physical recordings made an impression on Daniel, who was taken aback by its sheer size. One of his hosts would later recall how the entrepreneur browsed the records in amazement, an experience he later addressed on air.

"This record archive was the image I used when I tried to explain what it was we wanted to build. Just imagine everything that's in this archive—only on your phone," he said.

In his carefully scripted radio performance he mentioned his family, growing up in Rågsved, and his first few assignments in the technology industry. This radio show was where Daniel first described his time as a confused young man in search of an identity, during which he bought a red sports car and, for a short period, fell into a depression. He also relayed how he spent his teenage years pulling "virtual pranks" in various hacker chat rooms and how he, much later, found that he and Sean Parker must have been part of the same online circles as teens.

"At some point then, we realized that we had both been hanging out in the same chat rooms and talked to each other. Most likely something about taking over the world. That's how we were," Daniel said. He also offered some banter on the music industry, describing how he once witnessed a famous drummer trash his manager's office in New York.

Six years had now passed since he, as a twenty-three-year-old, had started Spotify with Martin Lorentzon. They now had 600 employees, enough for some of the reception staff not to know who he was.

"A couple of months ago I was almost denied entrance," he said during the radio show.

The Swede now had met many of his idols. He mentioned U2's frontman Bono and lingered on a particular anecdote about the singer-songwriter Neil Young. Daniel had just arrived in San Francisco, feeling dazed after trips to London, Singapore, and New York in quick succession. Neil Young stopped outside his hotel in a white Cadillac.

"He picked me up and we drove around for nearly two hours talking about music. Sometimes it feels like I'm living in a fairy tale," Daniel told the listeners. Neil Young himself would emerge as a fledgling entrepreneur in the music space. In 2012, he launched a prototype of his own triangular, portable PonoPlayer. An accompanying streaming service would follow a few years later.

During his radio appearance, Daniel also mentioned how he had lunch at the Beverly Hilton Hotel on February 11, 2012, the day before the Grammy Awards in Los Angeles. He was accompanied by Neil Young and the legendary record executive Clive Davis, father of the music lawyer Fred Davis, who helped Spotify during the early years. Clive had served as Whitney Houston's mentor for nearly thirty years. Now, she was due as the guest of honor at his annual pre-party ahead of the awards ceremony the following day. At one point during the lunch, Clive Davis answered his phone and quickly left the table.

"Neither I nor Neil Young understood exactly what had happened," Daniel recounts on the program. Soon, they saw paramedics run by. Whitney Houston had passed away in a different part of the same hotel. Clive Davis's pre-party turned into a wake, where those closest to the star gave *in memoriam* speeches and spoke openly of their grief.

Daniel could now move freely through the power structures of the music industry. During the same trip to Los Angeles, he posed for a photograph at an event hosted by Universal CEO Lucian Grainge, one of his main antagonists in the messy negotiations that led up to Spotify entering the US. Said to be uncomfortable at industry events, Ek was willing to show up and pay his respects to one of the industry's most powerful people. Several other well-known faces had made it to the same party, such as the rapper Ludacris and the Universal executive Jimmy Iovine.

By this time, Daniel had parted ways with his girlfriend, Charlotte Ågren. While he had been committed to their relationship, he was often several time zones away. Things are said to have ended amicably in early 2011. Around the same time, Daniel left London and moved back to Stockholm.

During the past winter, the Spotify founder had taken some much-needed time off, traveling to the south of Brazil with Shakil Khan, among others. According to the gossip site Gawker, Mark Zuckerberg and Sean Parker had both flown south to join the fun. They would appear to have left Florianopolis with colorful memories.

During the spring of 2012, Daniel had begun exploring his options as a single man. Several people would recall that he dated a Spotify employee who held a junior role at the company. Both warm and kind, the pair were said to have a natural chemistry. They would sometimes head home together after going out for drinks after work with a larger group.

Tellingly, much of their interaction was said to have occurred online. That was partly because Daniel travelled a lot, but also because the virtual Daniel had a different swagger about him. In person, the now twenty-nine-year-old CEO still gave a quiet and shy impression. But online, he was charming, funny, and brimming with the confidence befitting a world-famous entrepreneur. Despite his age, fame, and riches, Daniel would still only feel truly uninhibited in front of a computer. In that sense, not much had changed since he flirted with girls in high school over ICQ.

After the secretive fling, Daniel threw himself into a relationship with another woman. He would give her a shoutout in his radio program that summer.

"I have now met someone who is special to me. But I've also realized that I need someone pretty special to deal with all my darting back and forth," Daniel said during the broadcast.

He was referring to his future wife, Sofia Levander.

THE POWER OF LOVE

The romance began when Sofia, presenting herself as a freelance writer, asked to interview Daniel. While waiting for a reply, she wrote a long email lambasting the Spotify founder for not answering. Something about her attitude piqued Daniel's interest, as he would recall.

Before they had even met, Sofia Levander had shown the kind of unabashed confidence that was one of her defining traits. Like the Spotify founder, Sofia had grown up in surroundings that made her determined to get hers in the world. What she lacked in book smarts, she made up for in fearlessness, determination, and a captivating life story.

Born in late 1980, Sofia was two years older than Daniel. She had grown up in the affluent area of Djursholm, a suburb just north of Stockholm that was known for stately villas and a high concentration of power and money. Its residents included some of the most prominent names in Swedish industry and commerce, such as the Persson family, which had founded the fast fashion giant H&M shortly after World War Two. In Djursholm, children could grow up and become adults without once riding the Stockholm subway.

At school, Sofia and her older sister, Anna, mixed well with the children of the Swedish business elite. But unlike them, they did not come from a wealthy home. Sofia's father was a professor of psychiatry and her mother would later become a psychologist. When Sofia was four years old, her father moved out. Throughout her childhood and teenage years, Sofia, her mother, and her sister lived with her maternal grandparents, as two people would recall. The house was big enough for the five of them and they were never poor, but in an area full of millionaires, they felt like the have-nots.

The Levander family lived down the road from the E18 highway, which led straight into Stockholm. Like Daniel, Sofia and Anna grew up with a single mother. Whereas Anna studied hard and eventually graduated from the Stockholm School of Economics, Sofia—or "Cookie," as her close friends called her—chose a different path, one that often worried her loved ones. Soon after she graduated from the local high school, Sofia started studying abroad.

On September 11, 2001, while Daniel was in his final year of school, Sofia Levander was living in New York City. She was twenty years old and had just started studying PR and marketing at Pace University in lower Manhattan. Early that morning, she headed south from her apartment in the East Village, which she shared with three other people. The attack on the Twin Towers would leave an indelible impression on her.

"We're watching as both skyscrapers burn and I'm seeing people jump from both of the buildings," she told the Swedish daily newspaper *Aftonbladet* hours after the attack.

After leaving New York, Sofia studied media and communication at Stockholm University. Around this time, she starred as Nikki in the cable

TV show *Swedish Girls,* a kind of scripted reality show that sought to emulate HBO's smash hit *Sex and the City.*

"I can hardly stand watching her sometimes, she's such a fool," Sofia said about her character in a 2004 interview.

Talking to the reporter, Sofia was her candid self. She readily admitted that she was on the show to become famous, and that it would be "lame" to claim otherwise.

"But Nikki is extremely exaggerated. She might represent me at my worst state of drunken partying, like something that might happen once a year."

As Daniel started building what would become Spotify, Sofia spent some time in Libya. There, she helped sell and produce advertorials about the investment climate in the oil-rich country intended for publication in *Smart Money*, a commercial supplement to the *Wall Street Journal.*

At this time, Libya's dictator, Muammar Gaddafi, still ruled with an iron fist. It would be another few years before he was forced from power and brutally murdered following the Arab Spring. In her own book, *The Minefield Girl*, Sofia would recall how she, early on, found herself inside a Bedouin tent, where the all-powerful man gave her a creepy stare.

By some accounts, Sofia pounced on the opportunity to do business with the Gaddafi regime. She was said to have gotten close with one of the dictator's sons, Saif al-Islam Gaddafi, a widely influential power broker. A rule of thumb among Libya's business community was to keep one degree of separation from the ruling family. But Sofia Levander, now in her late twenties, was comfortable enough with Saif Gaddafi to call upon favors directly.

The details of Sofia's time in Libya would long remain unclear, but by late 2008, she appears to have left the country. At that time, tensions had begun to rise in Gaddafi's Libya.

"A series of events since last summer suggest that tension between various children of Muammar al-Qadhafi has increased," a US diplomatic cable from 2009, subsequently published by Wikileaks, would conclude.

"Much of the tension appears to stem from resentment of Saif al-Islam's high-profile as the public face of the regime."

After the NATO-supported uprising in 2011, the dictator's son would spend six years in prison. At the completion of this manuscript, he was wanted for crimes against humanity, and reportedly plotting a return to Libyan politics. His exact whereabouts were unknown.

Some of Sofia Levander's dealings in Libya appeared to bear fruit. During 2007 and 2008, she reportedly acted as liaison between Libyan authorities and a Swedish mine-clearing company, Countermine, landing them valuable inroads in the dictatorship. Countermine would later attempt a capital raise on the Swedish public markets that ended in a legal quagmire, with many of its shareholders feeling duped.

Sofia Levander would also spend time in Costa Rica with Moha Bensofia, a charismatic Libyan with a blinding smile and washboard abs. The two were an item for a time, according to several people. They also lived together in Stockholm, reportedly in Sofia's mother's city apartment. Later, Daniel and Sofia would help Bensofia flee Libya on short notice and settle in Stockholm, where he entered the couple's innermost circle.

In 2012, after Daniel received Sofia's fiery email, the Spotify founder replied. A quick Google search would have returned glamorous photos of the young Stockholmer, perhaps from her brief stint as a reality TV star.

The couple started to date, and the relationship progressed quickly. At the start of the summer, Sofia quit her job as an account executive for Microsoft's local ad sales team. By July, she and Daniel started posting pictures of each other on social media.

A few months later, Sofia Levander was pregnant. In June 2013, their daughter Elissa was born.

ANIMAL

As Daniel Ek settled into family life, Martin Lorentzon would remain a bachelor for years to come. The elder Spotify founder would never take formal employment with the company, preferring to focus on areas where he felt he could be useful for the time being. One day he might court investors, only to interview a candidate for a key position the next. He also took pride in planning extravagant company parties. Few people could say exactly what Martin was up to at any given moment. Spotify's largest shareholder followed his impulses and did not feel that he needed to prove himself to anyone.

As chairman, Martin would brief Sean Parker and the other board members ahead of each meeting. Many of the key figures that had built Spotify had come directly out of his personal network—such as the early investor and board member Pär-Jörgen Pärson, the company's CFO, Peter Sterky, and the music-license broker Niklas Ivarsson. Yet among Spotify staff, the forty-three-year-old was best known as the mischievous and quirky co-founder who might suddenly ride through the office on his unicycle.

During the fall of 2012, Martin would frequent Riche, a swoosh restaurant-bar near the square of Stureplan. He would regularly meet up with the political strategist Per Schlingmann, and often sought to discuss political issues of importance to Spotify with people in power. He would occasionally turn up with celebrity guests at Spotify's new headquarters. The Moderate politician Anna Kinberg Batra and Petter, a Swedish rapper turned entrepreneur, were two of many.

"Would you mind explaining what you're working on," the co-founder would ask a random employee, visitors in tow. When accompanied by journalists reporting on the hottest tech company in Sweden, he would strike a charming, boyish pose by the pinball machine, typically wearing a zip-up hoodie with a Spotify logo.

Martin exercised daily and would play squash, golf, and go cycling on his mountain bike. Most days, he would plan two outdoor activities. On one occasion, at the Jarla House headquarters, the energetic co-founder ambled over to one of Gustav Söderström's assistants with an idea.

"Let's go play golf," he said to the junior colleague, who quickly understood that he had no choice but to tag along for a round of golf in the middle of his workday.

People who have worked with Martin often tell stories of his sudden whims, restless enthusiasm, and pranks that register somewhere between childish and inappropriate. Many also find him funny. In the middle of a meeting where English was being spoken, he is said to have turned to one of his Spotify colleagues and explained to her, in Swedish and with a straight face, that he really needed "to take a poo."

"He won't sit still. It's impossible to get him into a room even for a short meeting," as one former co-worker would recall.

The same person suspected that Martin's goofy style was his way of deflecting the constant demands for his time, influence, and wealth, both at Spotify and outside the company. A conversation with Martin would often liven up his co-workers, even if it was hard to keep track of what he was trying to say.

"He is usually talking about five things all at once, jumping from one topic to the other. It gets confusing, but he always circles back to finish his points," as one former employee would recall.

As Spotify made inroads in the US, the company's press team began to see Martin as a liability, or a "loose cannon," in interview situations. His English wasn't great either. Underhandedly, they would lobby Daniel to dial back his co-founder's official duties abroad. Martin reluctantly accepted, seeing the wisdom in letting Daniel mature into the company's definitive spokesperson.

With time, Martin Lorentzon became known for his odd inside jokes. One weekend, he called a mid-level manager at the company who was out for a walk alongside his girlfriend. Startled by a phone call from Spotify's chairman, the employee answered immediately.

"Hi, Martin," he said.

"Squeal! Squeeeeal!"

For a second, the co-worker hesitated. Martin repeated his wish.

"I want you to squeeeeal!"

The Spotify chairman would not let up until his colleague made grunting animal sounds on the phone. His girlfriend wondered who the hell was on the other end of the call.

Over the years, Martin would ask many co-workers to squeal for him. He seemed amused by how everyone interpreted the request differently. Some were enthusiastic, others reserved. Some felt uncomfortable and that such behavior did not belong at an international workplace. Perhaps the squealing was Martin's way of getting them to let their guard down. Perhaps he thought the noise each person produced revealed something about their personality. Perhaps it was just a form of bullying. Regardless, he made the request to everyone, from the company's top managers to their personal assistants.

"Squeal a little, old boy," Martin once wrote to Shakil Khan in a tweet written in Swedish.

Much later, the Spotify co-founder would explain how this inside joke had started at Tradedoubler, where he used the Swedish word "gny" (squeal) to teach a French coworker the quirks of Swedish pronunciation.

While Daniel continued to polish his leadership style, his co-founder remained relatively unchanged. By now, Martin had founded two wildly successful companies and saw no reason to alter his personality.

HUSTLIN' DAZE

In the year following Spotify's US launch, Daniel Ek's close advisor, Shakil Khan, had begun to explore opportunities outside of the company.

In March 2012, he announced that he was leaving Spotify to join the nascent networking platform Path. He would be "head of special projects," based in London but with global duties. Daniel was sad to see his friend leave.

"I am kind of an introvert guy, and Shak is the definition of social, so he was the link to the rest of the world in many ways for me and for the company," Daniel told the tech website, AllThingsD.

By now, Shak's international network had grown, and the "global favor bank" he had amassed was proving useful. At a tech conference in Berlin, he would introduce his friend Nick D'Aloisio, a sixteen-year-old entrepreneur and programmer, to Yahoo! CEO Marissa Mayer.

In 2013, Yahoo! acquired D'Aloisio's company, a natural-language processing startup called Summly, for a rumored $30 million. Three years after Apple acquired Siri, Yahoo had purchased its own language technology—thanks in part to Shakil Khan.

As an investor in Summly, Shak made money off of the deal. Others said to have invested included the news mogul Rupert Murdoch, the British comedian Stephen Fry, and the world-renowned artist Yoko Ono. Several of the other shareholders—including Li Ka-shing and the actor Ashton Kutcher—had direct ties to Shak.

In the years that followed, Shak would invest in a host of other international startups, among them the crypto-currency news website CoinDesk and Bitpay, a blockchain-based payments provider.

Spotify would, however, turn out to be his most successful bet by a distance.

TAXMAN

For Martin Lorentzon, Spotify was still the only show in town.

"I put all my eggs in one basket and watch them carefully," as he would describe his investment strategy time and again.

Preserving his company's Swedish heritage was important to Martin. He played an active role when new employees traveled to Stockholm for Spotify's annual Intro Days, telling the streaming company's origin story in his typically lively manner. After one of these presentations, a group of new hires from Italy approached him. Martin lit up when they asked him for a group photo, as one attendee would recall.

All of Spotify's large-scale festivities were part of Martin's remit. He jumped at the chance to celebrate Spotify's collective achievements and forge a bond between the growing swaths of people representing the company across the globe. In June 2013, Spotify invited its roughly one thousand employees to Summer Jam, a days-long party that spared no expense. Martin Lorentzon is even said to have covered a part of the costs out of his own pocket. At Berns, where Spotify had held its first launch party in 2008, he roused his staff with a passionate speech. The week culminated inside a remodeled hangar at Arlanda Airport, where the British electronica band Faithless performed until the early hours.

Eventually, Martin began to take on commitments outside of Spotify. In April 2013, he took a position on the board of Telia, the telecoms company where he had spent some time as a trainee during the 1990s. His nomination to the board resulted in a media storm, after Swedish Radio reported that the Spotify co-founder had avoided paying taxes in Sweden by hiding his wealth in Cyprus and Luxembourg.

Familiarly, Spotify's press department met the news with silence. Martin's lawyer stepped in as spokesperson, claiming the ownership structure was established for "business" reasons. Eventually, the Spotify founder wrote a piece published in the opinion pages of *Dagens industri*, Sweden's leading financial newspaper. In it, he defended his decision to minimize his tax contributions in Sweden.

"I am proud to have contributed to building two strong Swedish companies that have created many jobs in Sweden and abroad," he wrote.

He claimed that he moved his money abroad because in the late 1990s, he had found it difficult to find Swedish investors willing to back his "crazy ideas." By placing his money in tax havens, he was following the example set by venture firms like Northzone and Creandum.

"I realized early on that in future ventures I would have to finance my ideas on my own. Hence my investment company in Cyprus."

The company, Rosello Company Limited, appeared to have struck few deals outside of Spotify. A few years later, Martin and Daniel would make an investment in their friend Shakil Khan's company Student.com, but other than that small holding, Rosello functioned as the largest single shareholder in Spotify. It was certainly a risky strategy, but Sweden's most successful serial entrepreneur in decades had put nearly all his faith in a single company.

While he enjoyed nights on the town, his other investments would remain modest for years to come. He was said to own an apartment in the northern ski resort of Åre. But Martin resided in the same apartment in Vasastan, a chic neighborhood minutes from the city center, that he acquired during his years at Tradedoubler. It was a modest abode for a man who, by 2015, would become a billionaire.

SPOTIFY TV

SPOTIFY WAS ALWAYS A HIGHLY secretive company. Licensing deals with the record labels were strictly confidential, and staff were often asked to sign nondisclosure agreements (NDAs). They generally remained loyal, and leaks were rare. This only made the press more eager to cover the goings-on at the rapidly developing streaming company.

In mid-2011, following the launch of Spotify in the United States, Daniel embarked on a secret pet project. He formed a new unit within the company, kept separate from all other departments. Details of the project would remain unknown to the outside world for years, and the full picture would not emerge until the publication of the first Swedish edition of this book.

In the fall of 2011, Daniel assembled a small team that he and his colleagues would internally refer to as Magneto. It was named for the figure in Marvel's *X-Men* series who, by controlling magnetic fields, could steer target-bound bullets, missiles, and trucks in any direction. Daniel's goal was to steer millions of music listeners toward a different media format: video.

"It was a stealth organization," as one source would put it.

DO IT AGAIN

Daniel Ek's plan of attack on the billion-dollar TV industry began with proprietary technology. The twenty-nine-year-old founder handpicked two exceptional software developers—known internally as Ludde and Andoma, after their user names in the company's chat rooms—to jump-start the effort. Ludvig "Ludde" Strigeus was the self-taught wiz kid known for single-handedly writing the front-end code for Spotify's first music player, and was the only programmer at the company who reported directly to Daniel. His partner, Andreas "Andoma" Smas, was a coder who joined the company in 2008 and had previously worked on video streaming technology.

Their goal was to reinvent online video. In keeping with Spotify's etiquette, the coders would not tolerate buffering; the stream could never pause to load. To assure a seamless experience, Strigeus and Smas created an entirely new file format, called Spotify Video. Abbreviated as .spv, the files carried a lighter load than the usual formats. Strigeus was meticulous and obsessed with saving computer memory wherever he could.

"Every time you waste a byte, God kills a kitten," he would muse to his coworkers.

Despite their best efforts, the Magneto team eventually abandoned the Spotify Video format for HLS, or HTTP Live Streaming, the only format that was compatible with Apple's iOS mobile operating system.

Daniel and his Chief Product Officer, Gustav Söderström, began the hunt for someone to lead their new foray into video. The Swedes said virtually nothing about the secretive project during interviews. Eventually, they tapped the Comcast veteran Mike Berkley for the role, and in the spring of 2012, he moved with his family from Silicon Valley to New York. He commuted to Spotify's Chelsea offices in the former Port Authority building on Eighth Avenue. There, a few floors above Google's New York headquarters, Daniel and Mike drew up a vision for their project.

"We are about to enter the Golden Age of Video," as an internal pitch described it in February 2012, just before Mike formally joined Spotify.

Daniel believed he had identified a potential gap in the TV market. He wanted to build a digital, on-demand alternative to linear broadcasts via cable and satellite. He was not looking to compete directly with Netflix— whose catalogue at this time consisted mainly of old movies and past seasons of various TV series—but rather to enter the same space as Hulu. Viewers of Spotify would be served live sports and news, current seasons of TV shows, and a selection of movies. Daniel instructed the Magneto team—which was to keep its mission secret even inside Spotify itself—to tailor content for each viewer.

"Your video service will be highly personalized. It will know your tastes and interests and your consumption patterns. It will anticipate what content you want and when you want it," the pitch stated.

By the end of 2012, Mike Berkley was able to show his bosses a prototype.

VIDEO KILLED THE RADIO STAR

Twice a year, Spotify's top brass gathered for the company's Strategy Days, where between fifty and one hundred executives and key employees would debate the future direction of the company. The meetings were held in spring and fall, either in the US or in Sweden. An invitation to the power meeting was a clear status symbol among lower-ranking staff.

In late November, the Strategy Days were held in an anonymous conference room in downtown Stockholm. It was below freezing, and many participants struggled to make it there on time.

"Nothing is impossible, except everyone being here at 8am," as one punctual attendee quipped on Twitter.

Mike Berkley, who had flown in from New York, took the stage in front of roughly sixty of his peers and told them that he saw video as an additional core business for Spotify. At this point, he and his team had spent around a year trying to create a new type of user experience.

Mike—a musician turned businessman—picked up an iPad with a 3G connection. He opened an app that not even Daniel Ek had seen yet. Suddenly the tablet started to broadcast live Swedish cable TV. Mike flicked seamlessly between channels; the shows were being transmitted live, but as soon as he tapped the screen, they restarted from the beginning. The app came with an instant playback mode. The interface was every bit as quick as Spotify's music player.

"It was a magical experience," as one attendee would describe the presentation.

By a feat of programming, the Magneto team had eliminated the loading time associated with digitally encoded TV. The app—eventually dubbed Spotify TV—could flip instantly between channels. For the second time in the company's brief history, engineers had built a product far superior to anything available on the market.

It felt like the finished product, but it was highly provisional. Spotify engineers had installed five small antennas in the southeastern corner of Jarla House, as close as possible to the twin antenna towers that formed a landmark in southern Stockholm. They were able to hack into around 30 Swedish cable channels, using the open source software Tvheadend to decrypt the signals and convert them into streams destined for Mike's iPad. Once again, a Spotify prototype had been built on pirated content. Daniel was impressed but, having grown weary of license negotiations, he wasn't convinced. At least not yet.

"I'm not worried about the product, I'm worried about the business case," he told people working on the project early on.

Mike and his team spent the next few years negotiating with a wide range of TV companies—from Swedish networks and cable companies to Time Warner, Fox, and CBS—to secure licenses for their content. They also drew up plans to build a digital TV receiver, Spotify's first-ever hardware product.

LIVING IN A BOX

During the fall of 2013, a group of Spotify employees traveled to Shenzhen, the epicenter of China's tech and hardware industry, across the border from Hong Kong. Shenzhen was home to factories that manufactured the iPhone, Dell's laptops, and headphones for Sony.

The Spotify team was in town to find a supplier for a small receiver and remote control that could be used with the Spotify TV app. On the surface, the blueprints looked much like the Apple TV system. The team told its Chinese counterparts as little as possible about the hardware, so as to not alert competitors. Back in Stockholm, Daniel Ek was mulling over questions of industrial design.

"We want to build our own hardware," he told Konrad Bergström, an energetic, forty-two-year-old Swedish entrepreneur with curly gray hair.

Daniel had chosen Bergström for the task because of his strong track record in hardware design. He was the co-founder of a Swedish startup called Zound Industries, which had struck gold designing headphones and speakers under its own brand, Urbanears, and by licensing the rights to the vintage audio brand, Marshall. Their colorful Urbanears headphones had already been featured in Spotify ads, forming a kind of counterpoint to the white-wired earphones that Apple had been working hard to entrench in popular culture ever since the launch of the iPod.

Spotify was already rolling out its own remote listening technology, Spotify Connect, which would let users switch seamlessly between connected speakers. The Zound co-founder, who dreamt of taking on Dr. Dre and Jimmy Iovine's Beats Electronics, now wanted to produce multiroom speakers together with Daniel Ek. A fruitful partnership, Bergström thought, would marry hardware and software in a way that could give Apple a run for its money.

Daniel, clearly a bigger fish than Bergström in the pond of Swedish tech, asked if Zound would be interested in designing a prototype for the streaming company's first piece of hardware. Bergström immediately accepted.

"I'll give you a good price," he said.

Over the coming months, engineers at Zound's Stockholm offices drew up designs for a black Spotify-branded remote and a receiver that plugged into the electrical outlet. From there, an HDMI cable ran straight into the user's TV to power Spotify's video offering.

The sleek remote carried the Spotify logo, with three wavy lines originally intended to represent audio streaming. The remote let the viewer navigate a grid of channels: up and down for sports, drama, and news; right and left for various programs within each category. Like Spotify's music player, the technology anticipated user behavior; as someone watched a certain program, the nearby channels would be on standby, streaming in the background at a low bandwidth. The move made switching channels as instant as on cable TV.

"It felt immediate," as one source would put it. Konrad Bergström took a number of meetings with Daniel Ek during 2013 and 2014. Zound spent hundreds of thousands of dollars developing the prototype, yet charged considerably less for the work.

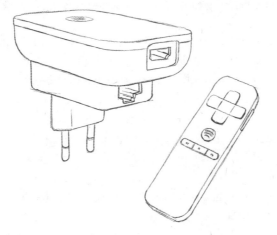

A sketch of a prototype for the hardware intended for the Spotify TV project. *(Sebastian Ramn)*

TORN

During 2013, Nordic TV executives were feeling the pressure. Younger viewers loved streaming TV series at their own convenience. Netflix had recently launched in Scandinavia. One appraisal showed that it had become the largest on-demand video service in Sweden within its first year. The local competitor Viaplay—which owned the rights to the national soccer league and to Spain's La Liga—had slipped to second place. The undisputed king of Swedish tech had no trouble booking meetings with executives in the TV industry. Five years after launching its service, Spotify was a clear success in the Nordics. Nearly half of all adults in Sweden had registered a debit card with the service. Decision makers in television knew that Daniel Ek could dominate their field as well.

The Spotify CEO was ready to invest tens of millions of dollars to explore a market that was many times bigger than music. He realized that his service could not stop at Swedish cable channels: it needed a rich American offering as well. Daniel wanted CNN, Cartoon Network, Disney, and ESPN to all be available. The Magneto team held discussions with a number of the large providers in the US, from Time Warner to Fox to CBS.

Daniel was said to be eager to secure the rights to soccer matches between his two favorite teams: AIK in Stockholm and Arsenal of North London.

In 2013, he took a meeting at Jarla House with Jonas Sjögren, the CEO of Discovery Networks Sweden, owner of the local channels Kanal5 and Kanal9. He was a former colleague of Spotify's new head of HR, Katarina Berg, who had made the introduction. Daniel began by asking a few basic questions about the TV business, and his counterpart delivered honest answers. His experience of startup companies, such as the Swedish online video venture Magine, was that they would usually try to weasel out of paying for content.

"So, we have two sources of income," Sjögren explained, detailing how TV networks made money both from commercials and by charging their distributors. Not a single distributor could avoid paying for content simply because they were able to attract new viewers. Sjögren was trying to imply that the same went for tech companies, regardless of the strength of their platforms. If a company like Spotify was given a discount, he explained, everyone else would start to haggle on the price. TV networks would see their business models upended.

Daniel also took several meetings with the network TV4. He was spotted in their offices in the Stockholm port district of Värtahamnen and received delegations of TV4 executives at Jarla House. His counterparts were both curious and skeptical. Viasat, a major distributor owned by Cristina Stenbeck's investment company Kinnevik, was openly resistant. Any new offering from Spotify would compete directly with their digital service, Viaplay. Skeptics in television circles saw Spotify potentially damaging the relationship between TV companies and their distributors, and worried that their brands would be diluted. If viewers start to consume a mix of content on Spotify, then channels like TV4 and Kanal5 could lose their luster. Outside the Nordic countries, television executives were even harder to persuade.

Even within Spotify, resistance to Daniel's pet project was spreading. As details of the product began to emerge, the flaws in the business model became clear. A thin slice of cable TV content would not match the abundant feeling users got from being served a global catalogue of recorded music. Yet a full-fledged digital TV app—with live sports, drama, and cable news—would require massive investments and require consumers to pay considerably more than the initial estimate of 300 crowns, or around forty-five dollars, per month.

MONEY FOR NOTHING

With time, Daniel Ek began to open up about Spotify TV, bouncing ideas off of his trusted lieutenants. In May 2013, during the company's Strategy Days in Uppsala, a university town north of Stockholm, he spoke about broadening the company's vision. He floated the idea that Spotify might become a hub for creativity in a wider sense, not just music. The idea was debated but never really took hold.

At the next strategy session, held that fall in New York City, Mike Berkley rolled out the vision behind Spotify TV. His team aimed to reinvent the TV industry, a vision that resonated with many of the attendees. Yet others had questions. The issue split Spotify's top employees into two camps. On Daniel's side were those who saw a fragmented TV market devoid of hard-hitting digital products. Neither Netflix nor HBO—which had recently acquired the local streaming offshoot HBO Nordic after a successful test run—had nailed their digital offering, they thought.

Others saw Daniel heading in the wrong direction. They believed that Spotify ought to focus on scaling up its music offering, and not risk diluting its brand by venturing into TV. Moreover, changing user behavior—from listening to viewing—was notoriously difficult. Why would a person who listens to music on Spotify be prepared to abandon their cable TV, HBO Nordic, Viaplay, or Netflix?

Some within Spotify's executive ranks had a crass view of the project. To them, Daniel's high-flying video ambitions showed that he was either growing tired of dealing with the record labels, or simply looking for a shiny new toy to show the company's investors.

The Spotify TV team had been isolated, partly to shield it from internal criticism. But by early 2014, as the service began to take on its final form, doubts had spread among some of the CEO's closest allies. By then, the team had grown to at least seventy-five full-time employees, working on anything from market research to partnership bundles with telcos. In salaries alone, the project had cost around $15 million.

A launch would require much more money than that. Three people would later recall how even a limited content package for the Nordic markets would have cost nearly $300 million to license. Payments for marketing and the hardware itself, which was to be free for the consumer, would then be added on. With live sports, the costs immediately soared beyond that figure.

"The sports totally killed the equation," as one source would recall.

In the end, even Daniel began to waver. The margins in Spotify's loss-making music business were troublesome enough. Either he could offer a TV product for around forty-five dollars per month, letting his investors foot much of the bill, or raise the fee substantially and risk losing potential viewers. He wasn't especially keen on either option.

But in August 2014—three years after he had set out to disrupt the on-line video market—the CEO gave the project one final push. Turning once again to a Google veteran, Daniel headhunted Shiva Rajaraman, who had spent several years on the product side at YouTube. Spotify's new Head of TV brought a handful of his former colleagues with him to Stockholm. His predecessor, Mike Berkley, left Spotify at the end of the month.

Soon, Shiva and his team had scrapped the hardware part of the project. The prototypes that had come back from China did not live up to expectations, especially the encryption standards. Tracking down a new supplier would be costly and time consuming—and time was no longer on Spotify TV's side. Apple TV had continued to grow, and Netflix was bigger than ever. Not to mention mid-size players such as Hulu and Roku, which were coming up in the US.

But perhaps, the re-assembled team thought, there was room in the market for an app that was compatible with third-party hardware, such as Amazon's dongle, Fire TV. Shiva got in touch with the network he had built while working for YouTube. He sought to construct an offering that could be launched in Scandinavia and the US simultaneously. But it quickly proved difficult. The costs shot up as soon as the US market came into question. During the fall of 2014, staff were gradually siphoned off the Magento team and relocated to other parts of Spotify. By the end of the year, one key member would recall, there was hardly anyone left.

HEARTBREAKER

The fateful message was delivered to Konrad Bergström during a lunch meeting with one of Daniel Ek's top lieutenants. The Zound co-founder stormed out of Farang, a swanky restaurant across the street from Spotify headquarters. The secret project he had spent months working on for little money suddenly looked like a fiasco. There would be no video-streaming hardware. And when it came to the multiroom speakers, Spotify would instead choose to deepen its partnership with the hardware firm Sonos, one of Zound's main competitors.

In early 2015, a cargo pallet arrived at Jarla House. A thousand leftover receivers and remotes had been shipped from China by boat. There was no longer any room for them at the factory in Shenzhen.

APPLE BUYS BEATS

T O FULFILL HIS PROMISE TO investors of large-scale success in the United States, Daniel Ek needed to offer more than a searchable music database. The blueprint he had inherited from Napster held a natural appeal to anyone who had sat by a desktop computer in the 1990s and browsed millions of music collections via online chat rooms. But Spotify's user base skewed young, and by the early 2010s, most teens had found alternate ways to discover tracks online.

A powerful player in the United States was Pandora, a steaming service that would switch on like car radio and play songs with similar musical traits. It would become clear that Spotify needed to expand its repertoire and offer more of a lean-back experience, as product designers in Silicon Valley would describe it. This was a clear departure from Daniel's original vision in which users were assumed to be actively searching for music, building playlists, and sharing them with others. At times, he seemed surprisingly reluctant to let that version go.

"We should never tell anyone what to listen to," Daniel told one of his colleagues as late as 2010.

Soon he would be singing a different tune. Spotify would revamp its radio feature and draw users toward activity-based playlists such as "Italian dinner" and "Dubstep workout." Slowly, it would build out an à la carte menu of playlists designed for specific moments in the lives of its users. Competitors—such as Jimmy Iovine's Beats Music—would push them further in that direction.

F M

In September 2011, while on vacation in Tennessee, the young programmer Erik Bernhardsson received a call from Spotify's CPO, Gustav Söderström. "We need a really strong radio function. And you know how that stuff works," Gustav told the twenty-seven-year-old over the phone from Stockholm.

The bespectacled coder had recently finished a brief stint at a hedge fund in New York City. There, he had used advanced math to help optimize the fund's high-frequency trading instruments, with the purpose of shaving milliseconds off of each trade in order to beat the market. Since leaving the hedge fund he had accepted a position at Spotify's North American headquarters in New York. While waiting for his new US work permit, he'd decided to travel south and, like Paul Simon in the famous song, stop in Memphis and spend a few hours at Graceland, the palatial home that Elvis once purchased in the late 1950s.

Just a few days in, Erik Bernhardsson's vacation was cut short. Gustav wanted him to head back to New York as soon as possible, promising to compensate him fairly once he had a work permit and could start receiving payouts. Spotify's head of product had just experienced a moment of clarity and was in a hurry to build a new genre-based radio feature. The idea was to start siphoning users from Pandora, whose listeners could simply pick a song they liked and lean back while being served similar music on an infinite loop.

Erik hopped in a cab and took the next flight from Memphis to New York. The next morning, he stood outside 111 Eighth Avenue, admiring Spotify's US offices in Chelsea. The massive brick building took up an entire city block and had, for decades, belonged to the city's Port Authority. Its new owner was Google, whose New York headquarters claimed several floors of the building.

Erik took the elevator to the eleventh floor and was greeted by a handful of colleagues in the otherwise empty office. Furniture and boxes lay in piles on the floor. Large windows ran along one side of the space, with the view stretching northeast over the landmarks of Midtown: the Empire State Building; the MetLife building, which appeared to shoot directly out of Grand Central Station; the piercing, metal spire of the Chrysler Building; and Rockefeller Center on 50th Street.

At this time, Pandora had thirty six million users who listened every month. That made their service three to four times bigger than their Swedish foe. On the New York Stock Exchange, the digital radio company was valued at over $2 billion, around twice as much as Spotify.

Erik found an available desk and got to work. The millions of user-created playlists, he figured, were a treasure trove in Spotify's growing data set. The title of each list might say something about the type of music it contained. A playlist called "Chillwave" would be likely to feature contemporary, electronic dream-pop while "Uptempo House" probably contained fast-paced dance music. Within a few hours, Erik had written code that analyzed playlist titles and the songs chosen to fit together in each list. He deployed the code and, as a first test, found eighty four songs that seemed to belong together. That morning, he laid the groundwork for what would become Spotify's new radio feature, which the company would eventually patent in the United States.

Three months later, at the Le Web conference in Paris, Daniel Ek walked on stage in a black polo shirt, carrying a water bottle. He launched the re-vamped Spotify Radio, explaining how users could now choose a song and ask the player to queue a selection of similar music. He made sure to point out that unlike Pandora, his new radio feature allowed for "unlimited skips and unlimited stations."

"It was a big use case that a lot of people were asking us for. Today, we've covered that use case," said the Spotify founder.

A few hours later, when the New York Stock Exchange opened, Pandora suffered a five percent drop in its stock price, wiping out around $70 million from its market cap.

Spotify Radio was not perfect. Over the coming years, picky listeners would mock the song selections, calling them predictable and simplistic. But the new feature did mark the beginning of the end of Pandora's dominance within digital radio in the US.

VIVA LAS VEGAS

While Spotify was testing the waters in the US, Jimmy Iovine was hard at work building a new type of streaming company, with its roots in the music business.

In January 2012, a few weeks after Spotify Radio launched, the Brooklyn-born record executive found himself in Las Vegas. The sun was shining on the City of Second Chances, and it was time for the annual Consumer Electronics Show, CES.

The board of Beats Electronics had convened in a conference room at The Wynn, a five-star hotel on the northern end of The Strip. One item on the agenda was "Daisy," the streaming project that was still under wraps and, for now, shared its name with Beats president Luke Wood's dog. Trent Reznor, frontman of the alternative rock band Nine Inch Nails, was seated at the table. He had been tapped as chief creative officer of the project and had worked on a conceptual pitch with the Swede Ola Sars, who was the chief operating officer of "Daisy."

The duo's presentation expanded on the concept of "human curation," with playlists by Beats-affiliated stars such as Dr. Dre, Will.i.am, and Gwen Stefani. One aspect that really piqued the board's interest was a feature called "the sentence," which Sars and his team had cooked up in Stockholm. The idea was that the listener would describe their setting and mood, and let the streaming client set the soundtrack. A listener who was "in a house," "with their friends," and felt like "starting a riot" might be served a rowdy song by The Beastie Boys or DMX.

The executives in the conference room were impressed. At this time, Spotify's partnership with Facebook was still fresh. The Beats concept felt like a natural next step. The room was in agreement: their blueprint was already better than anything those "robots in Sweden" had cooked up. The presentation ended in cheers, with Dr. Dre clapping loudly.

RUNNIN' DOWN A DREAM

In a matter of days, the elated mood in Las Vegas had dissipated. Jimmy Iovine seemed impatient and displeased since he, much like Daniel Ek, was only really at ease when things moved fast. The energetic music executive had thought that a Beats streaming service could be ready to go within a few months. That might be possible, Ola Sars would tell him, but only with non-interactive licenses. That would make Beats' new product a radio service in the style of Pandora, not an on-demand player that would compete squarely with Spotify.

Sars had, by this time, recruited his former colleague, the previously skeptical Fredric Vinnå, as the project's Chief Technical Officer. Vinnå moved to Los Angeles and quickly became close friends with Trent Reznor. The two had a lot in common—the long-haired Swede also liked to dress in all black and talk about product design. They would hang out in Reznor's modernist home in Beverly Hills and frequently return to the idea of a streaming service with a heart and soul. The duo convinced Iovine to take the time to build a fully functioning streaming service. They wanted to challenge Spotify, which the Beats team thought resembled a glorified FTP server: a modest improvement on file-sharing software like Napster, but too technical, and hardly culturally relevant.

Time was of the essence for the Beats team. To buy some, they figured they needed to acquire an existing streaming company. One option was Rdio, which had its head offices in San Francisco. Jimmy Iovine met with co-founder Niklas Zennström, the Swede who had recently cashed in spectacularly when Skype was sold, for a second time, now to Microsoft. Iovine is said to have left the meeting thinking Zennström wanted too much money for his streaming company. Instead, he and the Beats team decided on MOG, another San Francisco-based streaming service with forty employees. The company was founded a year prior to Spotify, yet didn't stand a chance against them. Beats acquired MOG in March of 2012 for around $14 million, which would be pocket change in the ensuing streaming wars. Ola Sars would take credit for landing the deal. But soon, the "Daisy" project would move into a new phase that would result in his departure from the company.

Fredric Vinnå, however, rose through the ranks. He was allotted shares in the company and became Head of Product, filling his team with top talent out of Silicon Valley. It was a perfect setup, but taxing work. In 2013, Vinnå lived in a swank apartment with a view of the San Francisco Bay, but he never had the time to furnish it properly. Most nights he would work until midnight, only to get up early the next morning and do it all over again.

Long before the product was finished, Iovine was in talks to sell his company. He met with Ted Sarandos, the Chief Content Officer at Netflix, who was quickly becoming one of the entertainment industry's top executives. One source would recall how Iovine also courted representatives from Google and the team at Microsoft's Xbox division in Seattle, which had inherited digital music distribution from the discontinued Zune project.

Many big technology companies had contemplated entering the music-streaming market at this point. Iovine's main goal, however, was to sell his company to Apple.

WE'RE NOT LIVING IN AMERICA

Despite its code name, Beats' intention to challenge Spotify was no longer a secret. By 2013, details of the project had begun to leak to the press. Among those who took notice were Spotify's founding duo, and one of them was especially annoyed.

"Trent? Damn him," Martin Lorentzon said during a meeting in Stockholm, having just been told about the rock star's influential role at what would eventually be called Beats Music.

Just a few years prior, the Nine Inch Nails singer was one of many influencers in the music world that helped promote Spotify in the United States. The way Martin saw it, if there was a dark side in the digital music space, Trent Reznor had just enlisted. He now worked for Jimmy Iovine, whose ties to Apple had been clear since he helped Steve Jobs launch the U2 special-edition iPod back in 2004.

The meeting in Stockholm had been requested by Ola Sars, who was about to start a new streaming company with Spotify as a major shareholder. Daniel Ek was also present to discuss the new venture. Soundtrack Your Brand would offer music streaming to shops and restaurants. But the conversation lingered around Sars's turbulent time with Iovine, Vinnå, Reznor, and the others. It had now been a year since he left Beats with just over a million dollars as thanks.

Martin floated the idea of getting Vinnå to come work for Spotify. Daniel seemed especially interested in how Beats Music was meant to work. Sars, bound by a nondisclosure agreement, painted a general picture of how their music curation—with playlists tailored for each user—would work once the service launched.

Spotify was already heading in the same direction. Besides Spotify Radio, they had launched a "Discover" tab with music recommendations served up by algorithms. But Daniel knew that he needed to program much more of the listening on his service if Spotify was to become a true hit in the United States. He had recently seen market research that showed Spotify lacking a unique advantage over their American competitors. Online radio listeners in the US had responded that their instinct was to turn on Pandora. Those looking for a specific song would tend to search for it on YouTube. Spotify was not the leading contender, not even for the lean-forward user case that it had always centered around.

The results fascinated several of Spotify's top executives, who had begun to realize the extent of the problem. They were too far-removed from the average music listener in the US. How might they reach thirteen-year-olds who just wanted to hear the latest cover track aired on *American Idol*? Spotify's new tagline—"Music for every moment"—was a roadmap of sorts. But exactly how they would deliver on it remained unclear.

Daniel had already tried to partner with third-party app developers, once again borrowing a page from Mark Zuckerberg's playbook. For around eighteen months, leading music magazines like *Rolling Stone* and *Pitchfork* had been building apps within Spotify that contained music charts and user reviews of new releases. Def Jam, an influential hip-hop imprint under Universal Music, served Spotify users their music in playlisted form. Other developers offered anything from touring schedules to dating services based on a person's music taste.

But the app that truly caught Daniel's attention was Tunigo. It had been built by a company with offices in a basement on a tucked-away stretch of Kammakargatan, a back street in central Stockholm. In workstations starved of daylight, coders and music editors had built playlists that fit into categories like "romance," "working out," "travel," and "partying." They had been heavily inspired by Songza, a startup based in Queens, New York, that would later be purchased by Google.

In May 2013, Spotify paid more than $6 million for Tunigo, the company's first acquisition since µTorrent in 2006. The new subsidiary was tasked with helping Spotify sift through the roughly twenty million tracks in its catalogue. Several members of the Tunigo team joined Spotify, among them the company's CEO, Nick Holmstén. He would become director of the section within the Spotify player called "Browse," where listeners could find new music.

"Tunigo helps users find great music for every moment," Nick said when the deal was announced.

The concept of "moments" would, over time, become central to Spotify's product strategy. The following year, in an interview with the *New Yorker*, Daniel would sound like he had found his edge.

"We're not in the music space—we're in the moment space," he told the magazine.

THINKIN BOUT YOU

As the battle for streamed music heated up, Jimmy Iovine was not alone in talking to potential buyers.

During 2013, Daniel Ek once again held several meetings with representatives from Google. This time, the stakes were higher—as were the dollar sums.

The Swede had had a complicated relationship with the search giant ever since he, as a teenager, was rejected for a job there. YouTube was now one of Spotify's core competitors. Many Spotify staffers were bothered by the fact that Google's sprawling video platform earned advertising dollars on music videos while paying the music industry considerably less than Spotify did.

Four sources would recall that Daniel spoke to Google about selling his company two years after the US launch. According to one account, Daniel flew to San Francisco to meet Larry Page, the revered co-founder whose crowning achievement—coming up with the "Page Rank" algorithm, the backbone of Google's search infrastructure—had since spawned an internet empire. By many accounts a problem-oriented, introverted person, Page was now serving as Google's chief executive, having taken over from Eric Schmidt two years prior.

Both Daniel Ek and Martin Lorentzon have remained tight-lipped about the discussions. One source, however, would describe how Daniel had seemed interested in a deal only if he could serve as head of both Spotify and YouTube, as a new online media division. A deal with Larry Page would need to include a grander vision about music and video.

"Daniel was interested in the deal," as one source would say, "but he didn't want Spotify to become yet another business unit within Google."

The Swede did not appear interested in cashing in on his company and joining Google only to leave once his entire payment package had matured, the way many acquisitions in the tech space tended to pan out. One forthcoming example was Facebook's $16 billion acquisition of the messaging service WhatsApp.

Daniel and Page didn't click, and Daniel left the encounter feeling slightly rejected. The numbers didn't meet his expectations either, according to two sources.

During the talks, Daniel was said to have asked for $10 billion and then lowered his ask to $8 billion, one source recalled. Google's representatives offered $3 billion, or maybe $4 to $5 billion, depending on the source. Regardless, the parties remained billions of dollars apart. The negotiations never amounted to a formal bid.

"Google knows all about advertising and weren't very impressed with that side of Spotify's business," one source in the record industry would recall.

In a regulatory filing from December 2013, Google wrote that it had "recently pursued but discontinued a potential buyout of a foreign company, with a valuation estimated in the range of $4 to $5 billion."

According to one source, Daniel would have had a hard time pitching Page on the idea that he would also run YouTube.

"That was the part of Google that everyone wanted to work at," the source said.

Daniel Ek once again had walked away from acquisition talks, meaning venture capital was the way forward. His finance team had been drumming up interest for a new round of funding that would bolster Spotify's valuation and allow its CEO to keep investing in growth.

It turned out to be a hard sell. The Spotify team met with a wide range of investors but did not have the metrics to show that their business would eventually yield major profits. To convince the skeptics, the Spotify team started making aggressive projections for its future mobile growth, one person would recall. They wanted to issue new shares amounting to 6 percent of the company in exchange for $250 million. That would indicate a total value of more than $4 billion for the company.

Ordinarily, a deal of that size would mostly be swallowed by one or two lead investors, with smaller shareholders sharing the scraps. But in this case, there was only one interested party: Technology Crossover Ventures, a fund based in Silicon Valley. To ensure its influence over proceedings at Spotify, TCV secured a board seat at the company.

The seat was taken by Barry McCarthy, a seasoned American media executive who, two years prior, had left his position as Chief Financial Officer of Netflix. The outspoken sixty-year-old would come to play an influential role at Spotify over the coming years.

Once again, Spotify had convinced an investor to take a leap of faith. Apart from their Facebook partnership in 2011, Spotify hadn't been able to dazzle venture capitalists with its growth figures. Success always seemed just a few quarters away. Daniel was running out of time to convince the market that Spotify would win the battle over digital music.

CALL ME MAYBE

During 2013, Beats Music's CTO, Fredric Vinnå, found himself in a meeting with Jimmy Iovine and Eddy Cue, who had been one of Steve Jobs's most trusted executives. Among countless other projects, Cue had helped create the iTunes Music Store in 2003 and the App Store in 2008. Given Apple's size, both innovations had helped spawn entirely new sectors in the digital economy.

Fredric Vinnå was still hard at work creating Beats Music with Trent Reznor and their team. But it had become clear to him that Iovine wanted to sell the company as soon as he could. The Swede found the negotiations stressful. His job was to build a strong product, and he still wasn't sure he would succeed. Once ready and launched, the app needed to find traction among digital consumers in the United States, who were spoiled for choice. The launch date, which had been set to January 2014, loomed ever closer.

Daniel Ek kept in touch with Vinnå throughout 2013, hoping to recruit him to a top position in Spotify's product division. Vinnå politely declined, preferring to stay at Beats Music at least until the launch, and braced himself for an intense push to finish the project. The final three months became a whirlwind of meetings, video conferences, and technological meltdowns.

THAT DON'T IMPRESS ME MUCH

On a cloudy Tuesday morning in San Francisco, Fredric Vinnå and Ian Rogers, the CEO of Beats Music, woke up in a conference room. They had been sleeping on the floor of what had served as the company's war room. A couple of hours must have gone by. The pair looked at each other, smiling wearily. It was January 21, 2014. Beats Music was live, but they both knew it wasn't really ready. The thought of how much work remained made Vinnå feel nauseous. An endless series of minor catastrophes had preceded the launch, but Jimmy Iovine had finally gotten what he wanted. Beats Music was out on time, and the app was more or less functioning.

Music journals such as *Rolling Stone* reported that Beats Music had succeeded in differentiating itself from Spotify, Pandora, and YouTube with its playlists by tastemakers and artists. At the core of the product was "the sentence," a feature designed to serve up the right music at the right time.

"I'm in a den and I feel like dancing to pop music," talk show host Ellen DeGeneres said in a commercial that aired during the Super Bowl halftime show.

New users began to trickle in, tempted by the free trial period. After that, the app cost ten dollars a month. Like all other streaming services, Beats Music lacked the unlimited free tier that was the key to Spotify's growth.

"Image is everything: Beats Music bets on style and celebrity to take on iTunes," the headline on the tech site The Verge read after the launch.

The staff at Spotify's offices in New York downloaded the Beats Music app immediately, but few were impressed by its features. The verdict from the engineers—the very technicians Jimmy Iovine had taken aim at—was that Beats Music was a disaster. They couldn't understand why Beats had acquired MOG instead of Rdio, a service they thought had far superior technology. As his colleagues roasted their new competitor, the designer Christian Wilsson was impressed by the Beats playlists. He joked that Dr. Dre's hip-hop picks felt considerably cooler than whatever was coming out of the Tunigo team back home.

A few days later, the Beats Music team celebrated their launch with a star-studded show at the Belasco Theatre, a historic building with a Gothic façade in downtown Los Angeles. On stage, Dr. Dre, Eminem, Diddy, Ma$e, Busta Rhymes, and Nas performed classic hip-hop tunes in a formation that was intended to resemble a human playlist. Drake, Selena Gomez, Macklemore, and Paris Hilton all made cameo appearances.

BEAT IT

A few weeks after the launch of Beats Music, Fredric Vinnå had had enough of the near-constant glitches, the many meetings, his duties as manager, and all the endless hours. His relationship with his girlfriend was in dire straits, one of his two brothers had recently passed away, and all he wanted was to spend time with his family in Sweden. Daniel Ek got in touch again, tempting him with a top job at Spotify, in a professional environment, with reasonable working hours. Martin Lorentzon jumped in to seal the deal.

"Listen, it'll be summer soon. We'll go out in the archipelago, eat pickled herring, and drink shots of schnapps," the Spotify Chairman said.

Something snapped inside of Vinnå. He wrote an email describing how he needed to resign "for personal reasons," and sent it to Jimmy Iovine, Luke Wood, and Trent Reznor. His deal with Spotify wasn't finalized, and he didn't mention his new job in the email. Regardless, his decision rocked the Beats leadership team.

"No one has ever done this to me before," Iovine shouted over the phone.

Vinnå's departure hit Trent Reznor the hardest. He took it as a personal betrayal. Vinnå eased his own guilty conscience by giving up his shares in the company, saying he wanted to move on with a "clean slate." It would become the worst financial decision of his life. But when the airplane rose over San Francisco, he felt relieved. His cell phone was off, his laptop tucked away. All he could hear were the engines roaring. For the first time in over a year, he felt free.

COME AS YOU ARE

As the Beats Music team was busy converting its trial subscribers to paid customers, it was crunch time over at Spotify. In April 2014, the product team presented a comprehensive redesign that had gone by the codename

"Cat," after Catwoman. A uniform, black background served to highlight album covers and song titles, and the overhaul received praise in the tech journals.

"We have this metaphor of stepping into a theatre—when you dim the lights, the content comes forward," Michelle Kadir told *Wired* after the unveiling.

The product developer with the unparalleled sneaker collection conducted a dozen interviews with foreign journalists. She had led the redesign with Rochelle King, who had arrived at Spotify from the product division at Netflix.

Underneath the hood, Spotify had shed additional weight. For several years, the company had spent millions of dollars upgrading the back end infrastructure. Now, Spotify featured nimble, web-based code, an area where its technology had lagged behind European competitors such as WiMP and Deezer. The new back end allowed Spotify's engineers to work in an iterative process of constant updates. The time from idea to deployable code had been shortened from six months to just a few weeks. Finally, Spotify's back end was snappy again.

Fredric Vinnå had joined the company, with an office right next to Daniel Ek's. News of his arrival did not reach the product division until Beats Music's former product head suddenly stood in front of them, ready to start working.

The new recruit, whose title was VP of Product, struck his coworkers as calm and empathetic. But, as two people would recall, his expectations did not sit right with the head of product, Gustav Söderström.

Some tech CEOs are hands on with the product themselves; others allow their deputies a high degree of autonomy. For the most part, Spotify fell into the latter category. Gustav had carved out a powerful position for himself that spanned from strategist to evangelist. His long, prophetic emails about where Spotify was headed could arrive at any time of day. Of the handful of members of Spotify's executive team, he appeared to be closest to Daniel. Spotify was a product-driven company.

On stage, Gustav was a natural communicator, often outshining Daniel with his enthusiastic delivery, articulate storytelling, and a few jokes. At thirty-eight, his once-blond hair had started to gray, but he'd started working out more frequently and his diet was healthier than before. Privately, he'd just moved with his family from central Stockholm to the suburban island of Ekerö. From there, he rode his Ducati motorcycle to work whenever he could. Outside of Spotify, he continued to invest in startup companies. He owned shares in the Swedish e-commerce platform Tictail, a competitor of Etsy, and in the visual technology company 13th Lab, which would soon be bought by the Facebook subsidiary Oculus VR.

At the Spotify head office, Gustav Söderström now began to work closely with Fredric Vinnå, developing new song charts, artist pages, and a new home screen for Spotify's mobile app. The Beats Music veteran had a high degree of respect for his new boss, but the process at Spotify failed to inspire him. He missed hanging out with Trent Reznor and talking about a music service with "heart and soul."

By 2014, Spotify had turned the entire product division into "squads" consisting of up to twelve people. The idea was that every unit would work independently of each other, like a small startup within a big company. Squad members could mix with others to form chapters, tribes, or even guilds, with the latter consisting of individual members from any number of squads. It was a radical reorganization, outlined later in an ambitious white paper that praised the agile method of software development. The document would quickly spread among management professionals online.

Yet in practice, Spotify was not the agile utopia it wanted to be. Many employees found the model chaotic, hard to follow, and overly focused on team autonomy. Cross-team collaboration may have been the intention, but it rarely succeeded. Some felt that the blog posts and white papers explaining the "Spotify model" of management were misleading.

"Ironically, the posts were thought to be great for recruiting," one employee who joined Spotify in 2017 would recall after leaving the company. With time, the former employee noted, the Spotify leadership began to revert to more traditional and hierarchical modes of decision making.

Fredric may have been a casualty of this management experiment. He struggled to form a team that was loyal to him and his ideas. Some departed Spotify staffers would claim that Gustav could have done more to empower his second-in-command. A few months after joining Spotify, Fredric Vinnå felt like he needed a longer break from work. He had, after all, only taken a few weeks off after abruptly quitting his job at Beats in California.

THE MASTERPLAN

Beats Music was now gaining considerable traction among influencers and tastemakers in the music business. Spotify's playlists did not have the same air of exclusivity, except for Sean Parker's popular list, Hipster International.

The contrast between Beats' celebrity-laden approach and Spotify's curation style was partly by design. Daniel Ek believed he could find a more scalable way, centered around technology, to bring users the right songs at the right time. The Swede wanted to use machine learning to automate music recommendation at scale, and he had his eyes on a small company outside of Boston that was on the same quest.

Starting in 2005, engineers at Echo Nest had analyzed several decades of recorded music and sorted it into microgenres such as "Basque rock" and "more contemporary country." The company, which had its roots at the Massachusetts Institute of Technology (MIT), had also developed a tool that would come to be known as "Truffle Pig" for its ability to sniff out gems in a vast music catalogue. Users looking for "angry" music from the 1980s with a low level of "acousticness" might be served a selection of aggressive synth tracks.

In March 2014, Spotify made its largest acquisition to date, buying Echo Nest for around $70 million in cash and stock options in Spotify. As part of the deal, the roughly sixty Echo Nest employees, including the three founders, would now start working for Spotify.

"You'll start noticing improvements pretty much instantly," Daniel told a reporter after the deal was announced.

But the integration would turn out to be challenging. Echo Nest's technology relied on comprehensive data scrapes of blogs, song charts, and a wide range of other online sources. Spotify's recommendations team, meanwhile, had built their work largely on data from actual listeners: whether they skipped songs, saved them to a playlist, or started perusing releases from similar artists. The methodologies clashed, and it took a year or two for the recommendations teams to get up to full speed again.

A few years after the acquisition, most of Echo Nest's sixty-odd staff had stopped working at Spotify. Daniel's biggest acquisition to date appeared to have been his worst.

TEARS DRY ON THEIR OWN

A few weeks after the Echo Nest acquisition, Tim Cook looked poised to steal the limelight with a music deal of his own. In early May, the *Financial Times* reported that Apple was in talks to buy Beats for $3.2 billion. The news—and the price tag—sent ripples through the music world.

As soon as he saw the headline, Fredric Vinnå sent a text to his former Beats partner, Ola Sars. Three months had passed since Vinnå had given up his shares in the company. He couldn't bear to calculate the millions he might have earned on Jimmy Iovine's dream deal. At one point, Vinnå had owned 0.5 percent of the company.

The former Beats product developer started to think about Trent Reznor, who wasn't returning his calls, and had unfriended him on Facebook.

Two days after the *Financial Times* broke the still unconfirmed news, Nine Inch Nails held a concert at Hovet, an arena just south of central Stockholm. Vinnå stood alone, in a sea of fans watching his friend perform. During the last song—the ballad "Hurt"—tears rolled down his cheeks.

BIG EGO'S

Around the time of Trent Reznor's performance in Stockholm, explosive details surrounding the Beats deal appeared online.

One evening in May, with the *Financial Times* story still unconfirmed, actor and R&B star Tyrese Gibson began filming himself while hanging out at a music studio in Los Angeles. Sporting a large pair of Beats headphones, he spoke directly into the camera.

"Oh shit, that mix is crazy!" he yelled into it, shaking the phone to simulate a heavy bassline.

By his side was Dr. Dre in a long-sleeved black t-shirt, laughing along. It could have been yet another product placement for the Beats by Dre headphones. But about a minute into the video, Gibson blurted out a few words that would make Jimmy Iovine very nervous.

"Billionaire boys club for real, homie. Fix your face, fix your face. The Forbes list just changed," Gibson hollered into the camera.

"You know that, you know that," Dr. Dre filled in.

Then he said it himself.

"The first billionaire in hip-hop, right here from the motherfuckin' West Coast."

After a few celebratory dance steps, Gibson shut the camera off. Neither he nor Dr. Dre had mentioned Apple. But once the video appeared on Gibson's Facebook page, the rest of the world began to see it as confirmation that the deal was done.

Later, Iovine would reveal how the short clip could have ended the whole arrangement. A landmark acquisition was something that neither Tim Cook nor Eddy Cue wanted to—or *could*—announce in an impromptu online video.

Three weeks later, Apple finally confirmed that they had purchased Beats for $3 billion. Iovine and Dr. Dre would now join Apple to work on their music offering. They posed for the cameras alongside Cook and Cue.

Jimmy Iovine would rake in around $800 million on the deal, according to Bloomberg's initial calculations. That figure would push him narrowly past the billion-dollar mark, in terms of personal wealth.

Dr. Dre didn't quite make it. The following year, Forbes estimated his net worth to be around $700 million. Trent Reznor and Luke Wood also cashed in. A few months later, Luke would buy the most expensive home in the Los Angeles neighborhood of Silver Lake.

Back in Stockholm, Fredric Vinnå continued to text his former colleagues, congratulating them on their achievement. But most of them didn't bother replying.

For a time, Apple's foray into streaming felt like the only conversation topic at Spotify headquarters. According to the trade journals, Beats Music had only acquired just over one hundred thousand users. Yet the price tag had made the company Apple's largest acquisition ever. The question was: had they paid for the headphones or the streaming service?

Ola Sars developed his own theory. He believed Apple had primarily bought Beats because of Iovine's unique position in the music industry.

Tim Cook appeared to offer a similar explanation, stressing that the company now had several new recruits with a deep understanding of music. He also said that Beats Music was the first subscription service that had really gotten it right.

"They had the insight early on to know how important human curation is," Apple's CEO said, having just raised the stakes in the war over digital music.

DEATH VALLEY

URING THE TWO YEARS LEADING up to the launch of Beats Music, Daniel Ek and his team had endured a prolonged existential crisis. Throughout the negotiations with Google, and the attempts to build Spotify TV, his startup had been scrambling to future-proof its business. It was urgent. The "mobile revolution" was already underway, and Spotify appeared to be on the wrong side of history.

The most promising technology company in the music space had entered the app era with what was essentially a desktop product. Spotify's mobile apps had launched as early as 2009, but mobile access was a perk reserved for paying customers. That meant that on the smartphone, Spotify could not deploy its most effective growth engine: recruiting young listeners through its endlessly free tier.

For the second time in Spotify's brief history, the service stopped growing. Daniel would describe this period as a near-death experience for his company.

The crisis originated in 2012, five years after Steve Jobs introduced the iPhone. Young people started viewing smartphones as a full-fledged alternative to the desktop computer. Mobile data was cheaper than ever, the phones had become faster, the screens bigger, and companies like Uber were able to build groundbreaking services that worked exclusively as apps. The "mobile first" era had begun, and investors were throwing themselves at yet another area of explosive growth.

Tech companies that lacked a clear mobile strategy began to be punished by the market. During the summer and fall of 2012, Facebook spent its first six months on the stock exchange. The share price was on a downward trajectory, largely because Mark Zuckerberg had not convinced investors that he could make money off of mobile advertising. Facebook's rocky IPO was a clear warning sign for Spotify. Its board members followed the stock price closely, worried about the implications for their own company. Their medium-term aim was, after all, to float Spotify on the stock exchange and sell their shares.

SINCE U BEEN GONE

On the front line of Spotify's mobile crisis was Henrik Landgren, a former McKinsey consultant who started learning computer programming at the age of six. The tall, handsome thirty-one-year-old, admired among coworkers for his dogged and selfless approach to problem solving, had joined Spotify in 2010 as one of Daniel Ek's assistants. Henrik had insisted that Spotify needed an analytics division, so Daniel had him create one and lead it.

At Jarla House in Stockholm, the analytics team had set up a wide range of dashboards visualizing the music service's performance in real time. Starting in early 2012, Henrik and his team watched as the inflow of new users switched from desktop—where they could listen for free—to mobile, where Spotify only offered a free trial for forty-eight hours. That clearly wasn't enough time to convert them into subscribers. Of the new users who tried Spotify on a smartphone, only a small percent would stay on and pay for the service. The conversion rate on desktop—the backbone of Spotify's business—was much higher. But that was of little comfort if desktop use would keep dropping dramatically.

Spotify executives would often describe the conversion process as a funnel where new users flowed in at the top, and a stream of paying subscribers eventually trickled out at the bottom. But if new users only stayed for forty-eight hours, there was no time for them to build playlists, discover new music, and become habitual users. In addition, the declining intake of free users on desktop meant that the top end of the funnel was growing more narrow. Henrik grew more worried. It was clear that Spotify needed to take a plunge into the mobile era. At the very least, the mobile app needed to have its trial period extended.

During the summer of 2012, music listening on Spotify plateaued as it usually did during the season. But when fall began, a growing number of users did not return. The analytics team suspected that a large number of them were now using their computers less often, opting for their phones instead. It was an early indication that the massive shift to mobile computing was beginning to pick up speed.

"The edge of the cliff was getting closer," Henrik would recall. "We didn't know when it would happen, but we knew it was coming soon."

BRIDGE OVER TROUBLED WATER

In May 2013, influential investor Mary Meeker published her insights on the smartphone revolution. Her annual *Internet Trends Report* had served as the tech sector's favorite slide deck since the early days of the dotcom era. In this edition, Meeker noted how the mobile trend had shifted from "rapid" to "aggressive." Young consumers appeared to abandon desktop computers and laptops faster than expected. Gustav Söderström flicked through Meeker's slides and drew the obvious conclusion: without a free version of their mobile app, Spotify's growth would stop, investors would flee, and the company would die.

At this point, Spotify's licensing team had spent more than six months negotiating deals for what they called a "mobile free tier." It was not an easy task. While the record labels were making hundreds of millions of dollars every year in payouts from Spotify, they still disliked the idea of millions of people listening to music without ever being forced to pay. Now, Spotify wanted to expand their free service to include all smartphones, not just the ones belonging to paying subscribers.

"We had to go back to the music industry and say, you know what, the thing we used to charge money for, *you* now need to give it to us for free," Daniel Ek would recall years later, on stage in Helsinki. "That wasn't an easy sell."

Spotify's talks were being led by its head of content, Ken Parks, now considered a master negotiator by his team. Among his aides was Petra Hansson, who had stepped down as general counsel but still served as the lawyer overseeing Spotify's licensing talks. They knew the labels wouldn't grant them a free tier without restrictions, but they also entered the negotiations with an informational edge.

From extensive internal testing, they knew precisely which limitations would serve Spotify best. What remained was a game of poker that they knew would span months, perhaps even years. Their strategy was to act like their preferred set of restrictions was a concession to the record labels, when in fact it was precisely what Spotify's product division wanted.

For months, the product and analytics teams had experimented with various trial versions of their mobile app on thousands of users at a time. One version offered unlimited access to the catalogue, but only for a few hours per month. Another version worked on Wi-Fi, but not with mobile data. The best results came when users could listen without a time limit, but only access a subset of the catalogue which would only play on a shuffle mode. The data showed that this offering would be strong enough to attract new users, yet weak enough that existing paying customers wouldn't downgrade.

While the Spotify delegation knew what they wanted, the record labels knew that stalled negotiations would weaken their opponent. Perhaps they could sense that Daniel Ek needed the free tier extended to mobile devices for his company to survive.

The data became more and more distressing for Spotify. In the late summer of 2013, more listeners went "mobile only," by now a common term. Smartphones now appeared to have become a real alternative to computers. Gustav Söderström would later describe this period as "the summer when Europe went mobile."

Spotify's number of active users—the lifeline that kept investors funding the company—was now shrinking. Internal estimates showed that Spotify's user growth nearly halted between the second and third quarters of 2013.

Daniel Ek felt like his company might be headed for a crash landing. He would describe the task of pivoting toward mobile phones as "switching out the engines mid-flight."

I WANT TO BREAK FREE

To get the record labels on board, Daniel Ek and Martin Lorentzon had to make concessions. In the fall of 2013, as the license talks continued, they extended the "schmuck insurance" agreement they had reached with Universal Music before launching in the United States. The founders and a select group of early investors in Spotify would have to shell out at least two percent of the purchase price in the case of an acquisition.

By this time, that would have amounted to at least $80 million. According to company filings in Cyprus, the deal was renewed in October 2013, around the time that Daniel Ek was talking to Google about selling his company.

The second-largest label, Sony Music, also gave their go-ahead for the mobile app, while Warner Music, as usual, were late to agree. The smallest label of the three majors had by now been taken over by Access Industries, a conglomerate led by the billionaire Len Blavatnik.

Blavatnik, who would later invest in the French streaming service Deezer, seemed eager to make digital strides with Warner Music. Spotify's negotiators hoped that Warner Music's new CEO, Stephen Cooper, would be more accepting of their business model than his predecessor, Edgar Bronfman, Jr. They were soon disappointed. Warner had not changed its hard-line stance on Spotify's free service.

During November, the Spotify team sat in seemingly endless meetings at Warner's offices in the upscale London neighborhood of Kensington. There, in the same white stone building that had housed EMI before the label was carved up and sold off, a small delegation of lawyers and product staff went over the terms line by line. The talks were progressing slowly. Spotify had a deadline by which they needed to launch the free tier, and it looked like they weren't going to meet it.

On December 10, the day before Spotify's free tier was due to launch, Stephen Cooper finally agreed to the terms at a meeting in New York. The Spotify free tier lived another day. A wave of relief spread through the upper echelons of the company.

The next day, Daniel Ek announced the news to a group of journalists in New York. The free app could only play music in shuffle mode with regular ad breaks. Unlike paid listeners, free users would not be able to listen offline. Daniel also revealed that Spotify would soon launch in six new European markets and fourteen countries in Latin America. Spotify would take the lion's share of the digital music market in Mexico, ahead of competitors such as Google and Deezer.

In an interview with CNN after the presentation, Daniel explained what he and his team had been trying to tell the record labels for years: the more music people listened to on Spotify, the more likely it was that they would start to pay.

"That is, ultimately, our business model," he said.

He also touched on the concept of ubiquity, one of Spotify's core strategies. The idea was to introduce the service on as many operating systems and hardware units as possible.

"We want to be everywhere music is. So we're building Spotify into more things, whether it's home stereos or potentially even wearable jackets. Who knows?" Daniel said.

IT'S THE MOST WONDERFUL TIME OF THE YEAR

A few days after Warner signed, Spotify threw a Christmas party in the Chelsea Terminal Warehouse, a building that once housed the legendary nightclub The Tunnel, where rap stars like Jay-Z would perform. The warehouse was a relic from an era in which goods traveled by rail through Manhattan and were transferred to freight cars that were floated across the Hudson River on barges into New Jersey. Now, it was where Spotify's staff celebrated a free mobile app that would catapult them back into their natural state of rapid growth.

It was enough to make the Spotify executives feel giddy. Gustav Söderström, who had built Spotify's first mobile app four years prior, was in a celebratory mood, thanking the colleagues who had sealed the deal. Ken Parks, not usually one to get emotional, gave one of his colleagues a big bear hug. Martin Lorentzon and Daniel Ek held court at opposite ends of the warehouse. Everyone was dressed up and elated that the mobile crisis had finally ended.

A few years later, Daniel would admit that Spotify would have gone bust within six months if things hadn't changed. To him, this was one of Spotify's crowning achievements. Originally conceived as a desktop product, the company managed to adapt to the mobile era—and they did it "mid-flight," under constant pressure from competitors and from the music industry, which at this time still swallowed around 80 percent of all of Spotify's revenues.

"This was our Netflix moment," one source would recall, referring to the company's pivot from DVD rental to online streaming.

FROM NASHVILLE
TO BROOKLYN

T HE NEW MOBILE APP BECAME an instant hit, with
Spotify growing like never before in 2014. With the success came a
number of high-profile detractors, including world-famous artists
such as Taylor Swift. As they turned against the Spotify model, Daniel Ek
also had to face an ever-growing array of competing streaming services.

The Spotify CEO was also entering a new phase in his personal life. His
daughter Elissa was rapidly approaching her first birthday. Daniel frequently traveled to New York, but spent most of his time in the family's
grand, 3,200-square-foot apartment on Birger Jarlsgatan near the Spotify
headquarters.

He rarely stayed late at the office playing games of FIFA or table tennis.
His colleagues noticed how he tended to head home daily around five p.m.
to have dinner with his family. Several former employees would recall how
life with Sofia seemed to gradually pull Daniel apart from the small group
of Spotify coworkers he had previously held close, and his drifting slightly
from co-founder Martin Lorentzon.

Spotify was going from strength to strength. During the first half of the
year, the service added around seventy thousand new users every day. This
was a turning point for the company. The growth curve had finally shot up

significantly, allowing Daniel to showcase the kind of hockey-stick graphs that had been fetishized for decades among tech investors as a sign of great things to come.

Spotify no longer had to raise money based on belief in the idea and future projections. There was now a track record that Daniel and his team could show off to investors. Moreover, Spotify's negotiators could point to hundreds of millions of dollars in yearly payouts to the record labels. Gone were the days when doubts lingered over the fundamentals of Spotify's business, when even Daniel had a hard time explaining the inner workings of the freemium model to his skeptics. There were now signs that his company might eventually turn a profit, and not just in Sweden. With time, Daniel would deepen his understanding of Spotify's business case, and how to apply it in countries with varying income levels and demographics. He would also begin to communicate the Spotify play more clearly to investors.

"Early on, neither Daniel nor Martin had a firm grasp of the business model and how we could make it work," one source would recall. That now began to change.

The growth team, headed by Alex Norström, was constantly deploying new tricks to engage new listeners. At their disposal was an increased budget for online ads. During 2014, Spotify spent more than $200 million on sales and marketing efforts to supercharge their newfound growth. But Daniel was impatient.

"Why aren't we investing more?" he asked one of his coworkers during a coffee break at the start of the year.

Daniel was after only the strongest developers, competing for talent with the Silicon Valley giants. Spotify's stature was growing, but many in the music business wanted to limit the extent of Spotify's power.

PASS THE MIC

In January 2014, Per Sundin, Universal Music's general manager for the Nordic countries, traveled to Los Angeles for the group's yearly leadership conference. Here, a hundred of the most powerful people within Universal would soon gather to discuss where their industry was headed.

After an early, jet-lagged rise, the fifty-one-year-old Swede headed out for a run along the beach, past the Santa Monica pier, down to Venice Beach and back. Sundin was staying right near the water, at the Fairmont Miramar Hotel and Bungalows, which also served as the venue of the conference.

At breakfast, he spotted several industry legends. The singer Neil Diamond was there, as was the now eighty-year-old Quincy Jones, who produced Michael Jackson's early albums. The fifty-six-year-old founder of Def Jam, Russell Simmons, walked around in a baseball cap, gray hoodie, and a necklace of wooden soul beads. His Def Jam co-founder, Rick Rubin, looked part Malibu beach bum, part legendary music producer. Rubin often remembered for his cameo in Jay-Z's video for "99 Problems," a song he had produced—sported a blue hoodie, shorts, and slippers. Later, during a panel discussion on stage, he would kick off his slippers, revealing his bare feet.

Universal's fifty-three-year-old CEO, Lucian Grainge, turned up in a collared shirt and slacks. Billboard had recently named him the music industry's second most powerful person, after the power couple Jay-Z and Beyoncé. The British label head had garnered support within Universal after successfully acquiring parts of EMI two years prior for nearly $2 billion. The group now owned music by The Beatles, The Beach Boys, and Frank Sinatra.

Another entrant on Billboard's power list was Jimmy Iovine, whose constant business moves had secured him tenth place. The short, charismatic New Yorker had shown up to the conference in worn blue jeans, with his cap turned backwards. Many in the industry saw the sixty-year-old mogul as a brilliant creator who was constantly reinventing himself. Others would mutter that he was using Universal artists as mannequins for his Beats headphones and the recently launched Beats Music streaming service—all on the company's dime. The talk among some of the label's bigwigs was that Iovine had made himself untouchable, as one conference attendee would recall.

Universal's power brokers gathered in a large lounge with patterned wall-to-wall carpeting and crystal chandeliers hanging from the ceiling. Seated around a few dozen oval tables with name plates and microphones, the label heads followed panel discussions on the stage. The room was a kind of miniature United Nations, with delegates from record labels and local regions within the group.

In Sweden, Per Sundin was an influential music executive, but at the summit in Santa Monica, he was a Chihuahua in a room full of Great Danes. His American colleagues knew him primarily as the man who had signed the Swedish EDM star Avicii, and as an early supporter of Spotify. He found himself seated at one of the tables farthest from the stage.

As the day progressed, Sundin would recall, criticism of Spotify mounted. Many thought the service's new, free mobile app risked putting a dent in Universal's digital sales via iTunes. CD sales were still falling, and the industry was headed toward yet another year of declining revenues.

As the Spotify skeptics took over the discussion, Sundin could not hold his tongue any longer. He pressed the button on his microphone and started to voice his support for Spotify in a thick Swedish accent.

"It's me again," he said from his invisible seat at the back of the room, going on to explain how Spotify was turning free users into paid users in Sweden, and in large parts of Europe.

"Look at the data! We're converting from free to premium. We've killed off piracy. This is the future, and you can't stop it," Sundin said, growing ever more agitated.

Many of the other participants started looking down and shaking their heads. They saw his intervention as a head-on attack on Apple, which remained the industry's most important digital distributor. During the break, Sundin was unsure his tirade had been of any use. But then his Universal colleague Rob Wells, who had now been living in Los Angeles for three years, came over to encourage him.

"That was amazing! Well done, Per," Wells said in his thick South London accent, putting his arm around the Swede.

"I'm gonna get fired," Sundin said.

The Brit laughed and promised that his friend would keep his job, as Wells would recall.

"This is a discussion we need to have," Wells said.

The next day, Wells made sure that the event staff seated Sundin closer to the stage. The Swede felt relieved when he noticed the upgrade. Wells took the stage for a presentation about the state and future of the industry. One of his slides showed how sales via iTunes had plateaued, while streaming services from the likes of Spotify, Pandora, and Google had a revenue growth of around 80 percent annually. Streaming had succeeded in Europe, he said, arguing that it would soon pick up speed in the US.

The European duo at Universal would be proven right. The following year, services such as Spotify would help the industry break its downward trend and return to growth, albeit in modest terms.

Jimmy Iovine was another beneficiary of the trend. The following year, after the Apple acquisition of Beats, he had climbed to fifth place on the Billboard music-industry power rankings. In the 2016 edition of the list, Iovine shared third place with his Beats partner Trent Reznor, as well as Apple's Eddy Cue and Robert Kondrk.

With time, Spotify's CEO began to make a mark on the Billboard rankings. At the time of Universal's conference in Santa Monica, Daniel Ek held the number twenty-five slot. Over the following two years, he would climb into twentieth place, and then tenth. Then, in early 2017, Billboard crowned him king.

OUT OF CONTROL

During the first six months of 2014, Spotify gained eleven million new free users, an increase of nearly 50 percent. Such strong growth would soon become a problem. As the proportion of non-paying listeners increased, so did Spotify's payouts to the record industry, dealing a new financial blow to the still-unprofitable company.

Daniel Ek, who had always been aggressively focused on user growth, had to act against his own instincts. In June of that year, he decided to hit the brakes. The CEO asked his Chief Revenue Officer, Jeff Levick, to send word through the Spotify ranks.

"All market launches are off," Jeff said over the phone to Axel Bard Bringéus, whose team had taken Spotify to nearly fifty countries over the previous two years. The team in charge of new markets was at an offsite conference on the island of Grinda in the Stockholm archipelago, plotting Spotify's expansion across the globe.

For about a year, they had been preparing to bring Spotify to Russia, and even hired a general manager based in Moscow. But several new laws in the country—including one that required internet service providers to store their data on Russian servers—had given the Spotify team pause. Then, in February of 2014, Russian troops invaded the Ukrainian peninsula of Crimea. Axel's team dropped their plans to enter Russia, much to Martin

Lorentzon's relief. Spotify's politically engaged co-founder still harbored a deep contempt for the Russian regime.

However, that had not ruled out launches in other countries. When Jeff called the new-market team, its members had been debating where to go next. Their short list included Japan, South Korea, several countries in the Middle East, and a few additional European countries. But now all of their plans were put on ice.

"We're taking a break," Jeff told Axel over the phone.

Spotify's free tier had become something of a liability. Every free user cost Spotify around one dollar per month in payouts to the record labels and publishing societies. That cost could be offset by advertising revenue. But, fresh from the extended battle to secure new mobile licenses, Spotify did not yet have a mobile advertising platform. That meant that the millions of new users discovering the music service also cost the company millions of dollars every month. This was the music industry's way of ensuring that even if Spotify's number of free users ballooned, they would keep getting paid.

The growth was straining Spotify's finances and its investors were asking a series of tough questions. In Daniel's quarterly calls with shareholders, he was frequently pressed on when their growth in paying subscribers would begin to catch up with the surge in free users, a participant would recall.

One especially critical investor was Barry McCarthy, who had recently joined the company's board. Only a few months had passed since his company, Technology Crossover Ventures, invested in Spotify. Now, Daniel was failing to meet his own forecasts. From his base in California, the Netflix veteran made his dissatisfaction clear, two sources recalled.

Daniel had no choice but to act resolutely. He pulled the plug on Spotify's imminent launch in South Africa, where they already had a bundle deal in place with the local operator Vodaphone. His concern was that the mix of Spotify listeners in South Africa would skew heavily toward free users, putting even more pressure on the company's finances. Daniel also instructed Gustav Söderström and his product team to build a mobile advertising platform so that Spotify could offset the costs of onboarding free users.

For the first time, Daniel had to reconstruct how he thought of Spotify's business. Since its commercial launch, he had conceived of Spotify as a fast-growing startup with a number of metrics signaling its strength—such as an increasing number of monthly active users, impressive user retention, and an ever-growing valuation. Now, the idea of Spotify as a paid subscription business using its free tier to convert new users into paying customers gained more prominence.

Daniel began to concede that Spotify's paid tier was the key not only to its longevity, but to its very survival. Growing the number of total users—Daniel's primary focus since the beginning—was important, but it wasn't enough to impress Wall Street. Daniel was becoming more pragmatic, mindful that a successful stock market float was the only way to fully satisfy his early investors.

To make an impression on Wall Street, the paid side of Spotify's business not only needed to grow, it needed to become a larger portion of Spotify's overall user base. Paid subscribers accounted for around 90 percent of Spotify's revenues and were the key to its future profitability. In addition, record labels, artists, and songwriters might start viewing Spotify not as a service giving away music for free, but as a tool to get more people to start paying for music.

To attract more paying subscribers, Daniel had to make concessions. For instance, he ended Spotify's three-year boycott of Apple's in-app payments system. Listeners would now be able to upgrade to Spotify Premium directly through the App Store. They were, however, forced to pay a 30 percent higher subscription price, to compensate for Apple's surcharge.

In the spring of 2014, Spotify's communications staff sent out a press release stating that the company had reached ten million paying subscribers. This was the first in a series of press releases that would signal subscription growth in the run-up to Spotify's stock market listing.

The record labels monitored the dispatches closely. They wanted to make sure the proportion of free tier users did not become too high. At times, Spotify would cook the numbers by downplaying the total number of users by around ten percent, several people would recall. That way, the paying subscribers appeared to make up a larger share of the total, keeping both investors and record labels happy.

By September 2014, Gustav Söderström's product team introduced video ads on Spotify's mobile app. Within a few months, advertising revenues had begun to pick up, which partly offset the costs of Spotify's free users.

But, just as the clouds were beginning to dissipate, Daniel Ek was thrown into his company's next crisis.

SHAKE IT OFF

In November 2014, Taylor Swift released her album *1989*, with the Swedish hitmaker Max Martin as executive producer. The album sold 1.2 million copies in its first week, more than any other since *The Eminem Show* in 2002. The success had come without the help of Spotify, where listeners could see only a list of blacked-out tracks that were still unavailable for streaming.

"We are working on it and hope they will change their mind soon," read a message from Spotify to users longing to hear Taylor Swift's hit record.

The Spotify content team had been in talks with Swift's label, Big Machine Records, and her distributor, Universal, for months. Initially, her team had asked to make the album available only for Spotify's paid listeners. As always, Spotify declined, refusing to differentiate the catalogue available on their free and paid services. That still seemed like a slippery slope that would lead to a much-weakened free service.

As the album release neared, Big Machine Records—whose CEO, Scott Borchetta, was rumored to be selling the company—threatened to pull all of Taylor Swift's music from Spotify. A week after the release of *1989*, the label made good on their threat.

The pop star, who had previously likened Spotify's free tier to piracy, withdrew all her tracks. She opened up about her decision in interviews.

"I think there should be an inherent value placed on art," she would tell *Time* magazine.

Daniel Ek had been dealing with recurring artist boycotts since Bob Dylan left Spotify in 2009. In 2013, Radiohead's frontman, Thom Yorke, removed some of his music from the service. He later fanned the flames of the conflict by calling Spotify "the last desperate fart from a dying corpse," in one of the most unflattering descriptions of the mainstream music industry to date. The British pop-rock band Coldplay and the DJ Deadmau5 had also temporarily boycotted of Spotify, but Taylor Swift's sudden departure was more impactful and more public than any previous conflict.

Swift's label, Big Machine Records, had a distribution deal with Universal Music. She proceeded to ask her fans to find her music through iTunes or two of Spotify's competitors in the streaming space: Rhapsody or Jimmy Iovine's Beats Music, which by this time was owned by Apple.

"With Beats Music and Rhapsody you have to pay for a premium package in order to access my albums. And that places a perception of value on what I've created," she said, echoing the feelings of many record-label executives in the US.

Spotify's deepest, and most memorable, public-relations crisis had arrived. About a week after Taylor Swift's defection, Daniel responded with an impassioned entry on the company's blog. He explained that unlike other free services—"from piracy to YouTube to Soundcloud"—Spotify paid artists and other rightsholders every time someone listened to a song. The Swede proceeded to offer a crash course in the business model of streaming. He emphasized that streaming paid artists over a long period of time, as opposed to an upfront fee when someone bought a CD or downloaded a song through iTunes. The Swede promised that his payouts to the industry would grow in tandem with his company.

"Here's the thing I really want artists to understand: Our interests are totally aligned with yours. Even if you don't believe that's our goal, look at our business," he wrote, before taking a swipe at both Apple and Google with, "We don't use music to drive sales of hardware or software."

The debate over Spotify's royalty payments deeply frustrated Daniel. He was running a loss-making company that was bound to return the music industry to growth. More than 80 percent of every penny Spotify made was still going to record labels and music publishers. Yet he and Spotify were consistently being portrayed as a thoughtless tech company that did not have the best interests of artists and musicians at heart.

Part of the problem, the Spotify top brass felt, was that it wasn't up to them how record labels and publishing societies handled their payouts. Spotify had little to do with that part of the equation. It was up to each artist and songwriter to broker a deal they thought would be fair.

"$2 billion and counting," read the headline to Daniel's blog post, a reference to the amount of royalties Spotify had paid out since it was founded.

Soon, that figure had become central to Spotify's messaging around this sensitive topic. In February 2015, one of us visited Jarla House to interview Jonathan Forster.

The charismatic Brit, who was now serving as head of the Nordic markets, turned sour as soon as Taylor Swift came up during the interview.

Pressed on the matter, Jonathan Forster repeated the same three words, over and over: "Two billion dollars."

A BILLI

Taylor Swift was not the only artist trying to renegotiate their position in the music-streaming landscape. One of many proposals landed in Ken Parks's inbox toward the end of 2014.

"Look at this shit," Spotify's content chief said as he showed a colleague the email.

One of Jay-Z's representatives had gotten in touch. In the email, the rapper offered to license his catalogue exclusively to Spotify for one billion dollars, the source would recall.

There was no doubt that the streaming market had heated up. First Apple had acquired Beats, nearly making Dr. Dre a billionaire. And now everyone from Neil Young to Brooklyn's most famous rapper was trying to find ways to capitalize on the new technology.

Spotify's leadership team was unfazed at the prospect of losing the rights to stream Jay-Z's music. The analytics team had looked closely at the effects of Taylor Swift's boycott. As far as they could tell, the pop star appeared to have caused a few hundred subscribers to leave—if that. It amounted to a round-off error, since Spotify now had around fifteen million paying users.

Ken politely passed on the offer from Jay-Z's people, but the rap star would soon make an even bolder move.

HOLY GRAIL

In January 2015, the share price of a Swedish-Norwegian tech company rocketed upward. That Friday morning, an acquisition bid had been made public. The presumptive buyer was Jay-Z, real name Shawn Carter, who had changed his strategy. Instead of licensing his catalogue exclusively to someone else, he wanted to buy his own streaming service. The rapper-turned-mogul had fixated on Aspiro, the company behind the Swedish streaming provider WiMP. Its premium product was called Tidal.

The forty-five-year-old had come a long way since he founded Roc-A-Fella Records in the mid-1990s and released his acclaimed debut album, *Reasonable Doubt*. By early 2015, his business interests ranged from French champagne to the basketball franchise the Brooklyn Nets, which had recently relocated to the Barclays Arena between Prospect Park and the Manhattan Bridge. Among rap stars, Jay-Z currently ranked as the world's third richest.

His company, Panther Bidco, had just offered $56 million for Aspiro. whose time as a credible challenger to Spotify was all but forgotten. The bid had already been accepted by the Norwegian media group Schibsted, which controlled a majority of Aspiro's shares. But a few smaller owners would soon begin to resist.

"We will recommend that our members turn down the bid," said Sune Karlsson, whose shareholder association Aspiro Aktiekraft represented just over ten percent of the company.

A group of elderly Swedish stock-market enthusiasts was suddenly in an unlikely staring contest with Jay-Z. But Project Panther Bidco, which was ultimately controlled by S. Carter Enterprises, did not blink. A week later, the acquisition was finalized. Aspiro would soon be known as Tidal.

FAMILY BUSINESS

A couple of months later, Jay-Z and Beyoncé made their way to a glass-covered industrial building in Midtown Manhattan. Tidal was hosting a press conference where it would explain how it planned to change the music industry.

"We are here to launch a platform which is owned by the artists," Vania Schlogel, Chief Investment Officer at Jay-Z's company Roc Nation, told the gathered journalists.

She announced that Tidal would cost ten dollars per month, or double for those who wanted a type of high-fidelity sound that wasn't offered by other streaming services. The service would contain video, exclusive content, and the ability to listen to music offline.

"We will reinstate the value of the music. And what's even more important: we will create a space that brings together artists and fans," she said.

Then, she introduced Tidal's owners, who got up on stage one by one. "Alicia Keys," she said, as cheers began to spread through the audience. "Win Butler and Regine Chassagne from Arcade Fire."

"Beyoncé!"

By now, the crowd was clapping wildly. Soon, sixteen shareholders stood side by side on stage. It was an A-list bunch: Usher, Rihanna, Nicki Minaj, Madonna, Jay-Z, Kanye West, J. Cole, Jack White, Daft Punk in their trademark robot helmets, Deadmau5, and the country singer Jason Aldean, another artist who had previously boycotted Spotify. Calvin Harris and Coldplay frontman Chris Martin had dialed in through video chat.

Taylor Swift was not present for the event, but she had granted Tidal the right to stream her entire catalogue except for her new album, *1989*.

On stage, Jay-Z pointed out that the artists behind Tidal were icons who had succeeded because of their love for the music.

"I believe this is one of the things which distinguishes us from a tech company that sells advertising or hardware," he said.

The launch drew massive media coverage and became a hot topic on both sides of the Atlantic. In the lead-up to the event, the musical heavyweights backing the company had draped their Twitter profiles in Tidal's aqua color, tweeting about a turning point for the industry using the hashtag #TIDAL-forALL. In their world, success in the music business still hinged on close relations with influential artists. And in that department, they believed they could beat Spotify.

Once again, forces within the industry had transformed a small streaming service into a contender. At Spotify's offices in Stockholm and New York, staff nervously followed Tidal's launch. As always, they felt confident in their own product. From their own testing, they knew that offering higher-quality audio did not impact listener behavior in a meaningful way. What worried them was that Spotify was going up against some of the most powerful names in the music industry.

Martin Lorentzon was fired up about the launch, one person would recall. The co-founder realized that Tidal's business model might become an existential threat to Spotify. If artists suddenly started demanding a stake in their distributors, and started releasing music exclusively, the market would change. Perhaps music catalogues would scatter across various streaming alliances, like the fragmented world of online video.

Things began to look even more contentious when—later the same year—the rock legend Neil Young, a friend of Daniel Ek's, pulled his music from Spotify but kept it available on Tidal, citing the inferior sound quality. Skeptics, however, figured Neil Young was only out to market his own service, PonoPlayer, which offered high-fidelity audio and music files for download.

Daniel also worried about the state of the rapidly changing market. He had always resisted a strategy based on artist relations and exclusive releases, yet that was precisely where both Apple and Tidal were now headed. The Swede thought that such a model would never scale. But he needed to find a way to distinguish Spotify from its growing number of US competitors.

BIG DATA

THE "WINTER" THAT SPOTIFY HAD long been anticipating arrived in the spring of 2015. Competition was now coming at them from all angles. Amazon and Google had expanded their streaming services, and while Tidal's subscriber base was well below the one million mark, its strong ties to genre-defining artists rendered it a constant threat.

In addition, a forthcoming launch from Apple—some sort of revamp of Beats Music—loomed on the horizon. The iTunes Store already had around eight hundred million customers, most of them with registered credit cards. While Spotify was the market leader in streaming, iTunes dwarfed their roughly twenty million paying subscribers.

Yet with size came scrutiny. Apple's ties to the major labels now faced more criticism than ever before. Four years after Spotify's dramatic entry into the United States, the tech giant was still suspected of counteracting streaming services. During the spring, the European Commission, the US Department of Justice, and the Federal Trade Commission were all reportedly looking into whether Apple had joined forces with the music industry to counteract offerings such as Spotify's free tier.

Meanwhile, Daniel Ek was busy sharpening Spotify's product. His latest pitch to users and investors was not only to serve up "music for every moment," but also for every mood.

"If we notice that you're driving faster than usual to work, we'll adjust the music to that mood," he told a group of investors visiting Jarla House in the spring of 2015, according to one person.

To achieve this, Spotify needed to know where their users were and whether they were standing still, running, or traveling by car. One of the latest catch-phrases in the tech industry was "big data," and Spotify was about to start gathering more information from their users' phones than ever before. Daniel understood the value in knowing more about the listeners. Spotify's extended data collection would form part of a big product launch, scheduled a few weeks before Apple was due to unveil its new streaming service.

While the vision for the revamp belonged to Daniel Ek, the execution largely rested on Gustav Söderström. Fully aware of the high stakes, the duo's aim was to offer their user base an entirely new way of using Spotify.

"This is do or die," Gustav told his team as the launch date approached.

YOU DON'T KNOW ME

The pending transformation of Spotify, where the interface would truly let the user lean back, had the working title "Moments." Whether users were partying, relaxing at home, or hosting a dinner, the new features were designed as a soundtrack to life's every moment. The idea was to cover as much of the listener's day as possible, with playlists like "Deep Sleep" and a brand-new catalogue of podcasts intended to secure user engagement outside of regular music hours.

The product team had strived to target their recommendations using location data. A user who appeared to be on vacation in Los Angeles might want to hear "Going Back to Cali" by Notorious B.I.G. For that to work, Spotify needed to ask users to hand over their GPS coordinates. One especially bold idea was to let Spotify play its recommended track instantly, as soon as the user opened the app. The product team was confident their music recommendations would hit precisely the right note.

The athletic Gustav Söderström was particularly excited about a new feature called Spotify Running. To develop it, his staff had turned a nondescript room in Jarla House into a test lab. A visitor peeking in would recall seeing a Spotify coworker running on a treadmill, wearing headphones, while colleagues studied a computer screen nearby. The employees were testing software that matched the music to the pace of the jog within a few seconds. Spotify Running, which was being developed together with Nike, fed off of sensor data showing how fast the user's smartphone was moving.

The wide-ranging update of the Spotify app, due to be presented at a dimly lit studio in Manhattan, was partly the company's answer to the music curation Beats Music had brought to the forefront. Beyond that, it was a way of thwarting whatever Apple was about to present after their acquisition of Beats one year prior. The final component in the "Moments" revamp was an integration of video into the app. Shiva Rajaraman—who had shuttered the Spotify TV project only a few months earlier—had licensed video content in both Sweden and the US.

While planning its most ambitious product launch to date, Spotify CFO Peter Sterky had been instructed to secure new funding for the company. Spotify was growing at a healthy pace, and Apple's acquisition of Beats had confirmed that streaming was the future of the industry. Investors were easier to come by than during Spotify's early years, but Peter approached them with a big ask: He wanted to double the company's valuation to a whopping $8 billion.

DANCING MACHINE

As Spotify rushed to launch Moments, a few of the company's most gifted coders found themselves without much to do. The tight-knit team, based at the company's West 18th Street offices in New York City, were specialists in machine learning. Some of them had conducted doctoral-level research before joining Spotify to build music-recommendation tools. Their algorithms powered "Discover," the section where listeners could find new songs and releases. But their remit had shrunk during the latter part of 2014. Most of the features they had overseen were now being developed outside of Boston, at the offices of Echo Nest, Daniel Ek's most recent acquisition.

Yet the AI specialists in New York were gifted and ambitious. They began to skunkwork—the tech world's term for engineers experimenting on pet projects without clearance from above. Toward the end of 2014, two likable, low-key team members—Edward Newett and Chris Johnson—began to delve deeper into one of the ideas. They wanted to package their usual music recommendations as a playlist. Now, they challenged themselves to test which of their methods would render the best selection of music, resulting in a playlist tailored to the taste of each user.

At their disposal were a handful of tested ways to recommend music. One way was to pair the user with a listener that shared a similar listening history. Their system, built on massive troves of listening history, in part resembled how Netflix would recommend films and TV shows, or how Amazon would rank all manner of physical goods on its website. Another way to recommend music was to analyze the waveforms of songs to match them with music of a similar tempo, structure, and intensity. But the third way to recommend music yielded superior results.

Just as when the team had constructed Spotify Radio a few years prior, it relied upon the now approximately 1.5 billion playlists created by Spotify listeners themselves. Most were a collection of music that somehow fit together, whether by sound, theme, or mood. When the recommendation team fed the engine with that data, it came up with a machine-powered selection of songs that somehow felt organic.

To confirm their findings, Edward and Chris placed a request to test the playlist in-house, on other employees. Their new boss, Matthew Ogle, moved the new, personalized playlist to the top of the employee-only playlists in the Spotify client. The decision paid off immediately.

"It's as if my secret music twin put it together. Everything in it is good," one of the early testers wrote. The recommendation team and a few product designers decided that the playlist could be released every week, like a personal mixtape. They trimmed it down from about one hundred songs to thirty songs, or around two hours of music, and called it "Discover Weekly."

Before launch, they would have to perform a live test on real Spotify users and study its performance. Just a few hundred thousand users scattered over the world would be enough. But the product pipeline appeared clogged, and the higher-ups seemed preoccupied with Moments. The skunkwork playlist would have to wait.

MOMENT 4 LIFE

Weeks prior to Apple's unveiling, rumors that Tim Cook was about to lower the price of streaming began to emerge. Several outlets reported that Jimmy Iovine and his team were looking at offering their service at five dollars per month.

Slashing the price of a streaming subscription in half would certainly be a hard sell on his compatriots in the music industry, but Iovine, the newly minted billionaire, was now working for Apple. Cutting the cost of streaming could boost their user growth and put the loss-making Spotify under even more financial strain. The pressure was mounting in what the tech world had dubbed the streaming wars.

Meanwhile, Daniel Ek entered a brick building on West 37th Street, a couple of blocks from the Hudson River. The Spotify founder was about to deliver his most important stage performance to date.

The event, held in a former warehouse that now served as a sleek studio space, occurred right between Tidal's launch and the forthcoming rebirth of Beats Music in Cupertino. More than six months had passed since Taylor Swift ditched Spotify, and Daniel's messaging around artist compensation was carefully crafted.

"Spotify is on a mission to bring all the world's music to all the world's music fans, in a way that's great for them and great for all the amazing artists and songwriters who create it," he said, after welcoming the scores of journalists present and hundreds of others watching around the world.

A string of neon lights lined the ceiling and floors of the otherwise dark studio. Daniel Ek, now thirty-two years old, underscored that Spotify was not a gang of hostile technicians from Stockholm, but rather a tech company striving to protect the interests of artists and musicians.

"We're a technology company by design, but we're really a music company at heart," Daniel said, before bringing a few members of his leadership team out on stage.

Yet it was the non-music elements of the presentation that stood out. Spotify users would soon be able to find podcasts and video clips from ESPN, MTV, and the young channel VICE News. Ilana Glazer and Abbi Jacobson—the star duo from Comedy Central's acclaimed TV series *Broad City*—made an on-stage cameo. Several Swedish media companies, among them Kanal5 and the newspaper *Aftonbladet*, were also on board.

The scattered collection of video clips had been costly. Two people familiar with Spotify's financials would recall that Daniel had to clear a licensing cost of around $50 million with the Spotify board. In addition, Daniel had licensed podcasts from the likes of BBC and NPR in order to capture listeners throughout their day.

"We want Spotify to help soundtrack your life," he said on stage.

As far as the music went, Daniel stressed that data was only a complement to what he might have dubbed Spotify's "heart and soul": the company's curators.

"Of course, we look at data to help figure out what our listeners like. But another key reason for our success is really that we have some of the most talented music experts working to curate the playlists that matter most to our users," he said, in what appeared to be a retort at the thinly veiled shots being fired from Jimmy Iovine's camp.

Spotify's curators had assembled playlists such as "Workout," "Party," and "Gaming" in order for the app to stay relevant in every context. After the presentation, Gustav Söderström told *Wired* that his team had targeted every slot in the average user's day.

"I'd like for users to start Spotify in the morning and not really pause it until they go to sleep," he said.

The market leader in streaming was now a music company offering video clips, podcasts, music curation, and a running feature. Afterward, industry journalists surmised that Spotify had tried hard to differentiate itself from Tidal and whatever was coming at Apple.

"Here are all the new features packed inside Spotify," the *Wired* headline read.

To fully launch all the new features, Spotify would soon request access to more user data than ever. Before that happened, Daniel Ek would watch as Apple unveiled its billion-dollar foray into music streaming.

RELEASE ME

Two weeks after Daniel Ek pitched the future of Spotify to journalists and investors worldwide, Tim Cook took to the stage in San Francisco—and he saved his best news for last.

"We do have one more thing," the Apple CEO said, quoting his predecessor's signature line to the audience's cheers.

Cook then cued a lavishly produced video chronicling the history of recorded music, from gramophone recordings to radios, and later to LPs, 8-tracks, cassettes, iPods, and iPhones. The viewer was then transported to the current year, 2015, and the Apple Music logo, prompting Cook to invite another speaker onto the stage.

"He has worked with fantastic artists, from Bruce Springsteen to John Lennon and countless others. We are happy to have him as a part of Apple's team. Please join me in welcoming Jimmy Iovine!"

The sixty-two-year-old Beats founder—sporting his signature blue-tinted glasses, a dark suit jacket, jeans, and dark sneakers—stepped onto the stage to cheers.

"Thanks, Tim," he said.

Iovine pointed out that he was a part of the iTunes Media Store launch in 2003, and that he now hoped to transform the industry one more time. Another artistic film promoting Apple Music, with shots from concerts and young people listening to music on their phones, was beamed from the projectors.

"There is a need for a place where music can be treated, not like digital bits, but more like the art it is," the narrator's voice said. "With feeling and respect and the desire to explore."

The voice belonged to Trent Reznor, who suddenly appeared on screen.

"This is what we will do with Apple Music," he said.

The new streaming service offered a complete catalogue, specially composed playlists and recommendations, and a new radio channel, Beats One. It would broadcast twenty-four hours a day and be hosted by DJs in Los Angeles, New York, and London. The heart of Apple Music was declared to be something called "Connect," where artists would be able to share remixes, photos, song texts, and other content with their fans. Apple's new service appeared to include a social network. The price was ten dollars per month, but there was also a free trial period of three months. Apple had not lowered the price point for streaming.

"At Apple Music we will give you the right tune, on the right playlist, at the right moment," Iovine said, outlining what every streaming service was aiming to do in 2015.

The price of Apple Music was on par with Spotify's paid service, although Spotify users who upgraded through the iPhone's App Store would have to pay three dollars more to make up for Apple's surcharge. A standing joke at the office was that Apple had made more off of Spotify's streaming than the company itself.

At Jarla House, it was long past dinner time on a Monday night. The sun was setting on Stockholm, yet many employees had stayed at work to follow the presentation. This was a moment they had been anticipating for years. Apple Music was only free for trial users, meaning Spotify had maintained its unique advantage of retaining users indefinitely without asking them to pay. During the presentation, Daniel Ek could not help but share how underwhelmed he felt on Twitter.

"Oh ok," he wrote, garnering thousands of retweets before he deleted the swipe at Apple's new service.

One thing that gave the Spotify team confidence was that Apple's software rarely made it big outside of the company's own devices. Spotify, on the other hand, was built to be ubiquitous.

"Still, we were nervous. The US market was important for the IPO," as one source would recall.

The Spotify staffer with the strongest ties to Apple's project, Fredric Vinnå, had recently left the company. A year later, he would be recruited to Apple by his former boss, Jimmy Iovine. That made "the Swede," as Iovine called him, the only person to move from Beats to Spotify and then back to his old gang, now at Spotify's arch rival, Apple.

In Cupertino, Vinnå would become Tim Cook's head of design for music, TV, and podcasts.

LOOK WHAT YOU MADE ME DO

The launch of Apple Music also drew the attention of regulators in Europe and the United States. Apple—which controlled the App Store, the sole distribution platform for apps designed for iPhones and iPads—now offered a competing service in the music space. And the company's ties to the music industry were still under scrutiny.

Soon after the launch event in San Francisco, the *New York Times* reported that the Attorneys General in New York and Connecticut were investigating whether Apple had broken antitrust laws in the US. Some of the investigating legal teams had previously brought the case against Apple that led to fines for colluding with book publishers to drive up the price of e-books, undercutting Amazon.

The suspicion was now that Apple may have put pressure on, or conspired with, the major record companies to counter "freemium" services such as Spotify. The new antitrust investigation bore similarities to those already underway in the EU and with US federal authorities. In a response to the reports, Universal Music's representatives commented that they had no deals in place with Apple, or any other record company, which would limit the availability of ad-funded music services.

Around the same time, Taylor Swift published an open letter with the headline "To Apple, Love Taylor" on her Tumblr page. In it, she explained why she had chosen to withhold her album *1989* from Apple Music, too. She wrote that Apple was set to skip royalty payments during their free trial period of three months. The letter implied that Apple had struck a much more favorable deal with the labels than Spotify, which had to pay every time a free user streamed a song.

"I find it to be shocking, disappointing, and completely unlike this historically progressive and generous company," Taylor Swift wrote.

What followed was an amicable dispute, in full public view, so formulaic in structure and tone that it appeared choreographed. Apple backed down the very same day. A few days later, just as Apple Music was about to go live, the parties had sealed the deal. Artists and songwriters would get paid, and Taylor Swift agreed to license the rights to *1989*, which neither Daniel Ek nor Jay-Z was allowed to stream.

"This is simply the first time it's felt right in my gut to stream my album. Thank you, Apple, for your change of heart," Taylor Swift wrote, this time on Twitter.

Later, Jimmy Iovine would tell the press about his efforts to get Apple executives to side with music creators.

NEW RULES

A couple of days after Jimmy Iovine had presented Apple Music, Daniel Ek took a short morning walk to Stureplan in central Stockholm. It was the beginning of summer and the Spotify founder wore a green polo shirt, jeans, and white Air Force One sneakers.

Earlier that year, on Valentine's Day, Daniel and Sofia had gotten engaged. A few weeks later, their second daughter, Colinne, was born.

As he stepped into the lobby of the Swedish telco Telia, Daniel appeared calm and reflective. He was there to meet three journalists from the Swedish financial newspaper *Dagens industri*. The Spotify CEO seemed happy to chat off the record, but appeared more guarded when the recording began. To one of the journalists present, he seemed to weigh his words carefully, eager to tone down the fact that Apple had just raised the stakes in music streaming.

"I don't think you have to be number one to succeed. For me, it would be enough to be one of the top three," Daniel said, showing a humility that many of his close coworkers and friends would not take at face value.

That morning, the financial press was awash with details of Spotify's latest round of funding. The company had raised more than $500 million. A significant part of the money came from Telia, which led to the interview alongside Telia's CEO. However, Daniel wasn't very interested in talking about the money he had just raised.

"I don't put too much weight on valuations," Daniel said when asked about Spotify's new price tag of $8.5 billion, which would be nearly four times as much as his loss-making company's revenue that year.

The sheer magnitude of Spotify's operation belied its CEO's humble talk during interviews. It was now a darling of the venture capital world, where being on top was the only game in town. Later in the interview, Daniel began to sound a little more confrontational. He expressed surprise at the fact that Apple's shift to streaming had taken so long and stressed that Apple Music was a sign that music streaming had finally become a household phenomenon in the US.

"It is a big validation of what we really have been saying for seven years, that the future is in streaming. Now the biggest company in the world is saying that they agree," Daniel said.

For many, Apple Music would initially prove a disappointment. About a week after the launch, *The Verge* reviewed the app, noting that the interface was messy and the loading times long. Jimmy Iovine would remain dissatisfied with the product for months, one person would recall. He would consider the first six months in the market a waste of precious time.

Meanwhile, Spotify launched two new batches of features over the summer of 2015. One of them—containing the more advanced parts of the Moments update—would turn out to be a flop. The other would become Spotify's most successful product launch to date.

DRESSED FOR SUCCESS

After a few frustrating months, Spotify's recommendations team in New York was finally able to test their AI-powered playlist on a larger group of listeners. In April 2015, they released Discover Weekly to nearly one million listeners around the world, and a few of them tweeted about the accuracy of the curation.

"Best 3 weeks of music I've ever had. Feel free to come back any time," one user tweeted after their three-week test run ended.

Daniel Ek, however, remained skeptical. He initially questioned the format of a curated playlist, and he was reluctant to allot more resources to the project team. But his doubts weren't enough to stop the wider launch. A few weeks into the summer, Spotify presented Discover Weekly to the world. It soon became a user favorite in Sweden and the US.

"It's scary how well Spotify Discover Weekly playlists know me," as one listener wrote on Twitter.

Within ten weeks, the new playlist had generated a billion individual streams. In the fall of 2015, Spotify surpassed Pandora in active users. After several years of experimentation, technology-powered music curation had paved the way for a new era in Spotify's history. Daniel Ek would soon celebrate the playlist on his quarterly call to investors.

Data from playlists created by users had once again proven their worth to Spotify. Discover Weekly ushered in a new era in which Spotify began to program an increasing share of the music listening on the platform. The following year, Spotify unveiled Release Radar, a playlist that sampled new releases tailored to the user's taste every Friday.

Several others would follow. Rap Caviar and Today's Top Hits would soon become Spotify brands in the music world, with the power to breathe new life into the careers of established artists and catapult newcomers to stardom. These were not the themed playlists intended specifically for "the gym" or "dinner parties," for which Spotify had previously been known. They were curated playlists, put together in part by algorithms and in part by Spotify's music editors around the globe. An outside observer would have to credit Beats for inspiring this development but—crucially, and true to Spotify's DNA—much of the work was done through automation.

By 2016, Spotify had become the preeminent tastemaker in digital music. Millions of listeners grew closer to the brand, feeling like Spotify understood their taste. In many cases, they no longer had to scavenge for the best songs. The best songs would now find them.

Spotify's product division drew valuable insights from the data that Discover Weekly generated. The machine-made selections carried a bias: The playlist tended to contain music from independent labels, rendering the major labels underrepresented compared to Spotify's catalogue as a whole. That meant that the product arm of the company had the power to greatly, and over the long term, influence outcomes within the industry. Not least, Discover Weekly could kickstart careers for unproven artists. Spotify could even use this power to replace the talent scouting that had traditionally been done by record labels.

The insights garnered from the new playlist machine would form a central part of Spotify's business strategy. But the coders in New York who had initiated the project in late 2014 felt they never received recognition, as one person would recall.

In the months that followed the launch, neither Daniel Ek nor Gustav Söderström reached out to the coders who had created the playlist. Over the next couple of years, the architects behind Discover Weekly would move on to other companies like Amazon and Google's artificial intelligence unit DeepMind. They left Spotify feeling like they hadn't been given credit for their work.

CREEP

Moments' collection of features was not fully launched until mid-August 2015. Spotify now went public with its new privacy policy, requesting access to photos, GPS coordinates, and contacts on the users' phones. In addition, sensor data would tell Spotify how fast the device was moving, and thus if the user was walking, running, or traveling on the subway.

Spotify's expanded data collection quickly garnered criticism in the media, with many users and experts viewing the new terms as intrusive. It was one thing, they would argue, to share one's location with Google Maps to navigate while driving. The necessity of sharing the same information with a music-streaming app was not nearly as apparent. *Wired* called the new policy "eerie," while *Forbes'* judgement was "real creepy."

The Swedish billionaire Markus "Notch" Persson, creator of the wildly successful Minecraft computer game, addressed his compatriot Daniel Ek directly on Twitter.

"As a consumer, I've always loved your service. You're the reason I stopped pirating music. Please consider not being evil," Notch wrote, referencing the infamous "Don't be evil" phrase found in Google's code of conduct.

Daniel had failed to gauge how sensitive the privacy issue was becoming. Concerns over aggressive data collection would not peak until after the 2016 US presidential election. Even so, the Spotify founder felt compelled to correct the misstep by publishing a post on the company's blog. He emphasized that the online furor over Spotify's new policy largely failed to understand that the company merely was *asking* for access, not demanding it. Spotify would only collect photos, contacts, and location data, he wrote, if the users expressly asked them to. The purpose, Daniel wrote, was for users to be able to customize the cover art for their playlists or find music that people nearby were listening to. The sensor data was intended to power Spotify Running.

During the fall, the product team began to roll out the Moments features that had been lavishly unveiled a few months prior. They started, as usual, by trying them out on about one percent of Spotify's now seventy million users. This test group could now view videos and use the app as their running companion. Members of the product team noticed two alarming signals in the incoming data: the users exposed to Moments were spending less time in the Spotify app, and tended not to return to it to the same extent as ordinary users. According to one person, users appeared to balk at Spotify instantly playing a song as soon as they opened the app.

"It's like the app starts playing something people didn't even want to hear," that person would recall.

In the end, only a small part of the Moments package reached Spotify's entire user base. The features that survived were Spotify Running and the themed playlists. The video clips, a $50 million outlay, appeared briefly for some users but soon disappeared completely. In Sweden, content from the popular TV duo Filip & Fredrik was only streamed a few thousand times, according to a person familiar with the figures. Many years later, the product department would scrap Spotify Running once and for all.

The botched revamp of the app did, however, mark the beginning of a new content strategy. Spotify's content team had, since late 2014, been talking about how to develop original material. Several early productions from Netflix—including *House of Cards* and *Orange is the New Black*—were showing significant promise. Netflix's stock had soared on Wall Street since they first began to air.

The head of Spotify's content team was now Swede Stefan Blom, who had taken over when Ken Parks left the company. Blom's team was mulling what kind of content Spotify might start to develop on their own. Betting big on exclusive music seemed like a dead end, and long-form video had its own limitations, as the failed Spotify TV project had proven. By late 2015, they also noted how the short-form videos included in the Moments update largely failed to gain traction.

There was, however, a growing media space that seemed appealing. Podcasts had been around for over ten years, but the medium had only recently begun to gain mainstream appeal. *Serial*—a pioneering title in the true-crime genre, which launched in 2014 by producers at This American Life—was the prime example. Another producer who had worked for This American Life, Alex Blumberg, was building the Brooklyn-based production company Gimlet Media. Suddenly, startups were popping up in the podcast space.

It would be years before Spotify began to pursue this opportunity with any urgency. Daniel Ek's ambitious but failed bets on video had forced him to focus on getting his core business in shape for the IPO. But once that was out of the way, Spotify would begin to add more podcast titles and start experimenting with exclusive launches. The idea was partly to distinguish the service from competitors, but also to start building a catalogue that could become more lucrative than music licensed from major record labels.

Soon, Daniel would enlist the help of one of the sharpest content strategists around. In the fall of 2016, Ted Sarandos—Netflix's long-serving chief content officer and one of the most powerful people in Hollywood—joined the Spotify board.

17

BRILLIANT SWEDEN

WHEN SPOTIFY CELEBRATED TEN YEARS as a company in April 2016, streaming had just become the largest source of revenue for the American music business. Growth had returned to an industry that had been shrinking nearly every year since 1999. Daniel Ek's promise to the label heads—that he would revive the industry— was now fulfilled. The music service founded in Rågsved in 2006 had thirty million paying customers, nearly three times as many as Apple Music.

Spotify's origin story often revolved around its celebrated founder Daniel Ek and his coming-of-age in Sweden. He would frequently laud his nation's public music education—where he learned to play instruments—and muse on how the means of distribution, which would save the music industry, came from the very nation where piracy had been so rampant.

Yet the Spotify CEO had an ambivalent relationship with his home country. He was operating in a global market and struggling to recruit the talent he needed in a country that didn't always make things easy for him. Stock options, a vital incentive for hirers in the technology industry, were taxed higher in Sweden than in other countries. Stockholm's persistent housing shortage was another constant problem in trying to lure talented programmers to the Spotify head offices.

Change was already underway. During 2016, Spotify's new CFO, Barry McCarthy, began to move the company's finance department to New York—where he planned to execute his still highly secretive plans for a public listing. Representatives for the Stockholm stock exchange, which was owned by Nasdaq, regularly courted Spotify to see if they would be interested in registering there. They even offered a dual listing in Stockholm and New York, but it was clear from the outset that the Spotify leadership had their eyes set elsewhere.

Meanwhile, a tug-of-war was underway inside the company over which cultural norms should be given priority. Two strong advocates for keeping the company's Swedishness were Martin Lorentzon and Katarina Berg, the head of HR. Katarina was not a typically Swedish, consensus-oriented leader—she often let underperforming employees go—but she was eager to preserve the company's Swedish heritage. And then there was Barry McCarthy, who ruled with an iron fist, American-style, and rarely held back in expressing controversial views. Daniel seemed to think Spotify could combine the two sets of values and forge its own style.

CHANGES

In June 2016, staff laid out a black carpet that circled the block of the swanky Grand Hotel on the Blasieholmen peninsula in downtown Stockholm. On it, pictures of a few dozen famous Swedes were imprinted: Greta Garbo, Zlatan Ibrahimović, Max Martin, Alicia Vikander, Hans Rosling, and many others. The carpet ran from the entrance to the hotel, across from the Royal Castle, up to its back entrance, leading into the lush Winter Garden event space, with its glass ceiling and stone pillars.

In a conference room on the first floor, Daniel Ek was about to welcome mostly foreign journalists to a celebration of Sweden's exalted position within popular culture and technology.

"For me, this is about paying it forward," the Spotify founder said, seated at the front of a lounge with powder-pink colored walls.

The thirty-three-year-old, by now an icon of the modern Swedish business world, had begun to understand how he might exert his influence. Over the coming years, Brilliant Minds would be his way of positioning

Spotify in the societal debate, while promoting Sweden as an exciting place to live and work. "Welcome to the creative capital of the world," read the banner behind him during this introductory press conference.

Tickets to Brilliant Minds were not freely available. The price, for those who had their applications accepted, was said to be thousands of dollars. But most participants had been specially invited by Daniel or his co-organizer Ash Pournouri, a music manager who rose to fame with Tim "Avicii" Bergling, another superstar of the contemporary Swedish music world. The guest list was handled by Natalia Brzezinski, the chief executive of Symposium, the annual week of events that culminated with two days of the Brilliant Minds conference. The trio had created a forum that brought together the upper echelons of Swedish corporate and cultural life, old and new. The three of them sat at a long table in front of the gathered journalists.

The room listened intently as Daniel spoke. He recounted how people abroad often would ask him how Sweden had managed to produce not only H&M and IKEA, but also a wave of young tech companies with valuations in the billions. He mentioned the Swedish gaming company DICE, which created Battlefield after being acquired by Electronic Arts, and Minecraft, created by Mojang at their offices in Södermalm. Switching to music, he brought up Spotify, SoundCloud, and Tidal.

"It's something in the culture, more than anything else," he said, pointing to Sweden's heritage within technology, tradition of wealth redistribution in politics, and appreciation for the importance of creative industries.

"The only way to experience it is by getting people to come here."

Attendees at Brilliant Minds 2016 included Google's former CEO Eric Schmidt, the Swedish actress Noomi Rapace, and Marcus Wallenberg, the chairman of the leading Nordic corporate bank SEB. The conference gave Daniel Ek the chance to showcase the business models of the future. Several Swedish startup founders, such as Zound's Konrad Bergström and Niklas Adalberth of the fintech unicorn Klarna, were also present. One constant theme was how Sweden's welfare system worked to encourage risk taking.

"The worst that'll happen is that you will fail, but still be able to live in your apartment and put food on the table. That encourages you to take risks. And some of those risks pay off as world-famous companies," Daniel said.

The CEO of Symposium, Natalia Brzezinski, had spent more than a year consulting in various roles promoting Sweden as a pioneer in her home country, the United States. She did it through interviews and conference appearances, drawing on the network she built while serving as the wife of the former US ambassador to Stockholm, Mark Brzezinski.

"Barack Obama said the world can learn something from the Nordic region. For us that was so powerful, and very much the thesis of what we're trying to do," Brzezinski said. She was well-positioned to carry out cultural diplomacy between the two countries. Her sister-in-law, Mika Brzezinski, was a renowned host of *Morning Joe* on MSNBC, one of the biggest morning shows in the US. Her father-in-law was the esteemed political strategist Zbigniew Brzezinski, who once served as National Security Advisor under President Jimmy Carter.

Sweden's ruling class was clearly present throughout Brilliant Minds '16, during which they mixed with international music stars. At a dinner party in the stately Djurgården home of the Bonnier family, heirs to a publishing dynasty, the former Swedish foreign minister Carl Bildt mingled with Prince Daniel, investors such as Kinnevik's Cristina Stenbeck, and the legendary music composer Quincy Jones. On another evening, Wyclef Jean was seen enjoying a meal alongside Fred Davis, the early Spotify advisor, at a restaurant overlooking the city.

The whole event was lavish but casual. In the Winter Garden at Grand Hotel, where the annual Nobel banquet was once held in the early 20th century, decorative spotlights lit up the symbol of Symposium: a large, human head in white plastic, built layer by layer as if created by a 3D printer.

On stage, Daniel Ek interviewed one of his heroes, pop star and music producer Pharrell Williams. But for the most part, the Spotify CEO stayed in the background, quietly exchanging words with friends and acquaintances. One of us, there to cover the event, watched as Daniel's confidant Shakil Khan moved through the room, offering warm greetings to many familiar faces. One of Soundcloud's founders, Eric Wahlforss, passed by in between panel discussions on leadership, artificial intelligence, and data-driven creativity.

As a young boy, Daniel had dreamt of becoming bigger than Bill Gates. He was now recognized as a pioneering business leader, and the world around him was interested in his thoughts about where society was headed.

How might new technology help prevent the root causes of disease, and not just relieve symptoms? What happens when machines make a hundred million people redundant within the transportation sector? No quandary seemed too far-fetched to consider.

"We're trialing six-hour work days, which I think is related to the future," Daniel said during the introductory press conference.

If more countries followed the example of the Swedish labor market, he added, parental leave would become more commonplace. That would in turn give people more free time to explore their creative interests.

"I think society would greatly benefit," Daniel said.

For several years, Daniel had spoken enthusiastically about innovation within the health-care sector. He would take frequent blood tests and once said that he underwent annual MRIs as a way of keeping tabs on his health. Some people said he had become a "health freak."

In 2016, he would also start frequenting fashionable fitness centers: Equinox in the US and Balance in Stockholm. Balance was founded by entrepreneur Daniel Westling, who would become Prince Daniel when he married the Swedish Crown Princess, Victoria.

Ek would often hit the gym with Moha Bensofia, whom he and his fiancée, Sofia Levander, had helped rush out of Libya a few years prior.

"Personal bests broken daily!" Bensofia declared on Instagram, as Daniel posed for a mid-workout photo, flexing awkwardly into the camera. He was still a little stodgy, but the transformation had begun.

The couple had welcomed Bensofia into their family, and would refer to him as an uncle to their two daughters.

That same year, Sofia Levander invested in the Swedish company Werlabs, whose tests measured anything from blood fats to vitamin levels. The money came from Daniel's new holding company which, like the one before it, was registered in Cyprus. A new parent company had been registered in Malta.

Daniel Ek had begun to free himself of the structures that Martin Lorentzon once helped him to put in place. According to some sources, Daniel no longer wished to be tied to his co-founder, who, according to one source, helped Daniel manage his personal finances in the early days.

Loyal above all to each other, Spotify's founding duo had always kept their disputes from the outside world. Yet Martin, while happy to dedicate himself to company parties, was said to sometimes question Spotify's lavish corporate culture, with teams flying across the world for internal conferences. But free spending had become the norm at companies such as Google and Facebook, and Daniel saw them as Spotify's peers. The CEO was anything but frugal in his approach.

"Perception is reality," as one of Daniel's favorite sayings went, according to one source.

To some, Daniel appeared to be levitating. Many of his old friends and coworkers had begun to wonder who truly remained in his inner circle. Daniel appeared isolated in Sweden outside of his family. On the rare occasion that he showed up when old friends were celebrating their birthdays or weddings, he would seem uneasy. And hardly anyone out of the old group of friends had been invited to his upcoming wedding in Italy.

"He seems to think everything he says will end up being published somewhere," someone who knew Daniel during the early Spotify years would recall.

Daniel Ek had matured in tandem with his wildly successful company, and was looking to broaden his horizons. He appeared to enjoy closed circles, rubbing arms with other business leaders and creators facing similar challenges to his own. The Swede's ambitions still knew no limits. He wanted Spotify to change the world of music and entertainment for generations to come. What mattered was "impacting culture," as he would describe it in interviews.

At the Brilliant Minds press conference, Daniel returned to one of his favored topics: successful Swedish entrepreneurs selling their companies to foreign owners.

"The thing that excites me about Stockholm is that we've had a couple of exits, you know, Minecraft and Skype," he said before offering some advice to Swedish founders.

"The number one advice I tell everyone is 'don't sell.' That's the number one problem we have. All of these things could go gigantic if they keep doing what they're doing."

It was the same argument he had put forth to tech journalist Kara Swisher in London seven years prior. Since then, he had negotiated with several tech giants, but had never been truly close to a sale. With the benefit of hindsight, the Spotify founder said he was tired of seeing US corporations gobble up the hottest startup companies in Europe as soon as they showed enough potential.

He had, however, begun to sell off some of his shares in Spotify. During 2013 and 2014, Daniel had sold shares for nearly $50 million via his holding company in Cyprus. The transactions were hidden from public view until one of this book's authors reported on them for the financial press.

Some of that money may have gone toward his new summer home on the island of Värmdö, southeast of Stockholm. In November 2015, Daniel paid more than $5 million for a waterfront villa that was nearly 4,000-square-feet, on a property spanning more than three acres.

The seller was Kalmar Investments Limited, a corporate entity registered in the British Virgin Islands. According to two people, it belonged to the Skype founder Niklas Zennström.

In the second row of journalists at the press conference, an American reporter with the news agency Reuters raised her hand. She asked Daniel to clarify what he meant.

"So, you're not going to sell?" she asked.

"Not going to sell, no," the Spotify founder said, with a coy smile.

WHATTA MAN

Spotify's tenth anniversary was marked by Celebration X: a week of festivities for the company's employees, in and around the Stockholm area. This was Martin Lorentzon's chance to showcase Swedish summer traditions to all of his staff. The co-founder took on the role of ringleader as over two thousand staffers celebrated Midsummer, a Swedish pagan tradition, with a ring dance at the Tele2 Arena in southern Stockholm.

Martin held court on a small stage in the middle of what usually served as a soccer field, surrounded by a Swedish folk band in traditional garb. As they played the Midsummer classic "Little Frogs," coders and product designers from around the world squatted and hopped along. Lorentzon gave an emotive speech in honor of his home country before everyone took a seat to enjoy pickled herring and aquavit schnapps in the sunshine, surrounded by thirty thousand empty seats in the stadium stands. Celebration X had quickly become a crash course in Sweden's unique and often drunken summer traditions.

Over the course of the week, Spotify's employees visited classic Stockholm establishments such as Operakällaren, an upscale restaurant behind the Opera House. One evening, they took ferries to the fortress of Vaxholm, a piece of early modern Swedish military history located on a strategically placed island in the archipelago. The staffers also sang karaoke, with hundreds joining in on a loud rendition of Queen's "We Are the Champions". Many got the chance to take selfies with Daniel Ek and Martin Lorentzon.

During the closing party, held at a warehouse location in southern Stockholm, loud cheers rang out as Justin Timberlake made a cameo on stage.

"I'm very happy to be here with Daniel and you guys. And as we say in Stockholm: skål, för fan!" he said, raising his glass for a toast in the local language. Backstage, the pop star learned to say "I raise my little hat" in Swedish, a feat that was documented and later uploaded to Instagram.

Closing out the last night of Celebration X were the electronic DJs Axwell & Ingrosso, two members of the Swedish House Mafia. As their hit, "Sun Is Shining," approached its climax, smoke began to pour out of cannons placed at the front of the stage. Laser beams began to flash, a costly array of pyrotechnics was triggered, and Spotify-green confetti rained down from the ceiling.

Martin Lorentzon's role at Spotify had become increasingly ceremonial. A few months prior to Celebration X, he had quietly stepped down as chairman. Daniel was now both chair and chief executive, a rare combination in Swedish corporate life, but common among publicly traded companies in the United States. By the fall, after discovering corporate filings in Luxembourg, the Swedish business weekly *Affärsvärlden* reported that Martin Lorentzon had stepped down to take a regular board seat. The Spotify co-founder had no choice but to address the matter publicly.

"I look forward to another ten years with Spotify as vice chairman, and the daily walks and talks with @eldsjal," he tweeted, in Swedish, tagging Daniel, whose nickname in most social media channels means "passionate enthusiast" or, more literally, "firesoul."

Over the following years, Martin's influence would decrease further. At the end of May 2017, he attended a seminar on politics on the tree-lined street of Strandvägen, which ran along the water and featured the grand apartment buildings that had been the homes of the Swedish business elite for more than a century. After the discussion, the Spotify co-founder was approached by Swedish Radio.

"I believe there is a shortage of two hundred thousand software developers in Sweden," Martin said during the interview.

Asked when Spotify's IPO was due, Martin dismissed the issue outright.

"We have not gotten anywhere at all and there is nothing to comment on about that," he said.

His answer did not add up. Over the past several weeks, newspapers such as the *Financial Times* and the *Wall Street Journal* had revealed details about Spotify's preparations to go public. Asked once again about the listing, Martin said the information had been taken "out of thin air."

"I guess you have to take the press with a pinch of salt. I'm not saying it's fake news, but half of what the media writes is usually correct, while the other half isn't," he said.

The headline—"Spotify Denies Listing Plans"—did not go down well with the company's communications team. Soon, Martin's comments were reprinted elsewhere. Within a few hours, the press department had sent out a retraction, noting that a public listing was, in fact, "a possibility."

"Martin is our co-founder and a board member, but not a spokesperson for the company," the press release read.

Only a few years prior, Martin Lorentzon could speak freely for Spotify, in which he was still the main shareholder. Now he faced the choice of reining himself in or having his impulsive statements corrected when the facts didn't line up.

The chatter among Spotify staff was that Martin's comments had upset and disappointed his co-founder. Both wanted as little public scrutiny of the company's finances as possible. Yet what Martin had claimed was simply too far-fetched.

The truth was that Spotify's finance department was about to finalize its application to be listed on the New York Stock Exchange. That work had been underway since the middle of 2015, when the music-streaming giant welcomed a new and outspoken CFO.

NICE FOR WHAT

"Why is Stockholm so shitty?"

The abrupt question put a stop to the regular small talk that had opened the meeting. Barry McCarthy had only been at his job for a few weeks, yet he already seemed disappointed with his new hometown. The recipient—a high-ranking Spotify staffer—struggled to make sense of the question. What did his new superior really mean?

Sure, Spotify expats would often complain about Stockholm being cold, gray, and full of people who would shove past each other in the subway without saying "excuse me." But this assertion—that Stockholm was simply "shitty"—was harder to make sense of, especially in mid-summer, with the city in full bloom.

The sixty-year-old Barry McCarthy, who had helped list Netflix on the Nasdaq stock exchange in 2002, would soon become well known for his rugged jargon. The American simply found Spotify's headquarters at Jarla House—a concrete slab in the middle of Stockholm—depressing. It was probably rough for Barry, who had left Palo Alto, where his home had a pool and a tennis court. In addition, the mission he had been brought in to carry out now appeared much harder than when he had signed his contract. Barry soon understood that Spotify was not ready to be listed—far from it.

The many problems varied. Spotify had grown quickly, and its organizational structure was, in places, haphazard. Its internal accounting system would have fit a medium-sized business operating in a handful of countries, but not a global market leader with business in nearly sixty countries. If a staffer in the finance department wanted to break down marketing costs for a single country for the year 2014, there would be no way of doing it.

Moreover, it was difficult for Spotify to accurately estimate its own costs. Over the coming years, the company would retroactively write up their royalty payments by more than $60 million due to accounting errors. Spotify had a hard time forecasting how the business would perform. During some quarters, subscriber growth came in well below its own estimates; during others, the number of subscribers surged past the growth team's targets.

Barry McCarthy knew that the stock market hated unpredictability. The new CFO had to get Spotify's reporting in shape quickly. He enjoyed the full confidence of Daniel Ek and showed his chief executive the proper loyalty and respect. Yet several coworkers would recall that Barry did not appear to take Martin Lorentzon seriously. According to one source, the original plan was for both Spotify founders to have adjoining offices in the splashy new headquarters being built on Regeringsgatan in central Stockholm, but once Barry had taken the reins as CFO, the Spotify board shelved the idea. By the time the building was completed in 2017, Martin's office was no longer part of the floor plan.

Barry McCarthy ruled Spotify's finance division with a firm hand. And with the stock market listing looming, a defining event for the young company, his influence extended further. Barry rarely shied away from bragging about his previous career achievements and was unsentimental in reorganizing the finance department, which partly meant letting staffers go.

Barry practiced what he liked to refer to as "radical transparency," a corporate trait he had taken with him from Netflix—essentially, he would freely and frequently speak his mind. Once, at an all-hands meeting, Spotify's employees got to witness it in practice.

"I don't give a shit about diversity," he said during a group discussion about representation at the company, according to one source. The CFO himself would later regret the comment and describe how he delivered it at a meeting with the North American sales team.

"Saying 'I didn't care' about diversity as a whole was sloppy and inaccurate. I realized that it was a very poor choice of words as soon as I got off the stage," Barry McCarthy said in an interview for this book. His point, he added, had been that diversity was subordinate to proficiency when building a team. Barry's comments would later be cited in a lawsuit alleging that Spotify underpaid female employees and allowed a culture of "boys' trips" involving drugs and strip club visits to thrive within the company's North American sales division. As of the completion of this book, the lawsuit was unresolved.

Ahead of the IPO, Barry set three firm priorities for the company. The first was to increase Spotify's margins, primarily through renegotiating better terms from the record labels. Spotify needed a significantly larger piece of the pie to eventually turn a profit. Not only would higher margins satisfy Wall Street, it was also in the major labels' own interest, as it would drive up the value of their own shares in Spotify. Second, he had to get the finance department's accounting on par with that of a publicly listed company.

Finally, Barry wanted the conversion to paying subscribers to become more predictable. The same applied to the company's financial forecasts, a task that he delegated to his predecessor, Peter Sterky.

The finance chief did not mince his words. In a pointed email to Spotify's executive team, Barry wrote that Peter had twelve months to sort out the company's forecasting, or else he would be gone. The email was written as if Peter weren't in the loop, but in fact he remained on the executive team's emailing list. A piece of radical transparency had just been delivered to the top of his inbox.

Another of Barry's email blasts was aimed at Henrik Landgren, the head of Spotify's analytics team. Shortly after he arrived, Barry wrote a company-wide email saying Henrik had done an "okay" job creating and running the analytics team; but it was now time for him to step aside in favor of Adam Bly, the founder of a data-oriented startup in New York that Spotify had just acquired. The announcement seemed to surprise Henrik, who had spent the morning in meetings and talking to colleagues about how to invest the money he was due to make from his stock options. He left the Spotify headquarters upset, to never return, as one person would recall.

Afterward, Daniel Ek followed up with an email praising Henrik for his efforts. Privately, Daniel then helped Henrik find the funds necessary to buy the shares allotted to him through his stock options, as one person would recall. The former analytics chief came away with a multimillion-dollar profit.

The unusual but widely praised corporate culture at Netflix would influence Spotify in several ways. At Netflix, numerous employees had access to its running tally of subscribers, information that was highly coveted by anyone trying to make stock trades. A wide group of employees was entrusted with knowing the subscriber count, and directors would sometimes learn of the company's financial performance before Netflix told the market. They were all entrusted not to leak the information.

Many years after Barry McCarthy's arrival at Spotify, Daniel Ek would claim that his company operated with similar levels of internal transparency, disclosing key financial information to many employees but, according to the Swede, never seeing it leak.

"You have to think hard about when to close the trading window for employees and board members," Barry McCarthy would recall in an interview for this book.

The way he put it, Netflix and Spotify opted to offer employees insight into key metrics, while also shortening the amount of time during which they could trade shares freely in between quarterly reports.

Bosses at Netflix were also known for frequent performance reviews of their employees. Nobody, not even a top executive, was indispensable. Every staff member had to meet exacting internal standards, knowing they could be fired at any time. The only exception, some would claim, was the Netflix CEO, Reed Hastings—though he would retort that he answered to his board.

In the late 2010s, the board members had few reasons to complain. Hastings had presided over a remarkable rally in Netflix's stock price that made the company not just Spotify's blueprint on Wall Street, but one of the giants of Silicon Valley.

As Spotify's new CFO, Barry McCarthy took several pages out of his old company's playbook. He was eager to install loyal lieutenants who would follow his orders, and he rarely backed away from firing people. He was disliked by many, but he was also resolute. And Spotify needed a firm plan if it were to enter the public markets. With time, Daniel Ek would pick up some of his leadership traits.

Early on, Barry drew up a plan to raise a billion dollars in funding, an eye-catching sum that he would frequently brandish in conversations around the office. On the ninth floor at Jarla House, staffers would ask themselves if the company really needed more money. After all, it had only been a few months since the former CFO and his team raised around $500 million.

Years later, Barry would say that he wanted the money to be able to weather some tough label negotiations ahead of Spotify going public. Another source would remark that the billion dollars might have been intended for acquisitions, to fend off Apple's advances within streaming. It also could have served as a safety net in case the economy went sour ahead of the IPO.

NEW KID IN TOWN

Spotify was now transitioning from a startup to a multinational corporation. Many of the early staffers who quickly advanced to senior positions had been forced to change roles. Some, like Jonathan Forster, the company's first head of sales, had stayed with Spotify, taking positions further down in the hierarchy. Others, like the marketing whiz Sophia Bendz, had left in acrimony, but kept her peace with Daniel. Then there was a rare cohort of employees who kept climbing the ranks of the company. Among them was Alex Norström, who would become one of Daniel Ek's most entrusted operatives.

During one of his few stage appearances, at the 2013 edition of the internet conference Slush in Helsinki, Alex explained how he viewed his mission.

"We're trying to build something that will last for more than a century," the head of growth said.

When he joined Spotify in 2011, he was met by a bunch of "long-term thinkers," he said, showing a photo of industrial-era businessmen who founded the Swedish engineering giant Sandvik in the 19th century.

"We want to grow fast, and we would like to be around," Alex said.

Alex valued his close ties to Daniel and was one of a few high-level managers who could make a joke at his CEO's expense. Initially, he was not part of the Spotify executive team, yet he managed to bypass the traditional corporate structure and report directly to Daniel.

"People like Alex Norström and Gustav Söderström know how to navigate Daniel's big picture ideas the best," as one former employee would put it.

Within a year or two, Alex earned his stripes as the head of growth. Daniel felt it was time for a promotion and, in the spring of 2015, he tapped him for a new role as vice president of subscribers. Alex's task was now to convert free users to paid subscribers.

Alex used a number of tricks straight out of the e-commerce playbook. One of his senior team members was Gustav Gyllenhammar, who had previously been head of Tradera, the Swedish subsidiary to eBay. Together, they identified customers who spent a lot of time inside the Spotify app without paying, and then inundated them with promotional offers. First, they would offer three months of premium listening for the price of one. If that didn't work, their follow-up would be a premium account for one dollar per month for three months. Families and students got their own discount plans.

Lowering the price that millions of users were paying caused the number of "subs" to grow even faster. Toward the end of 2015, nearly a third of all Spotify users were subscribers, up from a quarter a year earlier. Lower prices for some meant the average revenue per user would decline, but that did not matter. Once the new subscribers got used to music without ad interruptions, and a fully functional mobile app, chances were they would keep paying the full price. Alex continued to move up the ranks. In September 2016, his title was upgraded to chief premium business officer, and he finally joined the executive team.

To some, it was glaringly obvious that only men with a certain rapport with Daniel Ek were offered the opportunity to advance at Spotify. Of the dozen-plus people who made up Spotify's executive team and board, the HR boss Katarina Berg was the only woman. In conversations with employees, Daniel would acknowledge the problem, but also claim that the lopsided representation had been unintentional.

PIECE OF ME

In the fall of 2015, the Skype co-founder Niklas Zennström made a brief appearance in his old hometown of Stockholm. The Swedish Londoner, who had become a billionaire long ago, gathered a group of influential investors and entrepreneurs for a dinner party. One of its most prominent guests was Martin Lorentzon, who struck up a conversation with the head of a Swedish pension fund with over $30 billion at its disposal.

"I think it would be good for you to have more owners based in Sweden," Mats Andersson, the head of the Fourth General Pension Fund, told Martin.

Typically, Swedish public pension funds would only invest in listed companies. But Mats Andersson seemed prepared to make an exception. He explained that Swedish owners would stand firm in a crisis and prove more reliable than private equity funds elsewhere.

The message struck a chord with Martin. Soon, Spotify had agreed to terms with several institutional investors in Sweden. Even the Wallenberg Foundation—an investment arm of the Wallenberg Swedish industrial family, whose name was synonymous with the corporate elite—began to show their interest. It seemed that Swedish money would make up a large part of Spotify's next round of financing. But in January 2016, the plans they had drawn up leaked in the daily newspaper *Svenska Dagbladet*. The article clearly laid out that Spotify was looking for a convertible loan rather than equity funding, and that the plan was to float the company on the stock exchange.

The article infuriated Barry McCarthy. Rumors swirled that the leak had come from the Swedish bank Nordea, which was involved in brokering the deal. Fuming, the Spotify CFO insisted that he would not "deal with any Swedes ever again," as several people would recall.

The row caused a stir among the reputable Swedish institutions. A representative for the Wallenberg sphere called one of Spotify's Swedish shareholders to vent his frustration.

"You can't treat us like this," the representative said. He made it clear that the two heads of the Wallenberg family empire—the normally understated Marcus and his cousin Jacob—were not happy.

FALLIN' & FLYIN'

In February 2016, stock prices were falling in China, a hugely important source of growth for the global economy. Fear was spreading among investors that the global economy was headed for a contraction, and loss-making companies such as Spotify were especially vulnerable. Barry McCarthy saw Netflix's stock price drop over 20 percent within a few weeks. As a result of the market turbulence, one of Spotify's shareholders, the US mutual fund Fidelity Investments, would soon write down Spotify's valuation by 30 percent.

In a market plagued by uncertainty, the Spotify CFO saw even more reason to raise a large round of capital. The billion dollars he sought could get Spotify through a prolonged downturn. The idea was to borrow the money and let the lenders convert what they were owed into Spotify shares at a later date. The upside with a loan was that it would not let investors put a valuation on Spotify. That way, Barry could avoid raising funds at a lower valuation than before. In the tech world, so-called "down rounds" were to be avoided at all costs; it signaled a downward trajectory and irked earlier investors who would simultaneously see their ownership diluted and their shares drop in value.

Time was not on Barry's side. If he didn't act quickly to close the funding round, things might begin to look even worse. Representatives from TPG, an American fund which had invested in both Airbnb and Uber, had been in touch and proposed conditions. TPG wanted at least a 20 percent discount on Spotify shares when the company was listed, as well as interest on their loan.

"The terms were draconian," as one person would put it.

Barry revised his boycott of Swedish investors. The pension funds AMF, Folksam, and the SEB Foundation all joined in on the transaction. The prospective lenders found that the deal guaranteed them at least a 30 percent return once Spotify was listed. And chances were their profits would rise even more.

"We didn't understand how they could offer those conditions. It was too good to be true," as one source on the lenders' side would put it.

At the end of March 2016, the *Wall Street Journal* reported that Spotify was due to take a massive loan that would finance its path to the public markets. TechCrunch called it a "devilish deal," noting that Spotify needed all the fuel it could get "to win the race against Apple."

The terms of the loan were a major concession for Daniel Ek and Martin Lorentzon. Gone was the secrecy surrounding their intention to list Spotify, a piece of information they had kept under lock and key for years. The terms of the loan stated that a listing had to happen, and preferably within a two-year time span. If it didn't, the lenders would quickly start enjoying larger returns.

To the markets, it looked as if Barry McCarthy had painted himself into a corner, but the CFO appeared to see two primary upsides with the new arrangement. First, it gave Spotify a better negotiating position with the record labels and publishers. Since Spotify was now well-funded, the labels would not be able to put a "gun to [their] head" by stalling the licensing talks, Barry would recall. Second, the loan made it possible for Spotify to acquire companies.

Besides, the "devilish deal" had another, hidden benefactor. One of Spotify's lenders was Barry McCarthy himself, who put up $175,000 with the same favorable conditions attached. Within a few years, the Netflix veteran had made a tidy sum by lending his own company money.

LOSING YOU

Daniel Ek and Martin Lorentzon wanted Sweden to remain the base for Spotify's operations, but they felt that they lacked political support. In April 2016, they decided to voice their concerns.

"We need to act or we'll be left in the dust," they wrote in an open letter to Swedish politicians.

Former Moderate Party strategist Per Schlingmann, now a political consultant and personal friend of Martin's, helped draft the letter.

"It is madness to us that Europe, with a bigger population than the US, does not have a single company on a par with Facebook, Google, Apple, Microsoft, Amazon, or the other major American corporations. We want to show that it is possible!"

The founders wanted computer programming to be made a compulsory subject at school. They also demanded more rental apartments be built in Stockholm and for the tax on employee stock options to be lowered in Sweden. Spotify's personnel department was employing fewer people in Stockholm, preferring instead to create jobs in New York, where it was easy to arrange accommodation and advantageous stock options.

"If no changes are made, we will have to consider focusing our expansion on other countries than Sweden," the founders wrote. A few weeks later, a group of around sixty protesters from Stockholm's tech community gathered outside the Swedish Parliament demanding better conditions for fast-growing companies. "If Spotify leaves, Tidal wins," read one of the signs.

Spotify's founders would make good on their threat a year later, in February 2017, when the company signed an agreement with the City of New York to create one thousand new job opportunities. In return, Spotify would get $11 million in rent reductions.

The new US headquarters occupied floors twenty-seven and twenty-eight in 4 World Trade Center, just across from the Freedom Tower. Eventually, Spotify would extend the lease to occupy nearly six hundred thousand square feet of office space, becoming the building's second-largest tenant.

Through the panoramic windows in Daniel Ek's corner office, the Brooklyn Bridge looked like a miniature toy. It was a major outlay. Even before the extensions, rent for the new space totaled more than half a billion dollars over seventeen years.

The Spotify headquarters, however, remained in Stockholm. The new building on Regeringsgatan initially covered 215,000 square feet. Daniel Ek would have a corner office there, too.

PUT A RING ON IT

At the end of August 2016, Daniel and Sofia celebrated their wedding at Lake Como in northern Italy. It was an exclusive affair. Photographs of the many celebrity guests would soon make their way onto social media, and to news outlets across the world.

The ceremony took place outside, overlooking the lake. Daniel—dressed in a light beige linen suit, with a blue shirt and a little flower on his jacket lapel—stood at the head of the aisle next to the officiant, comedian Chris Rock.

Sofia, wearing a strapless wedding dress, walked down an aisle of pink rose petals to a piano version of "November Rain" by Guns N' Roses. One of the first guests she passed was Mark Zuckerberg, the Facebook multibillionaire, sporting a dark suit jacket, a white shirt, and a baby-blue tie.

Friends and family filmed the ceremony on their mobile phones. Shakil Khan, in a white Panama hat tilted to the side, looked on from his place close to the aisle.

The couple's two daughters—the three-year-old Elissa and one-and-a-half-year-old Colinne—had traveled with them from Sweden. Daniel's stepdad, Hasse, and his younger brother, Felix, both posed for photographs that were later posted online.

Martin Lorentzon was one of the few guests from Daniel's old group of friends in Stockholm, and only a handful of Sofia's old crew were there to celebrate.

When the ceremony ended, the couple walked back over the rose petals hand in hand to applause from the guests. Daniel was now married, and Sofia Levander was Sofia Ek.

"Drinks with Chris Rock in Como," Moha Bensofia, Sofia's old friend, wrote on Instagram beneath a photo of himself and the world-famous comedian. "Just your average Saturday with the Eks."

The joke rang true. Daniel Ek now belonged to a world of vaunted tech founders, famous musicians, and Hollywood stars.

"I don't know how many other Swedish CEOs have managed to penetrate that bubble," as one former colleague would put it.

Later that night, the pop star Bruno Mars performed for the scores of international wedding guests. Photographs from the event would soon end up in news outlets across the world. *Hello* magazine reported the news and posted pictures, as did *Vanity Fair*, trade journals such as *Billboard*, and business magazines like *Forbes*.

Mark Zuckerberg uploaded a photo that showed him and Daniel in conversation with Mark's wife Priscilla in the early afternoon sun, with Lake Como in the background. Priscilla wore a red dress with a beige scarf that matched Daniel's suit jacket.

"Many people know Daniel as one of the great European entrepreneurs—the founder of Spotify. I know him as a great friend and dedicated father," Zuckerberg wrote in the photo caption on Facebook.

Daniel Ek was now an international star. And, within a few years, he would become a Wall Street CEO.

THE
STREAMING WARS

S POTIFY'S TENTH YEAR AS A company was a phenomenal year for pop music. During 2016, artists like Beyoncé,
Drake, and Rihanna put out memorable albums—and they all did it
exclusively on either Tidal or Apple Music. Hit songs had now become a
weapon in the escalating war between competing streaming services. Daniel
Ek had returned the music industry to growth, but he did not appear to
have the artists on his side. He and Spotify now needed to forge closer ties
with the creators in the music industry. Luckily, they had a billion dollars
at their disposal.

In 2016, Spotify nearly acquired the Swedish-German outfit Sound-
Cloud, which was now becoming synonymous with emo-tinged independent hip-hop music, or SoundCloud Rap. Spotify also considered buying
Tidal from Jay-Z. Details of that deal would not emerge until the publication of this book. Together, the acquisition targets formed two sides of the
same coin. Tidal was close to many of the world's biggest music stars, while
SoundCloud was a platform where millions of musicians, big and small,
could upload music directly and challenge the major labels.

Meanwhile, Spotify would begin to wage a more public lobbying campaign against Apple's dual role as both competitor—through Apple Music—and distributor—through the App Store. American senator Elizabeth Warren would side with Spotify and publicly criticize Tim Cook.

EIGHT DAYS A WEEK

During the summer months, Daniel Ek spent much of his free time with his family. He and his children played in the family's new summer house in the Stockholm archipelago. Aside from that, he spent most of his time at work.

"I don't have a lot of free time," the Spotify CEO said in a live interview on TV4 in 2016.

The host, Casten Almqvist, lingered on Daniel's stint as a newly rich party animal in the early aughts. Journalists had frequently revisited this period of Daniel's life ever since he first described it on national television and radio four years prior.

"I had a really good time for about a year," Daniel now recalled. "But that wasn't at all something I was passionate about. It all comes back to the company and the music," he said, repeating the same story.

Several of Daniel's old friends and colleagues struggled to make the timeline of his origin story fit. Few remembered any stint of intense partying followed by a depression. The sports car he sometimes mentioned also seemed mysterious. It seems that Daniel first became rich in March 2006, when he sold Advertigo to Tradedoubler. Yet at that point, he and Martin Lorentzon had already begun recruiting employees for Spotify. Was that when he bought the red Ferrari? A few weeks after the Advertigo deal, Daniel and Martin founded the company that, according to Daniel's oft-repeated story, would become his purpose in life. It wasn't until that summer that he left his mother's old apartment in Rågsved for a new place in central Stockholm.

Where was he able to squeeze in "about a year" of partying and a bout of mild depression, followed by the insight that music and technology combined would be his calling? Like quite a few stories told by Daniel over the years, it did not seem to add up.

Now, live on TV, the tale was being revisited. Daniel stopped short of confirming any details or adding any new ones. Regardless, the larger point of the story rang true. The Spotify founder grew up in modest surroundings with a single mother, and probably spent some of his early money frivolously. The upshot of his "party boy" episode was that, at twenty-three years of age, he quickly matured and wedded his existence to Spotify.

Daniel Ek's appearance on TV4 was one of the few interviews he conducted during 2016. He had created his own playlist for the occasion, featuring new artists such as Tove Lo, Francis and the Lights, and Anderson.Paak. Spotify had just launched its new algorithmic playlist, Release Radar. The next ten years, Daniel said, would be all about bringing his company closer to artists.

"The barriers to creation have gotten much, much lower. You can use your cell phone to record an entire song," he said.

His new vision, based on a decade of studying the music industry closely, was that Spotify would become a marketplace where listeners paid for access to music, while artists paid to reach their audience. Casten Almqvist asked the obvious question: whether record companies would survive in such a scenario.

"We absolutely believe they have a role to play," Daniel said, before stressing that every part of the value chain had to reinvent itself in the new digital landscape.

NOT NICE

One of the grandest releases of 2016 was Beyoncé's *Lemonade*. The tracks had been interpreted visually in a longform music video that spanned the whole album and debuted in a primetime slot on HBO. The pop star rapped under water, danced with tennis star Serena Williams, and hurled a baseball bat through a few car windows to avenge a cheating partner. The release was an event that brought together millions of listeners across the globe, the way a new Michael Jackson video might have done on MTV in the 1980s.

Trendsetters like Rihanna, Drake, Kanye West, and Frank Ocean would all release new albums that year. Nearly all of them would top the Billboard album chart and feature prominently in critics' year-end summaries. The albums shared another common denominator: on their respective release dates, none could be found on Spotify.

Kanye West and Rihanna chose Tidal, in which they both owned shares, which carried their albums exclusively for a few weeks before they appeared elsewhere. Beyoncé's new album was initially only available on iTunes or Tidal. *Lemonade* would remain exclusive to those two outlets for years to come. In 2018, Beyoncé would rap about the episode, calling out Spotify by name and saying she didn't give "two fucks" about streaming numbers.

Frank Ocean and Drake inked expensive deals with Apple Music. Drake's contract, which gave Apple a few weeks' exclusivity, was said to have cost more than $10 million. According to the industry press, the architect of the deal was Larry Jackson, one of Jimmy Iovine's understudies, who, like his mentor, had moved from Universal Music to Apple. As Iovine and Jackson switched companies, so did their loyalties.

Within twenty-four hours in August of that year, Frank Ocean released two albums, both through Apple Music. One, an experimental album called *Endless*, was released via the Universal imprint Def Jam, apparently ending Ocean's contractual obligations with the label. The other, *Blonde*—containing a handful of hit songs—was under Ocean's own label, giving him a much higher share of the streaming royalties. Universal saw none of the royalties from *Blonde*, which would soon enter the *Billboard* album chart at number one. As *Billboard* magazine would note, it had taken Frank Ocean twenty-four hours to go from earning 14 percent of the royalties paid out, to earning the whole take from various streaming services, or around 70 percent. The deal, brokered by Iovine's Apple Music, reportedly left his former boss, Lucian Grainge, fuming.

As the streaming world fought over exclusive releases, Spotify was hardly in the mix. Jay-Z and Jimmy Iovine did what they were best at—striking competitive deals for new music—while Spotify had little exclusive content. In the fall of 2015, Spotify had the opportunity to premiere the video to Justin Bieber's song "Sorry," but, as one person would recall, the Spotify team could not get their technology up and running in time to do it.

Daniel Ek was uncomfortable with the prospect of artists shopping their material to streaming services, as if they were record labels fighting over the next hot album. He knew that Spotify needed to strengthen its position in popular culture and secure a strong catalogue to keep its user base growing. Therefore, as several sources would recall, he entered top secret talks with Tidal about a potential acquisition.

POWER

Stefan Blom, Spotify's content chief, led Spotify's talks with Tidal. He knew a bit about the industry, having previously served as Nordic head of the record label EMI.

During the meetings, Stefan sat across from Desiree Perez, one of Jay-Z's closest associates. A handsome woman in her mid-forties, Perez had long black hair, an unmistakable Bronx accent, and plenty of business acumen.

At Roc Nation, Desiree Perez had brokered deals that would define the interplay between artists and musicians. Recently, she had negotiated multimillion dollar deals with Samsung that helped both Jay-Z and Rihanna push their respective album releases to consumers. The money was not coming from actual music sales, but from sponsorship deals or investments—such as Jay-Z's stakes in anything from Tidal to the Brooklyn Nets basketball franchise.

"Selling music as a product is over," Perez once told an affiliate in the music industry.

Perez was used to delivering under pressure. In the 1990s, she acted as an informant for the Drug Enforcement Administration. For several years, she helped the DEA investigate drug-related crimes in Puerto Rico and Colombia. According to the *New York Daily News*, her work for the DEA had begun after she was sentenced for possession of thirty-five kilograms of cocaine. Perez had been Jay-Z's business partner since the early aughts, in charge of everything from music catalogues to nightclubs. And, in the summer of 2016, she was negotiating the sale of Tidal with a blond, bespectacled man from Sweden.

One thing was certain: Spotify had money. The Roc Nation team had read the reports of the company's billion-dollar loan. Perez set a price tag of $400 million, a hefty sum for a streaming service with a small user base still posting significant losses. That price would give Jay-Z around five times his initial investment. Stefan said he would consider a deal at half that price, but Perez did not back down. Stefan thanked her for her time and reconvened with the executive team at Spotify.

Daniel Ek could see the appeal of buying Tidal. It would get Spotify closer to Jay-Z and shareholders such as Madonna, Alicia Keys, Coldplay, and Nicki Minaj. Their goodwill could be worth billions in the long run.

Troy Carter, a forty-three-year-old African-American former music manager from West Philadelphia who was relatively new to Spotify, strongly advocated for the deal. Troy had joined the Swedish streaming service to handle relationships with artists and record labels. As a teenager, he was one of the members in the hip-hop group 2 Too Many, which for a short time was signed to Will Smith's record label Wiljam Records. Prior to joining Spotify, Troy had helped Lady Gaga become one of the world's biggest artists.

While some of his colleagues would belittle Jay-Z's business ambitions, Troy took the rapper seriously. He believed acquiring Tidal would raise Spotify's status in the music industry, not least in the African-American community.

"We don't have enough street cred," Troy told his colleagues, as one person would recall.

Daniel recognized the problem, but did not want to pay $400 million for a streaming service with inferior technology and a tiny user base.

"We're growing by several Tidals every month," one of the directors told Daniel.

Spotify eventually declined the offer from Roc Nation and Desiree Perez, but they did look at buying several other companies, people close to the discussions would recall.

Spotify's business development team, led by the handsome Canadian Sumit Varshney, also met with representatives from Deezer. The French competitor had recently pulled back from a stock market listing and seemed to struggle to grow. After several meetings, however, Spotify abandoned the effort.

Another target was one of Spotify's competitors in India. Both Saavn and Gaana Music were up for discussion, but Spotify's executives decided to launch conventionally in India once they had secured the music licenses to do so.

There was, however, one company that Spotify courted quite seriously over a long period. During the summer and fall of 2016, the streaming giant came very close to buying SoundCloud, which had plenty of street cred but a failing business model.

ON THE LOW

Late in the summer of 2016, Barry McCarthy stepped into Spotify's offices in Berlin, located a short walk from Potsdamer Platz, which had once been cut in half by the Berlin Wall during the Cold War.

Spotify Germany was far from its most important subsidiary. It ranked well below the Stockholm headquarters and the New York and London branches. The local staff wondered what brought the CFO to Berlin, as Barry had not given a reason for his visit. Things became clear when he asked someone to book him a cab to The Factory, a converted office building in the central Mitte district with brick walls and large glass windows. The Factory was home to a handful of well-known startups, among them SoundCloud, which by now had reached 175 million monthly listeners. Nine years had passed since Daniel Ek had sat down for coffee in Stockholm with the SoundCloud co-founder Eric Wahlforss. Since then, the pair had stayed in touch, with Daniel offering advice on keeping their stock structure as simple as possible so that investors did not gain outsize influence over their company, among other things.

SoundCloud had built an online community for musicians with a business model that exasperated record labels. The Spotify leadership saw potential in combining the two businesses. Together, they could create a European music giant with nearly 300 million users.

Only a select few were aware of the negotiations taking place. In fact, Spotify had already made an offer to buy SoundCloud the year before. At that time, SoundCloud's founders passed on the $500 million figure, mostly in Spotify shares. Barry was now about to make an even lower offer. He knew that SoundCloud, yet another music tech company struggling to convince investors, was on the ropes.

CLOUDBUSTING

By mid-2016, SoundCloud had become a pop-culture phenomenon. Artists like Kanye West and Justin Bieber would turn to the platform to premiere new songs.

It had also given rise to new genres, such as the unpolished songs with mumbled lyrics that internet users had dubbed SoundCloud Rap. Unlike Spotify, the Berlin-based service had a strong social component. It was a place where artists and music fans could interact. Some artists who had gotten their start on the platform had later turned into global stars. At its best, SoundCloud could kickstart careers that brought artists to the top of the music game.

In January 2017, Chance the Rapper won a Grammy for Best Rap Album. On stage at the Staples Center in Los Angeles, the young Chicagoan thanked God, his loved ones, and his distributor in Berlin.

"Shoutout to SoundCloud for holding me down," he said, as the audience cheered.

Yet for all its accolades, SoundCloud was a troubled business. Like YouTube, they were persistently being accused of making it harder than ever for musicians to earn money. A large portion of their catalogue was unlicensed. Between 2012 and 2015, SoundCloud made around $60 million in revenue, but ran up costs that were three times as high.

For a time, it seemed that SoundCloud would be acquired by Twitter. The price tag was rumored to be one billion dollars, which would have made it Twitter's largest acquisition to date. But, as two sources would recall, Twitter pulled out of the deal at the last moment. The social media platform's declining stock price had apparently caused its CEO, Dick Costolo, to reconsider.

Even Apple showed an interest in what SoundCloud was doing. Jimmy Iovine was charmed by Alexander Ljung, the SoundCloud CEO. As one person close to Iovine would recall, he saw that the Berlin-based company had a rare understanding of how to interact with the artist community. At the time of the meeting, Ljung felt his company was worth $800 million, according to the source. The valuation made Jimmy Iovine back down.

SoundCloud needed investment to keep their business running, and they were trying to avoid raising money at a lower valuation. A few years prior, they had promised several venture capital firms to chase higher revenues by launching a commercial streaming service with a complete, licensed catalogue. By 2016, when they finally secured the rights from the record labels, launching a competitor to Spotify and Apple Music looked like their only shot at offsetting their losses.

SoundCloud Go, which—like other streaming offerings—cost ten dollars a month, made a negligible dent on the competitive market. A year after launching it, SoundCloud reported losses of another $70 million.

MO MONEY MO PROBLEMS

Barry McCarthy's second offer for SoundCloud was 30 percent lower than his initial bid. This time, he offered $350 million of shares in Spotify.

SoundCloud's valuation had plummeted to a third of what it was in 2014, during the acquisition talks with Twitter. Yet a deal with Spotify would ensure the company's survival and give the founders tens of millions of dollars to share. Alexander Ljung and Eric Wahlforss swallowed their pride and accepted the bid, as two people would recall.

Before a deal could be struck, one obstacle remained. Spotify's team of experts had to examine SoundCloud's business in a due-diligence procedure. In the fall of 2016, Sumit Varshney traveled to Berlin with several colleagues, including Niklas Ivarsson, the licensing expert who, after serving nearly nine years at Spotify, had left the company to become a consultant. The team spent several days in a conference room in downtown Berlin. Eric Wahlforss, the SoundCloud founder, was there to answer any questions.

The narrative around the deal was nearly perfect: two companies, each with a pair of Swedish founders, uniting to fight Apple, Google, and Amazon. The Spotify team saw a number of strengths in SoundCloud's offering. Their user base was largely made up of music aficionados, the catalogue full of unique material and rare releases. By buying the company, Spotify could boost its indie credibility, get closer to artists, and, with time, challenge the record labels.

"Instead of record labels being the middleman, you'd have artist managers creating small record companies that would market their music directly on Spotify," as a source would recall.

Yet there were also several problems with SoundCloud's core business. Ivarsson balked at the company's recent licensing deals with the major labels.

"They're worse than the very first ones we signed," he said, referring to the draconian terms Spotify managed to secure in 2008.

Complaints against SoundCloud from music rightsholders were another concern. It was one thing for a smaller streaming service to slip up paying artists and songwriters for their streams; it was quite another for a market leader like Spotify, with plenty of cash on hand, to do so. To some, taking over SoundCloud's disputed catalogue would be tantamount to inviting publishers and labels worldwide to come after Spotify with lawsuits.

"That kind of stuff costs serious dough," one person would recall.

By late September, information about Spotify's latest acquisition target had leaked to the press. The *Financial Times* reported that Spotify was in "advanced talks" to acquire SoundCloud. Pundits began to speculate about what such a deal would mean. In New York, the potential deal had been discussed by both the Spotify board and executive team. At the very last moment, they decided to back out. Two people would recall that the Spotify top brass thought an acquisition of a controversial service might worsen relations with the record labels. Spotify was a year or two away from going public. It couldn't risk estranging the record executives ahead of the next round of negotiations.

"We came very close to buying them," one Spotify executive would tell one of his colleagues.

In early December, TechCrunch reported that Spotify had walked away from the negotiations. Daniel Ek needed to find his interactive platform for artists elsewhere. Martin Lorentzon did not seem particularly sentimental, later questioning SoundCloud's user numbers in a private conversation.

"What are we supposed to do with 175 million email addresses?" the Spotify founder asked.

It would be another six months before SoundCloud's future path had been set. Alexander Ljung laid off half his staff to bring in new funding from a group of investors that included Raine Group, where the former Spotify adviser Fred Davis served as partner.

With the stroke of a pen, SoundCloud's valuation was slashed to $150 million, less than half of Spotify's second bid.

WEAPON OF CHOICE

Rather than make a grand acquisition, Daniel Ek and his executive team began to work on their own way of approaching artists. They would devise a plan to let artists upload their music to Spotify directly, bypassing record labels and conventional distributors.

Meanwhile, the legal tussle with Apple intensified. Apple Music was growing quickly, unimpeded by the antitrust investigations into whether it had colluded to impede Spotify's freemium offering. None of the investigations had led to any fines or charges.

But Spotify had armed themselves by hiring a range of lobbying firms in Washington, DC, and Brussels. Their grievances with Apple were many. It was partly about Apple abusing its power as a distributor while operating its own service. Another issue was Spotify's insistence that proprietary voice technology, such as Apple's Siri or Amazon's Alexa, should be open to outside developers and not place services like Spotify at a disadvantage. After all, Spotify's strategy of being available on every device was dependent on accessing platforms controlled by other companies.

In June 2016, Spotify scored its first major lobbying landmark. Around lunchtime in Washington, DC, the Democratic senator Elizabeth Warren stepped into a large building with white pillars, around the corner from the White House. She was about to deliver a keynote speech at the New America Foundation, and one of her main talking points lined up nicely with Spotify's public affairs efforts.

"For markets to work, there must be competition. But today, in America, competition is dying," Elizabeth Warren said emphatically.

According to Warren, several large corporations were infringing on the competition in industries such as banking, food, aviation, and technology. Specifically, she name-checked Google, Amazon, and Apple.

"While Apple Music is readily accessible on everyone's iPhone, Apple has placed conditions on its rivals that make it difficult to offer competing streaming services," she said, stopping just short of mentioning Spotify.

At this point, Spotify had been available in the App Store for nearly seven years. During that time, 30 percent of the revenue from all of their subscription sales through that channel had gone directly to Apple. What critics would call the "Apple tax" made Apple's services business grow explosively.

At Spotify, frustration over Apple's model was widespread. The product division had long struggled to get their app updates approved and released in the App Store. Several times, Spotify staffers would recall, the process would grind to a halt until Gustav Söderström personally called California to make a complaint.

Gustav Söderström, Chief Product Officer at Spotify, in Stockholm, 2016. *(Jesper Frisk)*

Daniel Ek would hardly ever speak publicly about how difficult Apple was making life for Spotify, not to mention Steve Jobs' whisper campaign to thwart his company in the United States. Only once, during an on-stage interview in 2012, did Jobs' interference come up in stark terms. The online video footage of that interview shows Daniel tackling a touchy subject.

"There's another story I've heard, that Apple tried to keep you out of the US," the journalist and conference host Walt Mossberg says in the clip. "Is there any truth to that?"

Daniel glances silently at the audience, flashing an awkward grin. Several seconds pass. Finally, his stage partner Sean Parker interjects.

"You want me to answer this one?" he asks the Spotify CEO.

"Yeah, why not," Daniel mumbles.

"I can get away with saying things he can't get away with," Sean continues. "There was some indication that that might have been happening. It's a small industry in a lot of ways. Certainly a lot smaller than it was ten or twelve years ago," Sean says, chuckling at his cheeky callback to when his service, Napster, ruined the outlook for a music industry that had just hit its prime.

After a few seconds, Walt Mossberg starts to laugh, and several members of the audience join in. Even Daniel cracks a smile, flashing an admiring glance at his outspoken partner. Daniel would say that Sean was the only person he had met who had spent longer than him thinking about the digital future of the music industry.

In 2016, Daniel Ek still wasn't calling out Apple in public, but his company was in a stronger position to challenge the state of play behind the scenes. A few weeks after Apple Music was introduced, Spotify's press department sent out an email. The recipients were all Spotify subscribers who were paying thirteen dollars via the App Store. They were advised to end their subscription there and instead pay Spotify directly.

"You can get the exact same Spotify for only $9.99/month, and it's super simple," the email read.

Spotify had stepped up its campaign against the App Store. The following summer, Tim Cook finally tweaked the terms of his distribution platform, cutting Apple's revenue share to 15 percent after the first twelve months. But that did not mark the end of the legal squabble between Spotify and Apple.

Around this time, Spotify's product team was trying to get an update through the App Store. Despite several attempts, it wasn't accepted. Staff at Apple had noticed that somewhere in the app, Spotify asked users for their email addresses, which might let the Swedish company get in touch directly with users they had acquired through Apple, potentially tapping them to start paying Spotify directly. The hardware giant stopped the update.

At the end of June 2016, Spotify's general counsel, Horacio Gutierrez, sent a letter to his counterpart in Cupertino. He wrote that Apple was using its power as a "weapon to harm competitors." Apple's general counsel refuted the criticism.

The row over the App Store terms would continue for many years.

19

WALL STREET

B Y 2017, THERE WAS NO turning back. Spotify had to go public, and Daniel Ek dreaded it. Holding quarterly presentations and keeping investment bankers happy was not how he had envisioned leading a tech company. He had no desire to ring the opening bell on the stock exchange or give loads of interviews. But an IPO was the only way he could provide a lucrative exit for his early investors, while at the same time retaining control over his company.

Plenty of challenges lay ahead. Spotify had a loan, which risked costing them hundreds of millions of dollars a year in discounted shares, that needed to be paid off. The company had to get closer to turning a profit. Daniel and his CFO also needed to devise a strategy that would show Wall Street that Spotify was moving up the food chain, and becoming less reliant on the music labels—in other words, that their profits would grow substantially over time.

Some of this was familiar territory. The Spotify CEO had delivered quarterly briefs to a limited group of shareholders for years, and the company's stock had been trading through a variety of brokers in the secondary market. Big names were waiting for a chance to invest in Spotify. Many of the world's best-known names in finance and tech were already lined up, hoping for a piece of the action.

WORK

To reduce its losses, Spotify once again needed to improve its licensing terms with the music labels. The negotiations were led by Spotify's chief content officer, the mild-mannered Stefan Blom, who was based in New York. His goal was to ensure that Spotify would retain a larger portion of its revenue than before. The hard-hitting CFO, Barry McCarthy, had made his view clear: It was unacceptable that Spotify, when all the payouts to labels and publishers were complete, only kept around fifteen cents on the dollar.

Toward the end of 2016, negotiations with Universal were at an impasse, which took its toll on Stefan. Daniel Ek had provided the forty-four-year-old father with a luxurious four-room apartment on the Upper East Side of Manhattan, but his work was so demanding that he hardly had time to see his family. His life was essentially a series of nonstop flights to and from Stockholm, London, and Los Angeles to get the label deals over the line.

As usual, Daniel had impossibly high expectations of his executive team. Stefan Blom would rarely push back.

"His weakness was perhaps that he wasn't very good at saying no to Daniel," one of his colleagues would recall.

Despite having been in the US for six years, Spotify's free tier was still controversial. Stefan found himself caught between tough-talking label heads and his own demanding bosses. In the end, Barry McCarthy and Spotify's general counsel, Horacio Gutierrez, were said to have swooped in and dragged the deal across the line.

"I congratulate Daniel on Spotify's continued growth and innovation," Universal's CEO, Lucian Grainge, said in a written statement when the new deal was signed in April 2017.

The press release made no mention that the negotiations had stood still for several months. One of Spotify's main concessions to Universal was to let its major artists, like Drake and Taylor Swift, release albums exclusively to Spotify's premium subscribers for the first two weeks. For the record label, the arrangement was reminiscent of an age in which newly released albums were priced higher than the rest and still sold the most copies in record stores. For Spotify, however, it was another case of the free tier being diluted.

Stefan Blom signed similar deals with Merlin, the digital rights agency for independent record labels, and Sony Music. Then Warner Music, still the caboose of the negotiating process, agreed to their terms. The talks progressed partly because the music industry stood to gain from a successful IPO. The big three still owned more than ten percent of Spotify and understood that if the deals were welcomed by investors, their shares would go up in value.

Once the new licenses went into effect, Spotify went from earning fifteen cents to twenty-five cents on every dollar. The revenue split Spotify had aimed for—with labels and publishers taking 70 percent and Spotify keeping 30 percent—rarely worked out in practice. This was largely because the growth of the company's free service would end up costing it extra money every year. Under the terms of the new deals, though, growing the free tier of Spotify became considerably less expensive.

Stefan was relieved. He'd survived the most intense part of his professional career, but new challenges were just around the corner.

In December 2017, Daniel Ek gathered the senior directors of his content team. Spotify's CEO said that he was pleased with the new licenses, but he also questioned if Stefan was up for another tour of duty at the top of the company.

Daniel was now more comfortable making tough managerial decisions. He was inspired by Netflix, where leaders would refer to the company as a "team," not a "family," meaning underperformers could be swapped out at any time. Ek had also taken to a concept devised by LinkedIn's founder, Reid Hoffman, in giving his top executives time-capped assignments. Every "mission," as he called them, ran for approximately two years. After that, they could either take on new responsibilities or leave the company. In an interview, Daniel would explain that Spotify was the kind of shapeshifting growth company where it was hard for the top brass to manage more than two or three missions before moving on.

With the IPO just a few months away, the Spotify founder seemed unsure if Blom could take things to the next level. Daniel would describe how he asked his executive the same question over and over. Finally, Stefan produced the answer his boss was expecting. In early 2018, he put in his last day at Spotify after more than five years of service.

Daniel Ek—who would point to Stefan's departure as an example of his management style—personally took over his former colleague's duties and began to look for a successor.

Stefan's abrupt exit would stir up feelings not just among Spotify alumni, but also in the music industry. Ek did not say much about it until he, after the Spotify IPO, recounted the episode in an interview with Fast Company.

In the article, Ek appeared eager to show Wall Street that he could act resolutely if ever his top people were found wanting.

Yet few sources who had worked for Ek could recall any firing as dramatic as that of Stefan Blom. Many described how Daniel appeared to be
developing a ruthless edge as CEO.

"Daniel would sometimes let people hang themselves," as one source
put it.

But several former colleagues said that publicly airing out the argument
with Stefan—who had been "very loyal"—felt like an unnecessary move.

NOBODY'S CHILD

For decades, tech founders had tended to list their companies on the Nasdaq stock market in New York. This was true of Microsoft in 1986 and
Google in 2004. But after Facebook's tumultuous IPO in 2012, the trend
was broken. Twitter, Alibaba, and Snap all chose the New York Stock Exchange, with its famous pediment and columned facade on Wall Street.
That was Daniel Ek's first choice, too.

In the spring of 2017, Spotify recruited several new board members.
One of them was Cristina Stenbeck, principal owner of the Swedish investment company Kinnevik and seasoned tech veteran. Her track record
spanned from Avito, a Russian version of Craigslist or eBay, to the German
e-commerce giant Zalando.

Two other newcomers were Disney's former chief operating officer Tom
Staggs, and Shishir Mehrotra, a former product design director at YouTube.
The last new recruit was Padmasree Warrior, an old friend of Shakil Khan's
who had served on the board of Microsoft since 2015. She was now the
CEO of the US division of the electric car manufacturer NIO. All four were
independent board members, which meant Spotify now lived up to the
requirements of US financial authorities.

To make way for the new board, several people had to step aside. This
marked the end of Sean Parker's formal ties to Spotify, a company he had
made significant inroads for in the United States. He had arranged parties,
lobbied behind the scenes, and done countless interviews talking up streaming, and the Swedish service in particular. He even strongly defended

Spotify when Mark Zuckerberg wanted to limit its exposure on Facebook. But it had now been years since he argued Spotify's case in public.

As the IPO neared, Sean Parker's Founders Fund was not on the Spotify cap table, according to confidential documents. Sean, however, still held a small personal stake in the company. The other outgoing board members were Klaus Hommels, the angel investor and early Facebook backer, and Pär-Jörgen Pärson, who had followed Martin Lorentzon since the late 1990s. Soon, Pärson's venture fund, Northzone, would send record-breaking returns back to its investors.

Barry McCarthy would soon propose an unconventional way of going public. Instead of enlisting investment banks and raising a huge amount of capital by issuing new stock, he wished to simply register Spotify's shares on the stock market and have unrestricted trading begin.

It was called a direct public offering, or DPO. Barry explained that Spotify could save time and money by raising capital on the private market ahead of the float. Daniel liked what he heard. The company's shares were already trading at a record-breaking volume on the secondary market, so perhaps the company wouldn't need banks to prop up the share price during its first weeks on the New York Stock Exchange.

There was, perhaps, an added benefit to the direct listing. The "schmuck insurance" deal that Spotify had signed with Universal to enter the US market was still in effect, as one person would recall. That deal stipulated that if Spotify were sold or listed, Universal would receive an additional two percent of the purchase price. The money would come directly from Spotify's earliest shareholders. At this point, that percentage was the equivalent of $200 million, and the sum was about to grow.

But the secret agreement with Universal was never triggered. One person familiar with the details speculated it was because of the direct listing. In their unconventional process, Spotify's founders may have found a way to duck out of the costly and confidential arrangement.

JUST A FRIEND

As the IPO in New York drew closer, Spotify braced for the scrutiny that would come from authorities and media outlets alike. The Securities and

Exchange Commission would be looking closely at everything from business contracts to its accounting, and the background of every person with significant influence at the company.

Daniel Ek may have wondered whether that level of scrutiny would also apply to his close friend and adviser, Shakil Khan. During 2017, Daniel got drawn into a family feud between Shak and his older brother, Tanweer. The spat would create headlines in a range of international news outlets.

Tanweer, who felt that Shak had spoken ill of their father when he appeared on a podcast, was convinced that Spotify and Daniel Ek were not being forthright about the amount of influence his brother held at the company. He sent more than seventy emails to Shak, Daniel, and a Spotify investor claiming that the company was trying to tone down Shak's role ahead of going public.

Tanweer suggested that Spotify and Daniel were nervous about Shak's past, which included several convictions, one of them a "serious drug offense."

"Once a company moves onto the market, journalists have a habit of digging up in the strangest of places to find some very bizarre answers that can leave companies a little bit embarrassed," Tanweer wrote in one of his emails to Daniel.

Daniel did not respond, instead asking his general counsel, Horacio Gutierrez, to step in. Gutierrez stressed that their "patience had run out" regarding Tanweer's "unfounded claims and misguided threats."

"I'm hoping we can avoid the costly and protracted actions that will follow, including those involving your employer, so and [sic] I'm reaching out to you in good faith to discuss before we act," Gutierrez wrote.

According to Tanweer, Shak had described himself as Spotify's "head of special projects" on LinkedIn as late as 2018, despite having claimed to step down from that role six years prior. He would also point out that Daniel had tweeted, after Shak's apparent departure, that the Brit would soon be "hustling" for his company again.

In practice, Tanweer argued, his younger brother had been serving as Daniel's number two, effectively as co-CEO. A person with that amount of influence would ordinarily be declared openly in an IPO filing.

Tanweer wanted Spotify to "provide full details about Shak's background so that the reasonable investor can make an informed decision about whether to invest or not," according to court documents in the UK.

According to Shak, the conflict between him and his brother had begun when Tanweer was starting his company Carbaya, an online platform for selling used cars. Tanweer had described Shak as a key adviser to the company, which Shak denied.

"In fact, I had nothing to do with Carbaya," Shak said in his witness statement.

In early 2018, two months before the IPO, Shak brought his brother before the UK High Court, arguing that he was being harassed. Ultimately, the judge decided not to move forward with an injunction against Tanweer, arguing that the impact on Shak did not "go much beyond annoyance and distress."

The ordeal is said to have taken a high personal toll on Shak, who had already been shaken by a heart attack one year prior. As Spotify approached its listing, his LinkedIn profile stated that he was merely an "investor and advisor" to the company.

Once Spotify's dense IPO filing surfaced, amounting to 200-plus pages, the name of Daniel Ek's long-time consigliere was nowhere to be found.

C.R.E.A.M.

As signs of Spotify's listing started to spread, the company's valuation began skyrocketing on the secondary market. It reached its peak just before the IPO on Wall Street in April 2018. Rarely have shares in an unlisted company traded so intensively. Daniel Ek would soon seize on an opportunity to strengthen his control over the company.

Many of Spotify's early employees had become millionaires. Key figures such as Sophia Bendz, Mengmeng Du, and Jonathan Forster had converted their stock options and sold off large amounts of shares. Andreas Ehn, Spotify's first CTO, was said to have earned tens of millions of dollars on his stock options. In the early days, he owned one percent of the company.

The early employee with the largest uptick was Ludvig Strigeus, who held five percent of the company after he sold µTorrent to the Spotify founders back in 2006. His percentage had shrunk as new investors came in, but the share price kept rising. Between 2014 and 2017, the self-taught coder sold shares worth north of $30 million, but that was only a fraction of his total holdings.

Besides being a fantastic investment for venture capital funds, Spotify also enriched many influential private investors. One of them was Ian Osborne, who had advised companies like Uber and individuals such as the former UK Prime Minister David Cameron. Another was the US hedge fund tycoon Robert Citrone.

Throughout 2017, every new licensing agreement signed by Spotify sent the share price up. In April, when the deal with Universal was finally finished, the price jumped by 50 percent to $2,700 per share. Suddenly, Spotify was valued at around $10 billion, nearly four times what eBay had paid for Skype in 2005. For a Swedish tech company, Spotify's new valuation was enormous; yet this was only the beginning of a remarkable ascent.

The titans of the tech world had now begun to circle Spotify like sharks in shallow water. They followed its impressive growth in paid subscribers and saw how Netflix, another streaming service, was making a splash on the New York Stock Exchange. Masayoshi Son, the CEO of Japan's SoftBank, explored buying a large stake in Spotify, according to two sources. Softbank's Vision Fund was currently betting around $20 billion a year on tech companies like WeWork and, in late 2017, Uber. But according to one rumor, things had soured between Masayoshi Son and Martin Lorentzon, who had somehow managed to offend the sixty-year-old Japanese executive.

The global appetite for Spotify stock benefited swaths of brokers and bankers in Stockholm's financial district. Investment banks such as GP Bullhound would facilitate deals on the secondary market, taking a cut on every transaction. One person who tended to take the bait was Martin Söderström, an energetic young businessman whose wife Charlotte was the daughter of the clothing giant H&M's majority owner, Stefan Persson. The Perssons now had an investment fund, managed by Martin Söderström. In the fall of 2017, the fund held 0.7 percent of Spotify. Martin Söderström would constantly scoop up small positions under the banner of DIG Investment, a name that originally stood for Djursholm Investment Group, taking its label from the wealthy area where Sofia Ek had grown up.

By the time the licenses from all the major labels were in place, Spotify's shares had shot up to $4,000 each. The share price had doubled in just over six months. The closer the IPO came, the harder it was to find sellers. As one source would recall, Jack Ma, the founder of the Chinese tech conglomerate Alibaba, placed an order to buy at least $50 million of Spotify shares.

But by this time, its shareholders had started to exercise their "right of first refusal," which meant they had first dibs on any share sale. That effectively put an end to all transactions with third parties. By the time Jack Ma arrived, the game was gone.

At its peak, the secondary-market trading in Spotify was more intense than for any other unlisted tech company, as one person in finance put it. Shares in US tech companies like Uber and Airbnb would also be traded on the private markets, but in their case, rigid US shareholder agreements would block many of the deals. Daniel Ek could have stopped the secondary trades in Spotify, but he didn't—the trading put upward pressure on the share price, and it allowed his employees to cash in on their stock options. When reputable financial institutions got on the cap table, it also boded well for the IPO.

Some of the busiest buyers were the hedge fund managers at Tiger Global in New York City. When a large option package for Spotify's staff vested in early 2017, the company encouraged employees wishing to sell to turn to Tiger Global. The firm was an offshoot from Tiger Management, a hedge fund run by the legendary stock investor Julian Robertson between 1980 and 2000. During the fall of 2017, Tiger Global's managers asked various investment bankers to find Spotify shareholders willing to sell. Since they were being contacted by brokers representing different institutions, many got the impression that the demand was high. This may, in turn, have driven up the price.

"Tiger was sucking up as much as they could," as one source would put it.

Shortly, Tiger became one of Spotify's biggest shareholders. By December 2017, the fund owned six percent of the company, and they would soon come close to Daniel Ek on the list of the largest holdings. But the CEO had no need to worry. It would later be revealed that Tiger's top executives—the billionaire Chase Coleman and the internet investors Lee Fixel and Scott Shleifer—had transferred their voting rights to the Spotify founder.

It was the same trick that Yuri Milner had deployed when he turned Spotify into a unicorn in 2011. He'd invested tens of millions of dollars without taking a seat on the board. Daniel got the money he needed but didn't have to relinquish any formal control.

At this point, the billion-dollar valuation of Spotify from 2011 looked almost quaint. Yuri Milner's firm, DST Global, had sold its last shares in

Spotify just before Christmas of 2015, when the share price was $1,800. Two years later, the shares were worth more than twice that.

By the end of 2017, Spotify was valued at $16 billion on the secondary market. And Daniel Ek was about to push that figure even further.

EMPIRE STATE OF MIND

Signs of some new, mystery investor began to show in the spring of 2017, when Chinese delegations started visiting the Spotify headquarters at Jarla House. Employees began to hear the word "Tencent." The Chinese tech giant would soon become an important Spotify ally.

Tencent had been founded in November 1998 by Ma Huateng—better known as Pony Ma—and his four co-founders. Tencent's first product was an unapologetic rip-off of ICQ, the popular desktop chat tool that Daniel Ek once used to woo girls in high school.

In the late 1990s, Pony Ma had just enough imagination to call his version IOCQ. After complaints from AOL, the owner of ICQ, he renamed it QQ. Within a few years, the instant-messaging platform would attract hundreds of millions of users.

As Tencent advanced, Pony Ma became known for encouraging competition within the group. Sometimes he'd build several teams with similar assignments and let them duke it out in order to arrive at the best product.

In 2004, Tencent went public on the Hong Kong stock exchange. Its breakthrough moment would not come until seven years later, with the launch of WeChat. By 2017, WeChat had evolved into a social network that covered anything from payments to mobile games to news. It was quickly approaching one billion active users.

Like many Chinese tech giants, Tencent was controversial in the West. Chinese authorities would soon admit that they could erase messages in WeChat, which seemed to tie Tencent closely to the regime. Tencent had also launched a new streaming service, QQ Music, which had recently merged with China Music Corporation's two competitors, Kugou and Kuwo. The three music services had become one, and the new company would soon come to be known as Tencent Music.

Music streaming was only one area in which Tencent was gaining ground. In the 2010s, the company began to invest widely in the global tech sector. Within a few years, Tencent had invested heavily in Tesla, the ride-sharing service Lyft, and Epic Games, whose hit *Fortnite* swept over the world in 2017.

Like Yuri Milner, Pony Ma won favors by taking a passive role in his portfolio companies. In October of 2017, he bought twelve percent of the shares in Snap, which was listed on the New York Stock Exchange, and relinquished his voting rights. In the months leading up to the Snap deal, he had also been interested in acquiring all of Spotify, as two sources would recall.

Tencent's talks with Daniel Ek were said to have begun cautiously. The initial idea was a partnership between Spotify and Tencent Music. But over time, Tencent made it clear that they would be ready to buy the Swedish outfit for around $20 billion. The idea was to merge the two into one. According to one source, Daniel was offered the role of CEO of the new company. Spotify's Chinese counterpart already had hundreds of millions of users in China, but far fewer paying subscribers.

Publicly, Daniel had often proclaimed that he wouldn't sell Spotify. Privately, his stance was slightly more flexible. To his executives, he would maintain that selling would only become an option if the deal would provide a better platform to deliver on the company's vision. The proposal from Tencent, with him as chief executive, looked like it might fulfill his criteria. Yet the Spotify founder was hesitant, viewing an acquisition by Tencent as a backup plan, much as he had with Microsoft and Google in 2010, and with Google again in 2013. He and the Spotify board ultimately decided that they would rather take the streaming giant public, and remain independent.

"Daniel and Martin have always wanted to negotiate with companies like Microsoft, Google, and Tencent to understand the strategic value of the company. But I don't think they've ever had the intention of selling," one source would recall.

But the negotiations with Tencent did not stop there. In the fall, executives from both companies forged a new plan based on Spotify and Tencent swapping shares in each other's companies. Spotify would stay out of China, while Tencent would invest in Spotify at a high valuation and help the company clear its debts. The deal was finalized, and in mid-December, the Spotify press department sent out the press release.

"This transaction will allow both companies to benefit from the global growth of music streaming," Daniel said in a written statement.

In practice, Spotify was allocated shares in Tencent and Tencent Music worth a total of one billion dollars. Tencent acquired shares in Spotify worth just as much. Tencent also bought convertible loans from several of Spotify's lenders for around $600 million, and converted them into shares in the company. The lenders who sold to Tencent had thus seen their investments double in value. The remaining lenders would also convert their loans into Spotify shares.

Suddenly, Daniel had the kind of anchor investor that normally came with an IPO. Tencent even echoed a traditional listing by agreeing not to sell its shares within a certain time period. In this case, the lock-in wasn't a few months, but three whole years.

The new shares Spotify had issued to Tencent held a price of $5,300. That pegged Spotify's valuation at a whopping $25 billion. That share price had effectively set the floor for Spotify's listing, which was now only weeks away.

Within a year, Spotify had tripled its valuation. It was now worth more than the telecoms giant Ericsson, one of Sweden's largest public companies. Daniel Ek had paved the way for a grand entrance on the New York Stock Exchange.

WALK STRAIGHT DOWN THE MIDDLE

To please Wall Street, Daniel Ek and Barry McCarthy had started to identify a number of new ways to make money, even ones that would set them up for a clash with the major labels.

One of these ideas had been kicking around Spotify for a few years. It revolved around shifting listeners, even slightly, away from music owned by the major labels and toward songs that were less expensive to license. At scale, that could make a big difference to Spotify's bottom line.

Another project, grown out of the Spotify for Artists platform, was meant to bring the company closer to creators and producers. From a business perspective, it made sense for Spotify to move from being a distributor of music to becoming a destination for consumers and creators alike. This was a red flag to the major labels. So, Spotify would inch forward while drawing a firm line that they promised not to cross.

"We do not own rights, we're not a label, all our music is licensed from rightsholders and we pay them—we don't pay ourselves," a Spotify spokesperson wrote in an email to *Billboard* magazine in the summer of 2017.

Just a few days later, Daniel found himself under attack. *Music Business Worldwide* had published a list of fifty unknown artists whose music was trending on some of Spotify's major playlists, such as "Peaceful Piano" and "Music for Concentration." All together, the tracks had been streamed more than five hundred million times. Anonymous sources in the music industry railed against what they dubbed "fake artists."

It emerged that Spotify had licensed music from a Stockholm-based tech company, Epidemic Sound, who would sell access to a database full of music by no-name musicians to YouTubers and the film and TV industry.

The optics were bad. While Apple was signing multi-million-dollar contracts with huge pop stars, Daniel Ek seemed to be peddling a catalog of filler music. Spotify retained a larger portion of the revenue on the songs but had to face the criticism that they were watering down their catalogue. By July 2017, almost 1,500 tracks from Epidemic Sound had found their way onto Spotify. That number would keep growing.

"We've found a need for content," Spotify's policy and communications director Jonathan Prince said in a statement that appeased few label executives.

Daniel had also started taking an interest in a researcher named François Pachet, who had spent twenty years working at Sony. The Frenchman believed that hit songs could be created through artificial intelligence. His interpretive AI engine was used to scan dozens or hundreds of tracks in order to interpret and replicate their style.

Often, the computer would make independent decisions, such as inserting a few chords from the beginning of the Beatles' song "Michelle" into a bridge of one of its creations. In another project, François Pachet and his colleagues asked the AI engine to emulate pieces by Johann Sebastian Bach. A survey later showed that more than half of the listeners thought the AI-powered songs were Bach's own work.

In mid-2017, François Pachet became head of Daniel's new Creator Technology Research Lab in Paris. There, he would develop AI tools intended to help artists create new music. One of Pachet's colleagues was already producing AI music together with actual musicians. The band appeared on Spotify under the pseudonym SKYGGE, whose album *Hello World* got around ten million streams on Spotify in 2018. The AI engine didn't claim royalties, and never staged a Spotify boycott.

A few months later, just as Spotify was about to submit its IPO filing, Daniel made a move to get closer to independent artists. He announced the acquisition of Soundtrap, a startup that had spent the last six years moving from one run-down office to another in Stockholm.

Soundtrap's software let musicians create and record music collaboratively, in real time, without being in the room together. The service targeted amateur musicians and schools, which used it as a teaching tool.

At first, Daniel had sought a partnership with Soundtrap, but by the summer of 2017, his team was looking to buy the whole company. Soundtrap's users generally weren't fully-fledged artists but, Daniel figured, the better they got, the deeper their relationship to Spotify would become.

In the long run, the service could evolve into a new source of music for Spotify, helping the company become less dependent on the established record companies.

While it was low on revenue, Soundtrap had received nearly $8 million in venture capital. Among the owners were the local VC firm Industrifonden, and Spotify's former CFO, Peter Sterky. Daniel's executives had to make several bids, but Soundtrap relented when it became clear that Spotify would give them free rein once the deal was done.

"We share Spotify's vision of democratizing music," Soundtrap's CEO, Per Emanuelsson, said after signing the deal in November 2017.

The price tag was secret, but ended up being around $60 million, largely paid in Spotify shares.

Some of Soundtrap's shareholders would later brag about the price tag in private. They found it remarkable, given that the company had virtually no revenue.

WE WILL ROCK YOU

In March 2018, Daniel Ek and some of his top executives faced a gathering of Wall Street analysts for Spotify's Investor Day. It was a cool affair, held at Spring Studios in the trendy neighborhood of Tribeca, home to many celebrities in lower Manhattan.

"Please welcome to the stage: founder and CEO Daniel Ek," a voice thundered through the speakers.

Daniel stepped out in black jeans, a black suit jacket, white t-shirt, and a fresh pair of white Nike Air Force One sneakers.

"All right! Good afternoon, everyone," he said, welcoming the audience to Spotify's version of a capital markets day.

He spoke with the same conviction as when he pitched investors during Spotify's early years. But the balding, twenty-four-year-old founder in a bunchy pullover was gone. He now looked lean and fit, almost completely transformed from the Daniel Ek the US public had seen glimpses of over the years. He was now a handsome thirty-five-year-old whose boyhood dream had become worth $25 billion.

"For us, going public has never really been about the pomp and circumstance of it all. So you won't see us ringing any bells or throwing any parties," Daniel said, bashfully.

A few weeks earlier, Spotify had made its IPO filing public. Besides giving an exhaustive picture of the operations, the cap table revealed that several old timers—such as Martin Lorentzon's old partner Felix Hagnö and the coding genius Ludvig Strigeus—still owned shares worth hundreds of millions of dollars. It also showed that Sony Music was Spotify's fifth-largest owner, with almost 6 percent of the company.

Tencent had climbed past Daniel Ek and was now Spotify's second-largest shareholder, with just over 9 percent of the shares; but the CEO's influence had increased. Through stock bonus incentives and a certificate program, he and Martin—the largest owner, with 12 percent of the company—could control 80 percent of the votes. The setup resembled the dual-class voting structures that the founders of Google and Facebook had popularized.

On stage, Daniel addressed Spotify's reputation for secrecy by stating that the company had always acted transparently—just not toward the outside world.

"Transparency is really a key pillar of our culture. It's always been. It's just who we are and how we do things. We just haven't done it externally to the same extent as internally," he explained.

Then he laid out Spotify's new strategy for the first time: the company aimed to become a technology-driven layer between the fans and artists. This "two-sided marketplace" would allow the company to gain revenue from both listeners and creators alike. Spotify's constant stream of data revealed which tracks deserved a place in the programmed playlists, which now comprised almost a third of what people were listening to. This system could thus be used to control demand in the music industry.

The Spotify CEO underscored his point by mentioning Dermot Kennedy, who as recently as 2015 was still strumming his guitar on the streets of Dublin. The Irish singer-songwriter had uploaded a handful of songs to Spotify and, without the backing of any large label, gotten picked up by the algorithmic playlist Discover Weekly, reaching millions of listeners. Now he was touring all over the world and living off of his art.

In its IPO filing, Spotify also mentioned Lauv, an artist who was relatively anonymous until one of his songs ended up on the playlist Today's Top Hits. Millions of streams followed, and 70 percent of them came from playlists managed by Spotify.

"I think this is such an important part of the Spotify opportunity, because this is the part that nobody else is doing," Daniel said.

Then he proceeded to use a word with magical properties in the world of tech and finance.

"Some people say Spotify is disrupting the music industry. But I think we're really just part of the evolution of the music industry," he said.

Though neither he nor his audience knew it at the time, the buzz around the new marketplace strategy would soon fade. Its most aggressive feature—a service that let artists upload their music directly to Spotify, bypassing the traditional structure—only went live for a short time in 2019. Spotify may have ended the experiment as a concession to the record labels.

At Investor Day, the next speaker was Spotify's product guru Gustav Söderström. He stepped onto the stage in a dark-blue collared shirt, tight blue jeans, and brown leather shoes and explained that Spotify was sitting on 200 petabytes of data detailing its listeners' behavior.

Gustav described Spotify as a data-driven, scalable company to the room full of Wall Street analysts.

"Spotify is software. It's what we do. And we're good at it," he said.

Later, Barry McCarthy would spell out that Spotify was still putting growth before profits. As long as the company's total projected revenue per new user exceeded the cost of acquiring a new user, it made sense to expand.

Nine directors appeared on the stage that afternoon. All of them—except Danielle Lee, global head of partner solutions—were men.

When the lights went down, Spotify had done its best to put on a grand show for Wall Street. It was the company's last concerted performance before going public a few weeks later.

MORNING HAS BROKEN

On the Tuesday morning after Easter weekend, the sun stood low over the water in central Stockholm.

At eight thirty, Sophia Bendz was on her way to her office at the Alma members' club. Since leaving her role at Spotify's marketing department in late 2014, she had become an investor. Soon, she would become a partner at Atomico, the venture-capital firm founded by the Skype co-founder Niklas Zennström.

Walking across the Nybroviken dock, she took a picture of the sunrise over the Östermalm neighborhood. She was standing just a few blocks from Spotify's early offices. The temperature hovered around freezing and the sky was clear blue.

"Looks like a great day to list a company," she wrote, uploading the photo to Twitter.

Plenty of people shared her nostalgia. Magnus Hult, who sorted through Spotify's entangled metadata at the office on Riddargatan, liked the tweet. So did the former product developer Michelle Kadir and Pär-Jörgen Pärson, whose firm Northzone had been a shareholder in Spotify for nearly ten years.

Throughout the day, Spotify veterans would write to each other in an alumni group on Facebook. All of them waited anxiously for the trading to open in New York. April 3, 2018, was a big day, even if Daniel Ek would do his utmost to tone it down.

HARDER, BETTER, FASTER, STRONGER

A few hours later, it was morning in New York. Just before eight a.m., a security guard stepped into a small booth just inside the entrance at 11 Wall Street. Just over ninety minutes remained until the stock exchange would open, but the traders had already been taking orders for Spotify shares for an hour-plus.

The listing followed the stock exchange's usual routine. Journalists passed through the security checkpoint well ahead of time. Staff at the business channel CNBC prepared their studio for a live broadcast just below the podium with the bell that would open the trading. But neither Daniel Ek nor Martin Lorentzon would be standing on that podium. The night before, Spotify's CEO had explained why in an open letter.

"Of course, I am proud of what we've built over the last decade. But what's even more important to me is that tomorrow does not become the most important day for Spotify," he wrote as his company prepared for its big day.

In his signature, he once again quoted Daft Punk: "Harder, better, faster, stronger."

Unlike a conventional IPO, there was no predetermined price range for Spotify's shares. Instead, the intense secondary-market trading guided the stock traders setting the price. One of us, on assignment for the Swedish financial newspaper *Dagens industri*, was present that day. The traders on the floor said they had never seen anything like this process. This was the first ever direct listing on the New York Stock Exchange.

Outside, the cold morning wind swept over the southern tip of Manhattan. The front of the stock exchange was covered in a large black banner with the green Spotify logo in the middle. Underneath were three American flags, one of which was about to be replaced.

On the ground floor of the building, the security guard stood by a wall full of shelves with flags in cardboard boxes. He found the countries starting with "S," pulled a box off the shelf, and made his way to the second floor of the building.

LIVIN' IN THE FUTURE

About seventy blocks north, the man of the hour sat in a white leather chair. Daniel Ek had made his way to the western end of 57th Street, near the Hudson River, with his head of global communications, Dustee Jenkins. From here, *CBS This Morning* went live on air every weekday, drawing a full three million viewers.

Daniel, nursing a paper cup from Starbucks, made small talk with the host Gayle King. He was wearing a green polo shirt and an Apple Watch on his left wrist. On the air, he talked about how streaming was "not even a thing" before Apple Music launched. Now, his model was poised to take over.

"When you have all the world's music in your pocket, you start listening to a lot more music than you ever did before," Daniel said.

The last time the thirty-five-year-old was in this studio, Spotify had just introduced Moments, the unsuccessful music and video update that was supposed to follow users throughout their day. That was around the time of Taylor Swift's boycott of the company. Now, three years later, Spotify had just enjoyed a payback moment. Taylor Swift had recently sent out a greeting to her followers.

"There is a brand new video for 'Delicate' coming out, only on Spotify, tonight. So check it out," she wrote.

In the CBS studio, Daniel told the hosts how he had traveled "many, many" times to Nashville, Tennessee, to convince Taylor Swift to return to his service. A few days before Spotify's IPO, the service premiered her latest video.

The conversation turned to reports that Apple Music was about to surpass Spotify in the US in terms of paying users.

"Are you scared?" Gayle King asked.

Calm and prepared, Daniel said that Apple's presence only makes the streaming market grow further.

"As someone who grew up in a working-class suburb of Stockholm, I couldn't afford all the music. So back in '98–'99, I was really thinking about how I could get all that music, and do it in a legal way, while compensating all the artists," he said.

"So we're now a decade into that journey, and I really just feel like we're in the second inning," Daniel said, borrowing a baseball term that made Gayle King chuckle.

Daniel was repeating the lesson Martin Lorentzon once stressed: never let an IPO become the primary target of a company. Yet Daniel did admit that he would be glancing at the share price.

"I'll look at it when it opens. But my focus is really on the long term."

RED FLAG

During the tech boom of recent years, around a hundred companies had listed on the New York Stock Exchange every year. There were also about a hundred different flags stored in the lobby of the building. Around the time that Daniel Ek was being interviewed by CBS, the security guard stepped out onto the balcony and pulled down the American flag furthest to the right. He then hoisted a red one with a white cross in the middle.

A Swiss flag appeared next to the two American ones, under the gigantic Spotify banner. From the street below, one of us took a photo and posted it to Twitter.

News outlets from all over the world got in touch to publish the photo they had seen surface on social media. Reuters dubbed the story "the Swiss Miss," and it quickly spread all over the world. After a few hours, the stock exchange's press officers published a joke about Sweden and Switzerland in a tweet.

"We hope everyone enjoyed our momentary ode to our neutral role in the process of price discovery this morning," they wrote.

On the day of Spotify's IPO—April 3, 2018—a mishap on Wall Street saw the Swiss flag hoisted rather than that of Sweden. *(Sven Carlsson)*

MONEY, MONEY, MONEY

"Guys, the book is closing. 5.6 million, opens at 165.90!"

Spotify's IPO was almost four hours late. But at twelve thirty p.m., the order book closed. Sellers looking to offload 5.6 million shares had been matched with buyers.

At Spotify's offices in New York, the staff followed the initial trades on TV screens. The stock opened at a price that put Spotify's total worth at $29.5 billion, far higher than it had ever been.

Later that day, the stock price dropped. It closed at $149, which still made Spotify worth more than Snap, Twitter, and the Swedish clothing giant H&M. It also looked like Spotify had set a trend among tech companies preparing an IPO. Both Airbnb and Slack would reportedly explore the possibility of a direct listing.

Martin Lorentzon wasn't in New York for Spotify's first day of trading, but he did write several posts about it on social media. He also shared an article about the stock exchange raising the wrong flag, which appeared to amuse him. Of everyone celebrating Spotify's meteoric rise, the forty-nine-year-old had become the richest. He still owned 12 percent of the company, which came out to more than $3 billion. For his unwavering belief in Daniel Ek's idea, he was awarded nearly five hundred times his original investment.

Pär-Jörgen Pärson, the early investor, did not see as large a return. But Northzone's profits from the Spotify deal were the highest for any European venture capital fund to date. The Spotify deal had put Pärson on the international map. The day following Spotify's IPO, the Swedish investor visited the CNBC studio on the trading floor of the stock exchange.

The hosts asked him about the threat from Apple Music in the US market. Pär-Jörgen waved it off, saying that Apple remained strong within its own ecosystem, but weak outside of the world of the iPhone.

"It's been part of the Spotify strategy from the outset to be pervasive and work on all kinds of devices. With Apple's market share of about 20 percent, that naturally limits their reach," he said.

A few months later, both Northzone and another early Swedish venture investor, Creandum, had sold most of their shares in Spotify. In all, they had made more than $2.5 billion on the company.

The former Stardoll CEO Mattias Miksche, who hired Daniel Ek when Spotify was nothing but an idea, was praised for his part in the company's success. Early on, he had identified several of the young talents who would later build one of Sweden's biggest companies.

"Big shout out to you Mattias," the Swedish entrepreneur Alan Mamedi wrote on Twitter. Mattias Miksche answered him with a heart emoji.

By the end of Spotify's first day of trading, Daniel Ek's net worth was more than $2 billion. He wasn't the only shareholder with a reason to celebrate. The early investor Felix Hagnö, the ingenious coder Ludvig Strigeus, and hedge fund magnate Robert Citrone had all made hundreds of millions of dollars.

LIKE A ROLLING STONE

One hot-button issue ahead of Spotify's IPO had been how artists would be compensated if and when the labels sold their shares. The major labels owned more than 11 percent of the company, with Sony accounting for more than half of that portion. The generous stock option package Sony had been awarded ahead of Spotify's US launch had paid off handsomely.

When the first day of trading ended, the labels owned shares collectively worth around $3 billion. In a move some thought would distance the label from Spotify, Sony quickly sold around half of its stake. The label then promised to share the money with artists and partner labels regardless of what they owed in unrecouped advances. The largest label, Universal, appeared to keep their shares.

Warner, meanwhile, would gradually sell all of its stock for around half a billion dollars. Of that, artists received nearly $300 million after taxes, having had only $12 million deducted to account for unrecouped advances. The major labels' massive profits from Spotify shares were redistributed more fairly than many skeptics had feared.

ALL THE STARS

About a third of Spotify's now four thousand employees worked in Sweden, where the company had new headquarters. The newly constructed building, covered in copper-colored panels, spanned eight floors on Regeringsgatan in central Stockholm.

A few months after the IPO, Spotify invited members of the Swedish press to an "open house," to have a look around and meet some of the company's executives.

The lavish interiors included rooms for karaoke, pinball, ping pong, and even arts and crafts. It also featured a stage for presentations and performances, as well as a state-of-the-art music studio. Its sprawling roof terrace offered a view of the whole city; from the downtown skyscrapers to church spires in the Old Town and islands far out in the Stockholm archipelago. In the foreground was the Royal Palace and the island of Skeppsholmen, where Daniel Ek had taken countless walks to mull over difficult decisions with Martin Lorentzon and his top-level managers.

The gray, concrete high rises in Rågsved, where Spotify was given its name, were out of view. But looking northeast, the guests traced the journey from a small startup to a global company. Spotify's first offices—on Riddargatan, Humlegårdsgatan, and Birger Jarlsgatan 6—were all located in the upscale area of Östermalm. Looking north, they could see the spire from Johannes church in central Stockholm. Right behind it was Jarla House, where Spotify had matured and become the world's largest music-streaming service.

A few floors down, on the main stage, Daniel welcomed the visiting journalists. He sat down on a bar stool next to a delegation of his top directors and declared this an opportunity for a presentation followed by open questions. The few dozen journalists saw the moment as a shift for the notoriously secretive company; Daniel was said to dread press events, and rarely seemed satisfied with the published articles.

"We've talked about increasing the transparency within the company and for me, this is a step in that direction," the Spotify founder said.

His fluent Swedish bore a faint flavor of American corporate speak. The Spotify press department joked that the company's official language was "Swenglish," a peculiar mixture of Swedish with English phrases and syntax mixed in.

Some in the Swedish business world would argue that Spotify was in fact no longer a Swedish company. Its parent company was based in Luxembourg, Daniel's holding companies in Malta and Cyprus, and Spotify's New

York offices had recently outgrown the Stockholm headquarters in terms of headcount. And the company's stock was trading on Wall Street.

"In general terms, I don't find that very much has changed since the listing," Daniel said.

He explained that Spotify's IPO was the only viable alternative to selling the company. The early investors had to get their final payout.

"Ten years after launching, we felt it was time to honor that obligation," he said.

The soft-spoken Swede had caused another stir within his industry. A new policy, introduced a few months prior, had stated that music with lyrics containing hate speech did not belong on Spotify's curated and influential playlists. The policy also covered how artists conducted themselves outside of the studio.

Tracks by the R&B star R. Kelly, who had long been accused of sexual misconduct, were no longer being included in playlists like Discover Weekly. Another banished artist was XXXTentacion, who had been accused of assault, and Tay-K, a seventeen-year-old rapper from Texas who stood accused of two murders. It was not an issue of outright censorship. Their music could still be found in the Spotify catalogue.

To much of the hip-hop world, the policy made Daniel Ek appear culturally tone deaf. The label executive Anthony Tiffith—known within the industry as "Top"—would call the Swedish CEO and threaten to have his artists, among them the popular Compton rapper Kendrick Lamar, boycott Spotify.

The feud created fault lines between some of Spotify's executives. Troy Carter, its global head of creator services, an African American who had been molded by hip-hop culture, felt ready to leave the company if they didn't rescind the new rules. He was challenged by Spotify's public policy director, Jonathan Prince, a white Georgetown grad who had once worked at the State Department under Barack Obama.

A few days after the flare up, Daniel Ek dropped the part of the new policy that regulated conduct and artist behavior. One of XXXTentacion's songs made a comeback on the playlist Rap Caviar. But Spotify stuck to its decision not to promote music that contained hate speech.

When the issue came up at the press briefing in Stockholm, Daniel questioned whether he was the right person to decide what might be offensive to African Americans or other groups. He mentioned that Spotify had begun consulting organizations like the Southern Poverty Law Center, a US nonprofit known for its human rights work.

"My nirvana would be to take a concept that exists in Sweden, more like an ombudsman, and have an ethics board, and distribute the decision making so it's not just Spotify, but actually a broader group," the CEO said, adding that the issue was high on his agenda.

THE A TEAM

The conflict-averse Daniel Ek was now both a Wall Street CEO and one of the most powerful people in the music world. Criticism and controversy followed his every decision. The same applied internally, within a company that had once been dominated by engineers and small enough to fit in an apartment on Riddargatan.

As CEO, Daniel had been forced to evolve with his company. Conflicts came with the territory, particularly in a fast-growing, culturally impactful startup like the one he had co-founded. A number of sources interviewed for this book would describe how Daniel had a hard time knowing how to handle dustups among his lieutenants. Nearly a decade after Spotify started making big-name hires, many continued to recount how Daniel would let conflicts fester until the warring parties found their own solution. It was, still, a kind of natural selection in a corporate setting.

"The atmosphere is toxic at times. Daniel tends to give people overlapping responsibilities, then he lets them fight over who gets to do the work," as one person would recall.

Employees further down the hierarchy would sometimes post scathing reviews of Spotify on the employment portal Glassdoor.

"No one is actually accountable for anything because virtually all decisions must take place though a bewildering process of group consensus, where people who are ignorant of the topic at hand somehow have just as much of a say as the experts," one former employee at the New York office would post in November of 2019.

A handful of executives would depart Spotify following the IPO, among them Troy Carter, Jonathan Prince, Chief Marketing Officer Seth Farbman, and the long-serving communications director Angela Watts.

Yet many of the old guard remained at the company. Three of them—the chief R&D officer, Gustav Söderström; the head of premium, Alex Norström; and the HR boss, Katarina Berg—were present for the "open house" at the Stockholm headquarters that morning in August 2018. The host of the event was Dustee Jenkins, the company's new head of communications. She had roots in Texas and had previously worked for the retail giant Target, and for a Republican congresswoman in Washington, DC.

The number of female executives at Spotify had grown over the past few years. The global head of markets, Cecilia Qvist, was in attendance, as was the managing director for the Nordics, Jenny Hermanson.

Their message to the journalists questioning the company's constant losses was the same as it had always been: Spotify would keep burning cash in order to grow and retain its lead over Apple, Amazon, and Google's recently launched service, YouTube Music.

Spotify's free service had gone from berated to tolerated within the music industry, but relations were still tense. Touting Spotify's ability to convert users from free to paid, Gustav Söderström repeated the company mantra: "The more you play, the more you pay."

Then he did something that Daniel would normally avoid: Söderström mentioned several rivals by name.

"There's a competitor in the US called Pandora, which has its own challenges. You can't put YouTube Music in your pocket. As soon as the screen shuts down, it stops playing the music if you're a free user. Apple Music has no free tier whatsoever."

THE NOD

Three months after Spotify's "open house," Daniel Ek had his people set up a meeting that would kickstart the company's push into podcasting.

It was late November, the week of Thanksgiving, and two American entrepreneurs had rearranged their holiday plans to fly to Stockholm. The Swedish CEO began by showing the founders of the Brooklyn-based podcasting startup Gimlet Media around the new headquarters.

The Gimlet founders, Matt Lieber and Alex Blumberg, were two middle-aged finance and radio veterans. They were welcomed by Daniel—dressed casually in sneakers, jeans, and a black t-shirt—and shown into his office for an open conversation about Gimlet's business.

Lieber and Blumberg told him about the company, which had been founded in 2014 and had since built a catalogue of popular, expertly produced podcasts such as *StartUp*, *ReplyAll*, and *The Nod*. Gimlet had built a strong brand but was struggling with its finances and pressure from shareholders to drive up its valuation. The founders hoped that Daniel might be able to solve their problems.

Toward the end of the two hours, Daniel asked a question that caught his American counterparts off-guard.

"I just have one more question for you," he said. "What would you do if I gave you a billion dollars?"

The Gimlet founders were stunned, as they would recall in an episode of *StartUp*. They struggled to come up with strong ideas on the spot. Their boldest proposition, put forth by Alex Blumberg, was to get into the news industry and build an organization like the *New York Times*, but for audio.

Daniel clarified what he meant by the question.

"I want you to start thinking at that scale," Daniel said. "Because that's the scale that we play at."

A few months later, Daniel Ek announced the $230 million acquisition of Gimlet. It marked the beginning of an aggressive push into the US podcasting market, in which Spotify would spend a total of $600 million over the course of a year.

The strategy, laid out by Daniel in an open letter, was to make Spotify an "audio first" platform while competitors such as Apple and Amazon were expanding rapidly into video.

In 2019, Spotify would acquire the digital podcasting platform Anchor, the true-crime production studio Parcast, and, in February 2020, the ESPN veteran Bill Simmons' lauded sports and entertainment network, The Ringer.

EXIT

With the IPO fading from memory, Barry McCarthy's time at Spotify had begun to wind down. Toward the end of his tenure, in late 2019, the normally outspoken CFO started making statements that were even more bold than usual.

Now in his mid-sixties, Barry used his final months to talk up Spotify's underperforming share price and speak freely about his industry's dynamics. He revealed that Spotify aimed to double its share of ad revenues from ten to twenty percent. He also praised a beta version of a forthcoming streaming service being built by ByteDance, the parent company of the wildly successful social network TikTok. In a surprising admission, he said he had seen screenshots of the app ahead of Spotify's launch in India.

Barry presided over seven public quarterly reports as CFO. When the seasoned executive eventually stepped down in early 2020, Daniel Ek sounded fully comfortable on conference calls with Wall Street analysts. In fact, he sounded as calm and collected as the Netflix veteran who had schooled him.

THE HOUSE THAT
DANIEL BUILT

THE FIFTH EDITION OF BRILLIANT Minds was the most star-studded to date. On the first day, press photographers captured Daniel Ek, wearing a bomber jacket and sneakers, walking up the street toward the back entrance of Stockholm's Grand Hotel. It was June 2019, and the Spotify founder was now thirty-six years old, whipped into shape from all the hours at the gym, and nearly $3 billion richer than when he founded his company in a small office just a few blocks away.

A few paces ahead of him was Shakil Khan, the man who had once made Daniel his protégé. Despite any turbulence in his private life, Shak had remained one of Daniel's true friends. The Brit had shown him the glamorous world beyond Sweden at a time when Spotify's servers still hummed in an overheated closet. He had served as the trusted adviser who saw early potential in the Swede, becoming rich in the process. Shak's many years of air travel, business meetings, and partying had culminated in a heart attack two years prior. He had now recovered and was living a healthier life.

Daniel, too, had paid a price for his success. He was living under protected identity, a service that Swedish authorities offer to people subjected

Daniel Ek arrives at Brilliant Minds in June of 2019.
Ahead of him to the left is his friend Shakil Khan. *(Alex Ljungdahl / EXP / TT)*

to personal threats. A year had now passed since Spotify's much-publicized listing in New York. The share price had gone up during the first few months, only to fall back down as the stock markets began a general slide. Eventually, Spotify was forced to start buying back its own stock to stabilize the price. Since then, Daniel had delivered the company's first-ever profitable quarter. On any given day, Spotify's market value remained well above $20 billion, a level that had once been unthinkable.

Yet Spotify executives remained frustrated with their greatest competitor. A few months prior to Brilliant Minds, Daniel had initiated his first public campaign against Apple. He and the Spotify management had called out how the tech giant tilted the playing field to disadvantage smaller rivals. In February, they had filed a formal antitrust complaint against Apple with the European Commission in Brussels, and launched a campaign website called timetoplayfair.com.

Now, nine years after his shadowboxing with Steve Jobs, Daniel finally dared to call the Apple founder out by name.

"It's fairly widely known that Steve Jobs initially wanted only Apple content on the App Store," he said during a conference in Berlin.

Speaking to several heavyweights in European politics, Spotify's co-founder outlined his version of how the app economy came to be.

"What initially felt like a mutually beneficial partnership increasingly felt very one-sided. And it's now become completely unsustainable," he said.

Daniel Ek had unquestionably become a public figure. He nodded confidently and clasped hands with passersby before he and Shak vanished through the heavily guarded entrance, and out of the journalists' reach. A few hours later, the event's CEO, Natalia Brzezinski, would interview Barack Obama on stage. The former president was the reason security was extra heavy on this overcast Thursday afternoon.

The aim of Brilliant Minds—which was now financially supported by influential Swedish business families like the Stenbecks, Wallenbergs, and Olssons—had always been to create an environment similar to the World Economic Forum in Davos, but for people within tech and the creative industries. Yet unlike Davos, Brilliant Minds was now completely shut off to the media. Curious reporters had to rummage through Instagram to find shaky mobile footage capturing how the Swedish teenager and climate activist Greta Thunberg lambasted the participants for not taking global warming more seriously. A few hours later, the Wallenberg cousins hosted an exclusive dinner in their stately home on the royal island of Djurgården in central Stockholm.

The distinguished guest list led to extensive coverage in the Swedish press. The tabloid *Expressen* held a live video broadcast outside of the hotel entrance, catching glimpses of celebrities as they hopped into waiting cars. In-depth coverage was largely lacking. Several critics would turn against what they saw as a members-only club for the business elite. The contrarian columnist Johan Hakelius called the attendees "billionaire zombies."

Daniel Ek had revived a global industry and built Europe's greatest tech company. His work continued to inspire a generation of new entrepreneurs. Yet in his home country, the Spotify CEO was not a widely beloved businessman. His message, that millions of musicians should be able to make a living off of their work, had not taken hold. And his lifestyle often went against the grain of core Swedish values of humility and modesty. In Sweden, the ideal entrepreneur was still IKEA's late founder Ingvar Kamprad, famous for his "penny saved, penny earned" mentality.

THE SUBURBS

On the same day that Daniel and his friend Shak attended Brilliant Minds, Swedish newspapers were full of reports about the Spotify founder's new three-story house in Djursholm, the exclusive suburb where his wife had grown up. Recently, Daniel had applied to have the 430 square-meter villa, erected in the late 1800s, torn to the ground. Just before he arrived at Grand Hotel, word had gotten out that local authorities had rejected the application.

Daniel and Sofia had purchased the house a few months after Spotify was listed on the stock exchange. The price tag of more than $7 million made it one of Sweden's most expensive residential real-estate deals of 2018. Their arrival in Djursholm—an area comparable to the wealthy parts of Connecticut, outside New York City—would place the young couple right alongside Sweden's old-money elite. Several of the Swedish tech world's self-made billionaires would follow suit.

The house, located on a hill near the water, was crowned with a tower room offering a view in all directions over northern Stockholm. From there, Daniel and Sofia would be able to overlook the golf club to the north and the marina to the east. Looking west, beyond the Djursholm castle, was the area where Sofia grew up. The couple's daughters would go to school with the children of some of Sweden's most powerful families, just like Sofia once had. But unlike their mother, the Ek children would belong to one of Djursholm's wealthiest families.

News of the Eks' new home was soon reported in the Swedish press.

"When I saw the headlines, my first thought was that Sofia was avenging her time in high school," as one person would recall. "To truly do that, you have to be in the same environment, and play by the same rules."

Shortly after the deed was signed, Daniel and Sofia hired architects and builders to start renovations. Scaffolding was erected around the grand old building, but soon the work had ceased. Gossip intensified when Daniel and Sofia, in early 2019, bought an adjacent house for another $2 million. Would Daniel Ek, like Mark Zuckerberg in Palo Alto, start to buy up all of the adjoining properties?

Months later, the neighbors learned that unexpected flaws and water damage had convinced the Eks that they may as well demolish what locals saw as a landmark building. What now ensued was an age-old conflict between old and new money—or in this case, between millionaires and billionaires—a story pounced upon by the news media.

Many of Djursholm's residents felt strongly about preserving the area's character. The neighborhood had sprung up in the late 19th century, as academics, public-sector officials, and artists moved out of the city and into houses designed by some of Sweden's and Europe's most prominent architects. The suburb had gradually become the domain of the ruling class, but there had still been room for middle-class families, such as Sofia Ek's, to purchase a small home and become part of the community. The more people who moved in and transformed villas to modern mansions, the more homogenous Djursholm would become. Moreover, its cultural heritage would be lost.

Others looked at it from Daniel Ek's perspective. They argued that, unlike other wildly successful entrepreneurs like the Skype co-founder Niklas Zennström and IKEA's Ingvar Kamprad, Daniel Ek should be praised for choosing to remain in Sweden instead of moving abroad. He was still paying local taxes and contributing to the community. It was only fair that he do whatever he pleased with his new home.

The Spotify founder enlisted a small army of experts who argued that the house could be torn down while abiding by local building regulations. His consultants stated that the house had been erected in what was termed an "American" style in 1893, but later renovated with plenty of Art Deco details. By now, they said, the house was an architectural patchwork that had lost its cultural value. Yet the local politicians were not convinced.

"This is a landmark," said Claes Breitholtz, chairman of the local housing board, which struck down the application. "It is big and magnificent and has once been an extremely beautiful house."

Various publications would cover Daniel's proposed demolition. Stockholm residents would discuss it by the metaphorical water cooler, which in Sweden was more likely to be the coffee machine.

The villa in Djursholm wasn't Daniel's only headache. He was also looking to upgrade his summer house in the Stockholm archipelago. Among other things, he wanted to erect a tall, wooden fence to shield the property from onlookers. But that application was also rejected.

"A wooden fence has a restraining and privatizing effect," the local authority stated in its rejection letter.

On a metaphysical level, Daniel was now clashing with two core Swedish institutions: the "Jante law," a norm that promoted humility and discouraged boastfulness, and an actual law called "Allemansrätten," or the "right of public access," a wide-ranging and unique set of rights that let Swedes roam freely in nature. The latter made a fence shielding Daniel's property from outside view legally questionable.

Famously protective of their private lives, neither Daniel nor Sofia commented on the matter in the press. But Daniel had appealed the decision to stop the demolition. He eventually won that battle and in June 2020, builders started tearing down the house.

CHERRY PIE

While Daniel Ek's dream house was being razed, his business looked more solid than ever. When the American edition of this book was completed in the summer of 2020, nearly three hundred million people listened to Spotify every month. Over half of them did so for free, but the rest were paid subscribers.

At the negotiating table, the record labels often played the role of antagonists, but they knew that Spotify had served their industry well—by returning it to growth and lowering the cost of both distribution and marketing. Anyone looking for proof could check the labels' own finances.

In June 2020, Warner Music went public in the US. After the first week of trading, its valuation had risen to $16 billion, nearly five times what the company had been valued at in 2012. Just like Universal and Sony Music, Warner had seen its business flourish thanks to an idea in the mind of a twenty-two-year-old Swede.

There were plenty of other beneficiaries. Consumers across the globe clearly favored streaming, even if it meant paying around ten dollars a month. Thousands of employees and investors, from Shenzhen in China to Menlo Park, had become rich off of Daniel Ek's company. Every employee who spent significant time with Spotify had received stock options which, if they stayed for at least a few years, meant that they could buy a house or begin to invest in a startup of their own. Yet artists were, by and large, still unconvinced and unhappy with their share of the spoils.

In 2019, Spotify and several other streaming services had appealed a decision by the US Copyright Royalty Board to raise songwriters' payouts from streaming gradually, over the next handful of years. The appeal immediately drew criticism from the music community.

"Jeff Bezos is probably the world's richest man and Daniel Ek is on his way. They have created fantastic products, so why not support yet another great creation: songwriting," Kenny MacPherson, founder of the independent company Big Deal Music, told the press.

Apple—the only big streaming provider that did not appeal the decision—once again seized the chance to side with creators.

"Underneath the rhetoric, Spotify's aim is to make more money off others' work," Apple wrote in a statement, which partly served as a response to Spotify's antitrust complaint in Brussels.

"And it's not just the App Store that they're trying to squeeze—it's also artists, musicians, and songwriters."

FAKE ID

Another point of contention was the debate over fake or manipulated streams, a practice that diverted payouts from honest participants to those trying to game the system. The problem ranged from artists encouraging fans to stream tracks on repeat without listening, to people paying bot farms to stream music and help songs climb the Spotify charts.

One example surfaced in January 2020, when the pop star Justin Bieber allegedly republished a fan post on Instagram that detailed how to boost his new single, "Yummy."

"Create a playlist with Yummy on repeat and stream it. Don't mute it! Play it at low volume, let it play while you sleep," the post read.

The chatter about manipulated streams intensified, especially in Sweden. When a source in the music industry started claiming that the problem could be costing hundreds of millions of dollars per year, Spotify finally put its foot down.

"There is a lot of rumor and speculation out there," Spotify's Nordic director Jenny Hermanson told *Dagens industri*.

She then claimed that less than one percent of Spotify's streams had been manipulated during the fourth quarter of 2019.

By that time, Spotify was working actively to detect fraudulent behavior, weeding out tracks that had been manipulated and halting royalty payouts where they suspected cheating.

They also pursued the issue in court, such as when they countersued Sosa Entertainment in a legal battle over what Spotify described as a scheme involving "hundreds of millions of fraudulent streams."

LOVE IS AN OPEN DOOR

By 2020, Daniel Ek had mastered the art of answering questions about Spotify's podcast investments and user engagement. When he yielded to his new CFO—the jovial Paul Vogel, the former head of investor relations—it was more out of politeness than any uncertainty over the financials. He was also giving more individual interviews to news outlets.

In May, Daniel sat down for a lengthy interview with Emily Chang of Bloomberg TV. Speaking over video link, in a black t-shirt and a pair of white AirPods, Daniel gave one of his most candid media appearances to date. He touched on topics ranging from the ongoing pandemic to the kids' playlist "Frozen and Trolls," which he claimed to know all the lyrics to.

The conversation also covered many of the highlights of Spotify's fourteen-year history, from streaming pioneer to becoming the music industry's most important source of revenue. Its payouts since launch now totaled $16.5 billion.

Chang also delved into the thorny issue of Spotify's antitrust complaint against Apple. Daniel dug in, prefacing his answer by saying that the process was ongoing and that many details remained secret.

"Obviously, long term, we do expect Apple to open up," he said, speaking freely about his rival.

Soon, the European Commission would open a formal antitrust investigation into the rules of the App Store. During the interview, Daniel was able to list a number of encouraging signs, such as Apple allowing Spotify to use Siri for voice support and, more recently, to build products for Apple TV and the Apple Watch. Spotify would later be bolstered in their claims as the maker of *Fortnite*, Epic Games, rebelled against the payment terms in the App Store, launching their own legal fight with Apple.

"It's moving in the right direction, but we still have many many steps to go before we consider this an open and fair platform," Daniel said during the interview.

The conversation then turned to a touchy topic: Spotify's efforts in the video space. The reporting on Daniel's ambitious TV project that was scrapped in 2014 had already been published in an early Swedish edition of this book. An excerpt had followed in the US trade publication *Variety*.

"In all honesty, Emily, we experimented a lot when it came to video a few years ago. I think at the time it was less clear how the landscape of video would play out. You know, are we going to see long-form content, would we see short-form content like YouTube, or would we see something in between, and what would that look like?"

He then attempted to summarize the lessons learned from the secretive Magneto project.

"We pursued that opportunity, learned a bit. What we really ended up with was realizing that our key strategy is really around owning background moments, around owning, really, audio. It actually informed us, more than anything else, about the strategy on doubling down on audio."

In hindsight, Daniel seemed to view the tens of millions of dollars squandered as a small price to pay.

"I'm very happy with that today, when you look at a lot of these other media companies that have to invest billions of dollars in order to even be competitive with the likes of Netflix or YouTube."

Chang then asked if the Spotify CEO would consider selling his company, perhaps to Netflix? Daniel said no, adding that he was excited to be standing at the crossroads of an enormous consumer shift.

"The journey that Spotify is on is not just about entertaining people, it's about informing and educating them as well."

SHAPESHIFTER

In 2020, Daniel Ek seemed better prepared for his mission than ever before. He continued to close the gap between what he had always been comfortable doing—making bold bets, recruiting team members, recognizing when he needed to pragmatically cede to the record labels—and what he had to do to survive as CEO: navigate spats with the artist community, fire underperforming lieutenants, and communicate clearly and powerfully in interviews and conference calls.

Perhaps Daniel's greatest professional achievement was that he never stopped learning from the people he surrounded himself with. He had come to embody the traits of countless associates and former coworkers.

Martin Lorentzon had taught him how to keep the faith and stay the course; his friend Shakil Khan how to navigate social situations. His many lawyers and negotiators had helped him weed his way through the music industry, while Mark Zuckerberg had shown him how to think big and bold.

Daniel had come further than he had ever dreamed. He was now competing with some of the world's largest companies, which also meant he could not rest on his laurels.

Spotify remained vulnerable in many areas. YouTube Music offered a far superior search function, and a wide catalogue of music videos. Apple was growing in many directions, and would by the fall provoke Spotify by bundling their music offering with other services such as video, cloud storage and gaming.

For a time, it looked as though companies like Amazon might keep lowering the price of streamed music. A number of Spotify's challengers ran profits deep enough to keep subsidizing a loss-making music service. But with Spotify expanding into exclusive podcast content, it looked more likely that the company would raise its prices, at least in wealthier markets. The record labels expected as much, and Warner Music even mentioned it in their filing to go public in the spring of 2020.

Apple remained Spotify's archrival, as had been the case when Steve Jobs ruled digital music through iTunes. Yet Daniel was not only up against traditional streaming providers. The interactive video and music app Tik-Tok—used by young people to create and share short-form videos, often incorporating music—posted a reported $3 billion profit for 2019. That was the year its users made the rapper Lil Nas X's song "Old Town Road" go viral, transforming a meme into an international hit. The country-inspired rap track would later top the Billboard singles chart longer than any other song to date.

Many had begun to wonder what would happen if TikTok were to sign artists directly. It was not hard to imagine how a social media app with billions of users, which had already made huge strides in artificial intelligence, could start competing for talent with the labels, and challenge companies like Spotify, Apple, and Amazon on distribution.

"If the streaming services don't find a way to pivot and expand what they are, they'll be in trouble," as one industry veteran put it in early summer 2020.

Despite Spotify's early partnership with Facebook, Daniel had never fully capitalized on basic social features such as likes, comments, and shares. But he hadn't let go of the idea. Apple Music seemed in even worse shape, having let its original "Connect" feature fizzle out.

"They need to build tools for the artists to communicate with the fans directly if they're ever going to make any money. If you don't do that, you'll have nothing unique, and you'll go the way of iTunes," the industry veteran said.

In India, the challenge from TikTok's parent company, ByteDance, had already arrived. Its new streaming service, Resso, had a freemium business model and strong social features. The labels and publishers were all on-board, with the notable exception of Universal Music—perhaps because Tencent, a ByteDance competitor and Spotify partner, now held a 10 percent stake in Universal. New alliances were emerging in Asia, where a majority of the world's music consumers lived.

Chinese tech companies were under pressure. In the summer of 2020, the Indian government banned TikTok and fifty-eight other Chinese apps from operating in the country following a border dispute and concerns over security and privacy. In early August, as this book was being completed, President Donald Trump threatened to ban TikTok in the US, leading Microsoft and other tech giants into talks to acquire or invest in the social network's US operations.

Spotify's ownership ties to Tencent appeared more important than ever. Tencent Music, which was now trading on the New York Stock Exchange, had historically earned most of its revenue from interactive apps. One example was WeSing, a virtual karaoke service where users could donate money to artists doing live streams or pay influencers to sing a song just for them. Social interactions could prove key to engaging young listeners in countries like South Africa and Japan, and eventually in South Korea, where Spotify had yet to enter.

Spotify had passed on an indicative offer to be acquired by Tencent, yet a merger between the two remained a possibility. The tectonic plates of the music world were shifting. For Daniel, it was all about positioning Spotify before the next big rumble.

POD SAVE AMERICA

In mid-May 2020, a few weeks after his interview with Bloomberg TV, Daniel Ek took Spotify's podcast strategy to a new level, signing one of the most popular titles in the US.

The deal, reportedly worth more than $100 million, meant that his streaming service would soon become the only place listeners could find the *Joe Rogan Experience*, which had previously built a massive following on YouTube. Perhaps most famously, Joe Rogan had hosted Tesla CEO Elon Musk, who smoked marijuana live on air to the ire of some of his shareholders.

Following the announcement, Spotify's stock price shot up by eight percent on the New York Stock Exchange, bringing its market value to well over $30 billion. The next day, the share price rose another eight percent, and Spotify climbed past the $35 billion mark.

The same sequence would soon repeat itself. In June, Spotify signed exclusive podcasting deals with both Kim Kardashian West and DC Comics, with its stellar roster of superheroes like Batman and Wonder Woman. Spotify's stock climbed to new heights. By early July, the company was worth over $50 billion, a figure that had doubled in the space of a few months.

Spotify's transition into a media company—a kind of MTV for the digital age, the type of service Jimmy Iovine had once envisioned—was accelerating. And, finally, Wall Street was rewarding them for it. In the nascent podcasting world, there was still time for Spotify to form a Netflix-style service for podcasts, signing exclusive titles and producing their own.

Yet not everyone was convinced. Some stock analysts objected that Spotify was paying a lot of money for companies and content that would do little to improve their bottom line. In addition, the deal with Joe Rogan drew the kind of criticism from artists that had become a permanent fixture for Daniel.

"Spotify makes its name and builds its brand off music, which allows them to buy and license content from other creators," the rapper Phonte wrote on Twitter. "Meanwhile, the musicians who built the platform get paid micropennies."

In conference calls, Daniel defended his new strategy. A catalogue of podcasts within sports, true crime, and entertainment would help extend the amount of time users spent within the app. That would, in turn, lead to more paid subscribers, which would earn Spotify and the music industry more money. Embedding ads in an expanding catalogue of podcasts could also help Spotify grow their advertising revenues.

Apple and Amazon also intensified their work in podcasting, setting aside budgets to spend on original programming.

During its first two years as a public company, Spotify reported four profitable quarters. Daniel was eager to point out that the margins were now high enough that the company did not need further support from outside investors.

"We can now state that the business model works," he told the *Wall Street Journal* after one such profitable quarter.

Yet for the full year 2020, Spotify expected to post losses of around $200 million, largely due to money being spent on acquisitions in the podcast space. Daniel had returned to his strategy of putting growth over short-term profits.

DOGGFATHER

Daniel Ek was now gradually warming up to his public role.

As the COVID-19 pandemic spread through Sweden in the spring of 2020, he and Martin Lorentzon spent over a million dollars of their own money on providing testing to healthcare workers. Early on, Ek had asked Spotify's employees to work from home, an option they would retain until the end of the year.

"We all have an obligation to delay the spread of the virus and thus ease the expected burden on our healthcare system," Daniel wrote in a rare Swedish language tweet.

"I hope other companies in Sweden will follow suit," he added.

They soon did.

Daniel Ek was carefully looking after his own health. He had been known to limit his eating to between noon and 4 p.m. every day. Intermittent fasting was perhaps something he had picked up from his friend Moha Bensofia, whose regimen of "bio-hacking" also included weightlifting and personal therapy.

By 2020 Daniel was also mentoring up-and-coming entrepreneurs, particularly in the healthcare field, offering advice ranging from how to make it as a CEO to how to deal with burnout. The Spotify founder was also making private investments in the sector, such as paying around 18 million dollars for a small stake in Kry, Sweden's foremost digital healthcare provider, and bankrolling a secretive startup dedicated to preventative, AI-driven healthcare.

In late September of 2020, as this book was being typeset, Daniel raised the bar again by declaring that he was committing one billion euros ($1.2 billion), or around a third of his wealth, to invest in European start-ups or, as he put it, "European moonshots." The announcement was followed by a tweet indicating the involvement of Shakil Khan. It was picked up by Shak, who added: "I guess it's time to come out of retirement then."

A few days later, Daniel and Spotify board member Cristina Stenbeck invested in Northvolt as part of a $600 million equity raise to fund the construction of its gigafactories. The Swedish battery company had been started by Peter Carlsson, a Swede who had previously worked with Elon Musk at Tesla.

"Glad to be a small part of the journey and excited for Europe!" Daniel declared on Twitter.

THE FUTURE

Although music still engaged Daniel, the expansion into podcasting and long-form audio was perhaps the strategic matter at the forefront of his mind. Another was Spotify's responsibilities as a content platform.

In mid-2020, Daniel was thinking about how audio such as educational podcasts could make the world a better place. In an interview, he mentioned that Spotify was working to index and catalogue episodes to help people deepen their knowledge on a variety of subjects. Daniel called it a "knowledge graph" for audio-based learning. He was also readying an expansion into the market for audio books. Furthermore, recent patents indicated that Spotify was developing some sort of TikTok challenger, a karaoke function and technology for voice recognition and interaction.

Few questioned Daniel's ability as a technologist. But when it came to editorial decision making, he still appeared to be struggling. In September of 2020 he seemed confounded by an internal row at Spotify, with employ-ees reacting to what they described as transphobic content in some episodes of the Joe Rogan Experience. Despite media reports of the debate, Spotify's press department was slow to address the issue, including the fact that epi-sodes featuring controversial guests, such as the conspiracy theorist Alex Jones, were conspicuously absent from the platform.

The Spotify CEO was largely leaving daily operations to his executive team, of which he demanded more than ever before. He frequently asked why Spotify wasn't growing faster. Some executives felt that Daniel didn't credit them enough for their achievements. He was only thinking about the future.

How Daniel managed his team would define him going forward. His youth and unique experience suggested that he would remain in the chair for a long time to come.

Fourteen years after its founding, Spotify was still wrestling with a busi-ness built on low margins, and investors were still asking how Daniel might bring them up further.

Yet for him, the Spotify journey had barely begun. Streaming remained in its infancy, or in the second inning, as he liked to put it. As Daniel saw it, the battle over global audio consumption had already been decided. It was like a settled fact of future history. The rest of the world just needed to catch up.

ACKNOWLEDGMENTS

This book could not have been written without the help of dozens of people who have supported us over the past two years.

First and foremost we need to thank our many sources, speaking both on the record and anonymously. Many of you have gone against Spotify's corporate culture of secrecy, and taken personal risks, in order to help us get closer to the true story.

Thanks also to the many journalists—both Swedish and international—who have covered Spotify throughout the years. Many of you are included in the list of references and sources. We could not have put this together without your diligent work.

Thanks to our first publisher, Albert "Abbe" Bonnier of Albert Bonniers Förlag in Stockholm, who took a chance on us when this book was only an idea. Thanks also to the team at Bonnier Rights for helping us along the way and selling the book successfully to more than a dozen countries, including the United States.

The Spotify Play is the third edition of this book, and the first in English. It's been updated and improved with the help of several new sources. Kudos to them. Although the translation is our own, we owe a great degree of gratitude to our editor Keith Wallman at Diversion Books, and to our copyeditor Elisabeth Evan.

We need to thank our loved ones for putting up with us, and our bosses at *Dagens industri* and Swedish Public Radio for allowing us to pursue this project.

Lastly, we'd like to thank Daniel Ek and Martin Lorentzon for starting the company and giving us such a great story to cover.

REFERENCES
AND SOURCES

PROLOGUE

Three anonymous sources who heard Daniel Ek talk about Steve Jobs.

1. A SECRET IDEA

Interview with Mattias Miksche, former CEO of Stardoll. Stockholm, March 2018.
Interview with Andreas Ehn, former CTO at Spotify. Stockholm, July 2018.
Six anonymous sources who were close to Daniel Ek and Martin Lorentzon during this period.
Interviews with five sources who worked at Tradedoubler in 2006, including the former CEO,
 Martin Henricson.
Leijonhufvud, J. "Dockor ett riktigt klipp" *Svenska Dagbladet.* August 8, 2006.
Gripenberg, P. and H. Rosén (2013) "Historien om Spotify—så erövrades musikvärlden" E-singel,
 Dagens Nyheter.
"Sommar i P1. Daniel Ek." *Swedish Radio P1,* July 12, 2012.
Date for establishing Rosello Company Limited, Enzymix Systems Limited, and Instructus Limited.
 Open Corporates, 2018.
"Sommar i P1. Martin Lorentzon." *Swedish Radio P1.* August 1, 2020.

2. THE ENGINEERS

Friman, C. "Den osynlige." *Filter,* June 8, 2011.
Company documents from the spring of 2007. Luxembourg Business Registers.
Interview with Andreas Ehn, former CTO at Spotify. Stockholm, July 2018.
Interview with Fredrik Niemelä, former CPO at Spotify. Phone conversation, August 2018.
Interview with Per Sundin, manager of Universal Music's Nordic division. Stockholm, April 2018.
Interview with Pär-Jörgen Pärson, partner at Northzone. Stockholm, April 2018.
Three anonymous sources about the period at Riddargatan.
"Sommar i P1. Martin Lorentzon." *Swedish Radio P1.* August 1, 2020.

3. RÅGSVED

Tv4 Morning News (2013). Spotifygrundaren Daniel Ek om musiken, pengarna och idéerna.
 YouTube, January 2014.
"Daniel Ek från Spotify," parts 1/4 and 2/4. *YouTube,* January 2010.
The Swedish Tax Authority. Information about Daniel Ek's home address.
"Sommar i P1. Daniel Ek." *Swedish Radio P1,* 12 July 2012.
Interview with Gert Sävkranz, Daniel Ek's computer science teacher in high school. Rågsved,
 September 2018.

Interview with Micke Johansson, former recreation leader at the youth center in Rågsved. Bandhagen, October 2018.

Five anonymous sources from the time at Rågsvedsskolan and IT-Gymnasiet.

"Spotify's Daniel Ek on the state of streaming, tenacity, transparency, competition, what's next." *YouTube*, September 2015.

Gripenberg, P. and H. Rosén (2013) "Historien om Spotify—så erövrades musikvärlden." E-singel, *Dagens Nyheter*.

4. PARTY LIKE IT'S 1999

Interview with Pär-Jörgen Pärson, former CEO of Cell Ventures. Stockholm, April 2018.

Three anonymous sources about the period at Tradedoubler.

Lundell, S. "Miljonärer på internet-idé." *Dagens industri*, November 9, 2005.

"Daniel Ek from Spotify, part 3/4." *YouTube*, Jan 2010.

Elofsson, J. "It-branschens Greta Garbo." *Affärsvärlden*, March 2, 2014.

Interview with Edgar Bronfman Jr., former vice chairman of Universal Vivendi. Phone conversation, July 2020.

Interview with Thomas Hesse, former President, Global Digital Business and US Sales/Distribution, Sony Music. Phone conversation, October 2018.

"Apple Music Event 2003—iTunes Music Store Introduction." *YouTube*, November 2007.

"Apple Special Music Event 2003—Steve iChats With Artists." *YouTube*, April 2006.

5. BETTER THAN PIRACY

Interview with Fred Davis, music industry lawyer. Phone conversation, June 2018.

Interview with Rob Wells, former digital director at Universal Music Group International. Phone conversation, June 2018.

Cassel, F. "Inside the dusty brains of the first backer of Spotify—looking at how we were right and wrong about Spotify in 2007." *Creandum's company blog*, March 15, 2018.

Six anonymous sources about Daniel Ek's negotiations with the record companies, the state of the record industry, Spotify's financing, and the period in the Riddargatan office.

One anonymous source about Shakil Khan's past.

"The Om Show. Ep. 1 — Shakil Khan." *SoundCloud*, May 2017.

Interview with Eric Wahlforss, one of SoundCloud's founders. Stockholm, June 2018.

Holmström, L. "Hej! 2007 Live Updates." *Citizen Media Watch*, April 21, 2007.

"Sommar i P1. Daniel Ek." *Swedish Radio P1*, July 12, 2012.

6. "WEALTH-TYPE MONEY"

Interview with Joe Cohen, former CEO at Seatwave. Phone conversation, April 2018.

Interview with Pär-Jörgen Pärson, partner at Northzone. Stockholm, April 2018.

Three anonymous sources on Spotify's financial situation.

Four anonymous sources on Spotify's negotiations with Warner and Universal.

Carlsson, S. "Accel-toppen: 'Folk trodde att Avito-grundarna var ett skämt." *Dagens industri*, June 8, 2017.

Interview with Per Sundin, former head of Sony BMG Sweden, later Nordic head of Universal Music. Stockholm, June 2018.

Company documents filed in the spring 2008. Luxembourg Business Registers.

"The Om Show. Ep. 1—Shakil Khan." *SoundCloud*, May 2017.

7. ALL MUSIC FOR FREE

Leijonhufvud, J. "Svenskar Apples mardröm." *Dagens Nyheter*, October 30, 2008.

Interview with Ola Sars, co-founder of Pacemaker. Stockholm, June 2018.
Interview with Jacob Key, former business developer at Warner Music. Stockholm, April 2018.
Interview with Andreas Liffgarden, former business developer at Spotify. Stockholm, May 2018.
Interview with Joe Cohen, former CEO of Seatwave. Phone conversation, April 2018.
Interview with Per Sundin, former director of Sony BMG Sweden, later Nordic head of Universal Music. Stockholm, June 2018.
Startuppodden. "#21 - Gustav Söderström, Spotify, Kenet Works." October 29, 2014.
Interview with Rory Cellan-Jones, technology correspondent at *BBC*. Phone conversation, April 2018.
Scribd.com. Sean Parker's Email to Spotify's Daniel Ek. August 25, 2009.
Unknown author. "Sveriges supertalang nr 1." *Veckans affärer*, September 9, 2009.
Interview with Samuel Arvidsson, previously with Sony BMG. Stockholm, May 2018.
Greenburg, Z. "Dr. Dre's $3 Billion Monster: The Secret History of Beats." *Forbes*, March 8, 2018.
Jerräng, M. "Så fick Spotify skivbolagen med sig." *Computer Sweden*, August 7, 2009.
Sundberg, M. "Magnus Uggla arg på Breitholtz—lämnar Spotify." *Expressen*, August 13, 2009.
Adegoke, Y. "Global Music Sales Down 8 Percent in 2008: IFPI." *Reuters*, April 21, 2009.
Three anonymous sources about the launch party at Berns, Gustav Söderström's military service, and the celebration of Spotify being accepted in the App Store.
Two anonymous sources about negotiations with the record labels.

8. BRIDGE TO AMERICA

Interview with Thomas Hesse, former President, Global Digital Business and US Sales/Distribution, Sony Music. Phone conversation, October 2018.
Swisher, K. "Spotify's Daniel Ek Talks About Music Start-Up." *AllThingsD*, September 22, 2009.
"Sommar i P1. Daniel Ek." *Swedish Radio P1*, July 12, 2012.
Company documents filed spring 2008. Luxembourg Business Registers.
Interview with Andreas Liffgarden, former business developer at Spotify. Stockholm, May 2018.
Interview with Jacob Key, former business developer at Warner Music. Stockholm, April 2018.
Interview with Fredrik Niemelä, former CPO at Spotify. Phone conversation, August 2018.
Bradshaw, T. "Spotify defends business model." *Financial Times*. March 2, 2010.
"Daniel Ek, Keynote Interview point 1." *YouTube*, October 2010.
Three anonymous sources on the rumor that Google was negotiating to buy Spotify in 2010.
Seven anonymous sources about Andreas Ehn's exit, Daniel Ek's leadership style, things Daniel Ek would say about Steve Jobs, Spotify's financing, and the negotiations with Microsoft.
"Steve Ballmer & Daniel Ek @ KTH, Stockholm." *YouTube*, October 2010.
Dan Rose (drose_999). "In 2009, an unknown investor from Russia came out of nowhere to make one of the greatest late stage venture bets in the history of Silicon Valley. Why did FB choose an outsider to lead our Series D round? Here's the inside story:," May 26, 2020, 4:55 a.m. Retrieved from https://twitter.com/drose_999/status/1265114361900589056.

9. "SCHMUCK INSURANCE"

Interview with Thomas Hesse, former President, Global Digital Business and US Sales/Distribution, Sony Music. Phone conversation, October 2018.
"Sean Parker on Apple's Monopoly." *YouTube*, October 22, 2010.
Lauria, P. "Sean Parker and Steve Jobs Go to War Over Spotify, Apple." *The Daily Beast*. October 28, 2010.
Documents from Spotify that describe the settlement surrounding Sony's stock options.
Singleton, M. "This was Sony Music's contract with Spotify." *The Verge*, May 19, 2015.
Three anonymous sources on the negotiations in Europe, Spotify's financing, and negotiations with Universal in the USA.
Three anonymous sources familiar with Steve Jobs' conversations with senior executives at Universal.

Kamps, G. "Jimmy Iovine and Doug Morris Reminisce About Their Wild Late-Night TV Show 'Farmclub': 'We Didn't Know How to Do Television, We Just Did It.'" *Billboard*. September 18, 2015.

Sisario, B. "For U2 and Apple, a Shrewd Marketing Partnership." *The New York Times*. September 9, 2014.

"A Brief History of Spotify: Gustav Söderström." *YouTube*, January 2019.

Annual Report for Instructus Limited, 2013. Department of Registrar of Companies and Official Receiver, Cyprus.

"CNET News: Steve Jobs introduces iCloud." *YouTube*, June 2011.

Three anonymous sources with insight into Spotify's negotiations with Warner Music and Spotify's launch party in the US.

Sisario, B. "New Service Offers Music by Quantity, not by Song." *The New York Times*. July 13, 2011.

Bruno, A. "Rob Wells Named UMG President of Global Digital." *Billboard*. October 28, 2010.

Staff Writer. "Universal Music Group Takes Full Ownership Of GetMusic." *Cbronline.com*. April 24, 2001.

10. SEAN & ZUCK

Three anonymous sources with insight into Spotify's cooperation with Facebook.

PBS Frontline. "The Facebook dilemma." 2018.

"F8 2011 Keynote." *YouTube*, September 2011.

Hoe, P. "Billionaire Sean Parker throws Monster Party for Spotify." *San Francisco Business Times*, September 23, 2011.

Interview with Ola Sars, former director at Beats Music. Stockholm, June 2018.

An anonymous source about Beats' visit to Stockholm.

11. "WINTER IS COMING"

Four anonymous sources speaking on Spotify's growth strategy.

Interview with Axel Bard Bringéus, former director of expansion at Spotify. Berlin, May 2018.

Skavlan. "Interview with Daniel Ek." Swedish Television, SVT. March 5, 2012.

Interview with Teymour Farman-Farmaian, former CMO at Spotify. Over the phone, October 2020.

"Sommar i P1. Daniel Ek." *Swedish Radio P1*. July 12, 2012.

Edgecliffe-Johnson, A. "Lunch with the FT: Daniel Ek." *Financial Times*. September 27, 2013.

Three anonymous sources on Martin Lorentzon's role at Spotify.

Three anonymous sources on Daniel Ek's private life and work trips for Spotify employees.

Three anonymous sources on the life of Sofia Levander.

"Sommar i P1. Martin Lorentzon." *Swedish Radio P1*. August 1, 2020.

12. SPOTIFY TV

Eight anonymous sources with insight into Spotify's TV project.

Interview with Jonas Sjögren, former CEO of Discovery Networks Sweden. Stockholm, August 2018.

Edgecliffe-Johnson, A. "Lunch with the FT: Daniel Ek." *Financial Times*. September 27, 2013.

13. APPLE BUYS BEATS

Anonymous source who spoke with Daniel Ek about Spotify's recommendations.

Interview with Erik Bernhardsson, former developer at Spotify. Phone conversation, May 2018.

Interview with Ola Sars, former director at Beats Music. Stockholm, June 2018.

Interview with Fredric Vinnå, former CTO/CPO at Beats Music. Former VP of Product at Spotify. Phone conversation, July 2018.

Sherman, E. "Apple's $100 million U2 debacle." *Cbsnews.com.* September 17, 2014.

Press statement and annual report from Spotify about the purchase of Tunigo and The Echo Nest.

Four anonymous sources with insight into Spotify's negotiations with Google.

Gradvall, J. "The Tech Genius the Giants are Fighting Over." *Di Weekend*, September 8, 2016.

An anonymous source with insight into Beats Music's operations and merger negotiations in the USA.

An anonymous source at Spotify's New York offices.

Three anonymous sources with insight into the work at Spotify's product division in 2014.

Startuppodden. "#21 - Gustav Söderström, Spotify, Kenet Works." October 29, 2014.

"Dr. Dre Hip Hop's first Billionaire Celebrates with Tyrese Gibson." *YouTube.* May 10, 2014.

14. DEATH VALLEY

Interview with Henrik Landgren, former Chief Analyst at Spotify. Stockholm, September 2018.

Four anonymous sources about how Spotify built the free app and negotiated with the record companies, and two on the Christmas party of 2013.

Internal documents showing Spotify's growth in 2013.

Annual reports from Instructus Limited and Rosello Limited. Department of Registrar of Companies and Official Receiver, Cyprus.

Startuppodden. "#21—Gustav Söderström, Spotify, Kenet Works." October 29, 2014.

"Daniel Ek, Niklas Zennström, Ilkka Paananen: How We Failed our Way to Success." *YouTube*, November 2016.

15. FROM NASHVILLE TO BROOKLYN

Two anonymous sources on Daniel Ek's new habits and eagerness for growth.

Interview with Per Sundin, former director of Sony BMG Sweden, now Universal Music. Stockholm, June 2018.

Interview with Rob Wells, former digital director at Universal Music. Phone conversation, June 2018.

Interview with Axel Bard Bringéus, former director of expansion at Spotify. Berlin, May 2018.

Two anonymous sources on Jay-Z's offer for exclusive licenses and Martin Lorentzon's view of Tidal.

Carlsson, S. "Spotify: A Music Streaming Service going for Broke." *Business Insider.* March 11, 2015.

Leijonhufvud, J. "Jay Z vill köpa Aspiro." *Dagens industri.* January 31, 2015.

"Jay-Z's Tidal Opening Official Launching!!!" *YouTube.* March 30, 2015.

16. BIG DATA

Two anonymous sources on Daniel Ek's conversations with investors, Gustav Söderström's internal rhetoric, and Spotify Running.

Two anonymous sources on how Discover Weekly came about.

"Shop Talk: Product // Spotify Discover Weekly." *YouTube*, February 2016.

"Spotify. Media Even." *YouTube*, May 2015.

"Apple - WWDC 2015." *YouTube*, June 2015.

Interview with Fredric Vinnå, former VP of Product at Spotify. Phone conversation, July 2018.

Goldberg, D. Daniel Ek om Apple Music: "Man måste inte vara nummer ett." *Dagens industri.* June 10, 2015.

Atkinson, C. "Competition Commission Probing Music-Streaming Services." *New York Post*, April 1, 2015.

Wiggers, K. "Apple Pushing Music Labels to Kill Free Spotify Streaming Ahead of Beats Relaunch." *The Verge*, May 4, 2015.

Chen, Brian X and B. Sisario. "Apple Music and Labels Investigated in Two States." *The New York Times*, June 9, 2015.

Three anonymous sources about the rollout of Moments.

Two anonymous sources on Spotify's evolving content strategy.

17. BRILLIANT SWEDEN

Global Music Report. *IFPI*, April 2016.

Three anonymous sources about Daniel Ek's, Katarina Berg's, and Barry McCarthy's leadership styles as well as Martin Lorentzon's role at Spotify 2015–2017.

Carlsson, S. "Daniel Ek: Jag kommer inte sälja." *Dagens industri*. June 9, 2016.

Carlsson, S. "Daniel Ek has sold shares in Spotify for 300 million." *Dagens industri*. May 19, 2017.

Interview with Sören Granath, reporter at Swedish Radio. Via email, September 2018.

Granath, S. "Spotify förnekar börsplaner." Swedish Radio P1, June 2, 2017.

Two anonymous sources about Barry McCarthy's initial time at Spotify.

Three anonymous sources about Alex Norström's advancement.

Three anonymous sources about the Fourth Swedish Pension fund's courtship, the Wallenberg family's irritation, and the conditions of Spotify's billion-dollar loan.

Social media posts from Daniel Ek and Sofia Levander's wedding. Instagram and Facebook, 2016.

Molla, R and Peter Kafka. Episode 1: "Netflix is a team, not a family." *Land of the Giants*. June 23, 2020.

#Ensakidag (a Swedish podcast). "435. Ett samtal med Daniel Ek om Spotify och livet - igår, idag och imorgon." June 24, 2020.

Several friends and former colleagues on Daniel Ek's wedding and new lifestyle.

18. THE STREAMING WARS

Roettgers, J. "Streaming Overtakes Downloads, CDs as Top Music Revenue Driver." *Variety.* March 22, 2016.

Daniel Ek. "Så ska Spotify utvecklas kommande 10 år." *TV4 Morning News*. August 13, 2016.

Two anonymous sources, who got to know Daniel Ek before he started Spotify, speaking about his origin story.

Four anonymous sources speaking about Spotify's conversations about Justin Bieber's video, negotiations with Tidal, and negotiations with SoundCloud.

Three anonymous sources on SoundCloud's development 2012–2016.

One anonymous source on Spotify's reason for wanting to buy SoundCloud.

"Senator Elizabeth Warren's Keynote | America's Monopoly Problem." *YouTube*, July 2016.

Four anonymous sources about Spotify's lobbying in Washington, DC, and delays in the App Store through the years.

US public records on Spotify's lobbying activities.

Weich, C. "Spotify Urges iPhone Customers to Stop Paying Through Apple's App Store." *The Verge*. July 8, 2015.

Love, J. and M. Shanley. "Apple Fires Back at Spotify over Music Streaming Claims." *Reuters*, July 1, 2016.

19. WALL STREET

Four anonymous sources on Stefan Blom's work in 2017.

Safian, R. "Spotify's $30 Billion Playlist for Global Domination." *Fast Company*, August 6, 2018.

Khan (formerly JMO) v Khan (formerly KTA) [2018]. England and Wales High Court 241 (QB). February 15, 2018. Retrieved via: http://www.bailii.org/ew/cases/EWHC/QB/2018/241.html

Six anonymous sources about the former staff members' share profits and gray market trade in Spotify's shares.

Two anonymous sources on Spotify's negotiations with Tencent.

Internal documents on Spotify's cap table and the transaction with Tencent.

Contract between Spotify, Tencent, Daniel Ek, and Martin Lorentzon, dated December 15, 2017. SEC, April 2018.

Ingham T. "Spotify Denies it's Playlisting Fake Artists. So Why are all these Fake Artists on its Playlists?" *Music Business Worldwide*, July 9, 2017.

Three anonymous sources on Spotify's strategy to raise its margins and the acquisition of Soundtrap.

Carlsson, S. "Spotify bought Swedish App Company for Half a Billion." *Dagens industri*, January 2, 2018.

"Investor Day—March 2018." Video presentation, 2018. Spotify.

Ingham, T. "Revealed: How Sony's $750m Spotify equity cash will be shared with artists and indie labels." *Music Business Worldwide*. June 14, 2018.

Three sources on the subject of Stefan Blom's departure.

Official information from Spotify, Sony, Warner, and Universal.

An anonymous source about Anthony Tiffith's conversation with Daniel Ek.

Rys, D. "Top Dawg Explains how he Warned Spotify's CEO that Kendrick Lamar, Others would Pull Music over Conduct Policy." *Billboard*, June 1, 2018.

"Spotify CEO Daniel Ek | Full interview | Code 2018." *YouTube*, May 2018.

Blumberg, A. "Exit." *StartUp*. October 11, 2019.

Dance, G., M. LaForgia, N. Confessore. "As Facebook Raised a Privacy Wall, It Carved an Opening for Tech Giants." *The New York Times*, December 18, 2018.

20. THE HOUSE THAT DANIEL BUILT

VanDerWerff, T. "Trump Signs the Music Modernization Act, the Biggest Change to Copyright Law in Decades." *Vox*. October 11, 2018.

Anonymous source about Spotify's legal situation in the United States.

Digitally China Podcast. "Tencent Music vs. Spotify." January 3, 2019.

Public records concerning Daniel and Sofia Ek's home and building projects. Danderyd municipality and Värmdö municipality, 2018.

S1 filing, Warner Music. May 26, 2020. Retrieved via: https://www.sec.gov/Archives/edgar/data/1319161/000119312520150678/d833365ds1a.htm.

#Ensakidag (a Swedish podcast). "435. Ett samtal med Daniel Ek om Spotify och livet - igår, idag och imorgon." June 24, 2020.

Two anonymous sources on Martin Lorentzon's thoughts during 2018.

Two anonymous sources on Daniel Ek's leadership in 2018.

Dredge, S. "Spotify countersues Sosa Entertainment alleging stream fraud." *Musically.com*. May 19, 2020.

Ingham, T. "Spotify execs praise TikTok owner's new Spotify rival . . . while trashing Apple and Amazon Music's reach." *Music Business Worldwide*. November 20, 2019.

Leijonhufvud, J. "Spotify om fusket med fejkade lyssningar: Mindre än en procent." *Dagens industri*. February 17, 2020.

Deahl, D. "Justin Bieber told fans to game Spotify and iTunes to give him a chart-topping song." *The Verge*. Jan 10, 2020.

Ek, H. "Han räddades från döden av Daniel Ek och blev tech-sfärens 'legosoldat.'" *Dagens industri*. May 23, 2020.

Gurman, M and Emily Chang. "Spotify CEO Expects Apple to Further Open Up After Complaint." *Bloomberg.com*. May 5, 2020.

Dredge, S. "Spotify CEO talks Covid-19, artist incomes and podcasting." Musically.com, July 30, 2020.

REGARDING QUOTES AND EVENTS

With the exception of taped conversations and cited interviews, the quotes in this book are recollections by one or several sources who participated in, witnessed, or have first-hand knowledge of the actual conversation. The presentation of all quotes, events, and factual occurrences, gathered from anonymous and on-record sources, reflects the best journalistic efforts of the authors.

INDEX

ABOUT THE AUTHORS

SVEN CARLSSON is a tech journalist based in Stockholm. He is currently the technology correspondent for Swedish Radio News. He has a master's degree from Columbia Journalism School and previously worked at the daily newspapers *Dagens industri* and *Svenska Dagbladet*.

JONAS LEIJONHUFVUD has been a business journalist in Sweden since 1998. He interviewed Jeff Bezos when the tech bubble was about to burst, and Spotify founder Martin Lorentzon when it first launched. He has a BA in Media Arts from The University of Arizona and is currently a tech reporter at *Dagens industri*, Sweden's leading business newspaper.

The Spotify Play was updated and translated from Swedish by the authors themselves.